T0330292

The Changing Landscape of Food Governance

The Changing Landscape of Food Governance

Public and Private Encounters

Edited by

Tetty Havinga

Associate Professor in Sociology of Law, Faculty of Law, Radboud University Nijmegen, the Netherlands

Frans van Waarden

Professor of Policy and Organization Studies, Faculty of Social Sciences and University College, Utrecht University, the Netherlands

Donal Casey

Lecturer in Law, Kent Law School, University of Kent, UK

Edward Elgar
PUBLISHING

Cheltenham, UK • Northampton, MA, USA

Published by
Edward Elgar Publishing Limited
The Lypiatts
15 Lansdown Road
Cheltenham
Glos GL50 2JA
UK

Edward Elgar Publishing, Inc.
William Pratt House
9 Dewey Court
Northampton
Massachusetts 01060
USA

A catalogue record for this book
is available from the British Library

Library of Congress Control Number: 2014952158

This book is available electronically in the **Elgar**online
Law subject collection
DOI 10.4337/9781784715410

ISBN 978 1 78471 540 3 (cased)
ISBN 978 1 78471 541 0 (eBook)

Typeset by Servis Filmsetting Ltd, Stockport, Cheshire
Printed and bound in Great Britain by T.J. International Ltd, Padstow

Contents

Figures

Tables

Contributors

Gabriele Abels holds the Jean Monnet Chair for comparative politics and European integration at the Institute of Political Science, University of Tübingen, Germany. Her research interests are European integration, theories of European integration, role of parliaments in the EU, political participation, biotechnology regulation, food safety policy and gender studies.

John P. Burns is Dean of the Faculty of Social Sciences and Chair Professor of Politics and Public Administration at the University of Hong Kong, China. Burns researches public administration in China, including Hong Kong, focusing on civil service reform, party-government relations, public policy and governance issues.

Federica Casarosa is Research Fellow at the Centre for Judicial Cooperation at the European University Institute, Department of Law, Florence, Italy. She has worked as a consultant for FAO and as a Jean Monnet Fellow at the Robert Schuman Centre for Advanced Studies. Her research interests focus on private regulation in the food sector and new media law and regulation.

Donal Casey is Lecturer in Law at the University of Kent, Canterbury, UK. His research interests lie in the area of food regulation and in the issues of legitimacy and accountability. His research has been published in the European Law Journal, the Journal of Law and Society, and Regulation & Governance.

Neil Collins is Dean of the Graduate School of Public Policy, Nazarbayev University, Kazakhstan. He is a past president of the Political Studies Association of Ireland and a former Centennial Scholar at the American Political Science Association in Washington DC. He is the author of several books, including *Understanding Chinese Politics*, Manchester University Press, 2013.

Vanessa Constant Laforce has been working as a Researcher and Teaching Fellow in Law at the University of Abertay, Dundee, UK. She has also worked in France as a Parliamentary Assistant for Chantal Berthelot, French Member of Parliament. Her research interests include EU market access issues for agricultural food products from developing countries.

Robin van Dalen works for the Philips Africa innovation center, Kenya. Her passion is adventure, connecting people, business and human development. She worked for NGOs in Ecuador, Kenya and India, researched the halal market, and developed the medical software business in the Middle East. She is a Cambridge University graduate in organization studies.

Gareth Enticott is Senior Lecturer in Rural Geography at the School of Planning and Geography at Cardiff University, UK. His research explores the social impacts of animal disease policy, principally bovine tuberculosis, on farmers and veterinarians in the United Kingdom and New Zealand.

Elena Fagotto is Director of Research at Harvard Kennedy School's Transparency Policy Project, Cambridge, Massachusetts and a Ph.D. candidate at Erasmus University, Rotterdam, the Netherlands. Her research focuses on regulatory policy, information disclosure, and democratic governance. She is currently examining the role of private actors in food safety regulatory regimes.

Doris Fuchs is Professor of International Relations and Sustainable Development at the University of Münster, Germany. Her research focuses on the structural and discursive power of non-state actors (especially transnational corporations), sustainable consumption, financialization, energy, climate, and food politics and policy.

Marco Gobbato is a business consultant at Studio Tosi, Venice – Vicenza, Italy. He has worked as a Max Weber Fellow at the European University Institute, and as a teaching assistant at the University of Trento. His research interests focus on contract law, inter-firm networks and private regulation. His works have appeared on several books and journals.

Jörn-Carsten Gottwald has been Professor for East Asian Politics at Ruhr University Bochum, Germany since 2011. Prior to this appointment he worked at the Centre for Chinese and East Asian Politics at Free University Berlin, at the Department of Political Science, University of Trier and the Irish Institute of Chinese Studies, National University of Ireland, Cork.

Tetty Havinga is Associate Professor at the Institute for Sociology of Law of the Radboud University, Nijmegen, the Netherlands. She is interested in relations between industry and law with a view to the public interest. Her research explores the development and effects of private and public food regulation.

Agni Kalfagianni is Assistant Professor for Global Food and Environmental Governance at the Institute for Environmental Studies (IVM), VU University of Amsterdam, the Netherlands. She is also Senior Research Fellow of the international Earth System Governance Project (ESGP). Kalfagianni has published extensively on issues of effectiveness, legitimacy and justice of global food and environmental governance.

Alexander Kobusch is Junior Lecturer at the Institute of Political Science, University of Tübingen, Germany. His research interests are European integration, food safety in the EU, network governance and social network analysis.

Robert Lee is Professor of Law at Birmingham Law School, UK. Between 2001 and 2012 he was Co-Director of the ESRC Research Centre on Business Relationships, Accountability, Sustainability and Society (BRASS) at Cardiff University. His wider interest is in regulatory issues particularly in areas of health and environment.

Jing Li is Junior Research Fellow at the think tank, China Finance 40 Forum, where she researches food safety regulation and regulatory institutional arrangements. After conducting research at the Sun Yat-sen University she joined DemeterSoft, an IT company focused on food regulation, seeking to link the academic and practical worlds.

Peter Oosterveer is Associate Professor at the Environmental Policy Group, Wageningen University, the Netherlands. His work is in the field of globalization and sustainability of food production and consumption. Peter is particularly interested in global public and private governance of food, promoting sustainability and the role of consumers therein.

Haiko van der Voort is Assistant Professor at Delft University of Technology, Faculty of Technology, Policy and Management, the Netherlands. He earned his PhD with an extensive study on co-regulation. His research is about decision-making on norms in and among organizations. Related topics are regulation, enforcement, certification, and risk management.

Frans van Waarden is Professor of Policy and Organization Studies at Utrecht University, the Netherlands, and Fellow of Utrecht University College. His research interests are in phenomena at the boundaries between politics, economics, law and history, seen through the eyes of a sociologist: the governance of markets, regulation and its enforcement, and political institutions.

Xiaoqi Wang is Assistant Professor at the Department of Politics and Public Administration, University of Hong Kong, China. Wang's research interests include public administration, civil service reforms in China, and policy analysis of food safety and waste management. She has published a book and several journal articles about reforms and policies in China.

Abbreviations

AGES	Austrian Agency for Health and Food Safety
AH	Albert Heijn
AID	General Inspection Service of the Ministry of Agriculture (the Netherlands)
ANIME	Agenda-setting; Negotiation; Implementation; Monitoring compliance; Enforcement
AQSIQ	Administration of Quality Supervision, Inspection and Quarantine (China)
BAES	Federal Office for Food Safety (Austria)
BMG	Ministry of Health (Austria)
BMLFUW	Federal Ministry of Agriculture, Forestry, Environment and Water Management (Austria)
BRC	British Retail Consortium Global Standards for Food Safety
BSE	Bovine Spongiform Encephalopathy or mad cow disease
bTB	bovine tuberculosis
CB	Certification Body
CCP	Chinese Communist Party
CCTV	China Central Television
CDIC	Central Discipline Inspection Commission (China)
CFDA	China Food and Drug Administration
CiNGO	civil society NGO
CoC	codes of conduct
Codex	Codex Alimentarius Commission
CPCC	Control Points and Compliance Criteria
CPE	Inspection Office for Poultry, Eggs and Egg Products (the Netherlands)
CSR	corporate social responsibility
DCs	developing countries
Defra	Department for Environment Food and Rural Affairs (UK)
DO	denomination of origin
DPP	Democratic Progressive Party (China)
ECHR	European Convention on Human Rights

EFSA	European Food Safety Authority
EHEC	Enterohaemorrhagic Escherichia coli or E. coli
EPA	Environmental Protection Administration (China)
EU	European Union
EÜM	Ministry of Health (Hungary)
EUREP	Euro-Retailer Produce Working Group
FAO	Food and Agriculture Organization
FDA	Food and Drug Administration (US)
FMD	foot and mouth disease
FSC	Forest Stewardship Council
FSL	Food Safety Law
GAQSIQ	General Administration of Quality Supervision, Inspection and Quarantine (China)
GFL	General European Food Law
GFSI	Global Food Safety Initiative
GİMDES	Turkish Food Auditing and Certification Research Association
GlobalG.A.P.	Global Partnership for Good Agricultural Practices
GM	genetically modified
GmbH	limited liability company (Germany)
GoNGO	state NGO
GRASP	GLOBALG.A.P. Risk Assessment on Social Practice
HAC	Halal Audit Company
HACCP	Hazard Analysis and Critical Control Point
HCC	Total Quality Halal Correct Certification
HIC	Halal International Control
HQC	Halal Quality Control
HVV	Halal Feed and Food Inspection Authority
ICB	Industry and Commerce Bureau (China)
IFA	Integrated Farm Assurance Standard
IKB ei	quality control system for egg production (the Netherlands)
JV	Swedish Board of Agriculture (feed safety only)
KMT	Guomintang or Nationalist Party (China)
LD	Ministry of Rural Affairs (Sweden)
LNV	Dutch Ministry of Agriculture
MaNGO	market NGO
MÉBIH	Hungarian Food Safety Office
MGSZH	Central Agricultural Office (Hungary)
MIIT	Ministry of Industry and Information Technology (China)
MoA	Ministry of Agriculture (China)

MOH	Ministry of Health (China)
MRL	maximum residue level
MSC	Marine Stewardship Council
NÉHIB	National Food Chain Safety Office (Hungary)
NFU	National Farmers' Union (UK)
NHFPC	National Population and Family Planning Commission (China)
NOP	Dutch poultry farmers' organization
NVP	Dutch poultry farmers' labour union
NVWA	Netherlands Food and Consumer Product Safety Authority
OECD	Organisation for Economic Co-operation and Development
OIE	Office International des Epizooties (World Organisation for Animal Health)
PBO	Dutch statutory trade association
PFSS	Private food safety standard
PHB	Provincial Health Bureau (China)
PPE	Commodity Board for Poultry Farmers and Eggs (the Netherlands)
PPP	plant protection products
PRC	People's Republic of China
PVV	Marketing Board for Cattle and Meat (the Netherlands)
RASFF	Rapid Alert System for Food and Feed (EU)
RSS	regulatory standard-setting
RvA	Accreditation Council (the Netherlands)
SAIC	State Administration for Industry and Commerce (China)
SFDA	State Food and Drug Administration (China)
SFP	Single Farm Payment (EU)
SLV	Swedish National Food Administration
SPS	Sanitary and Phytosanitary
SQF	Safe Quality Food
SVA	Swedish National Veterinary Institute
TAR	territory, authority and rights (Sassen)
TNC	The Nature Conservancy
TOC	Toezicht op Controle or Oversight of Controls (the Netherlands)
USDA	US Department of Agriculture
vCJD	variant Creutzfeldt-Jakob disease
VM	Ministry of Agriculture and Rural Development (Hungary)

VWA	Food and Consumer Product Safety Authority (the Netherlands)
WG	Welsh Government
WHO	World Health Organization
WTO	World Trade Organisation
WWF	World Wild Fund for Nature

PART I

Introduction

1. Changing regulatory arrangements in food governance

Tetty Havinga, Donal Casey and Frans van Waarden

1.1 INTRODUCTION AND SUMMARY

The leading position of nation states in food regulation has been displaced by novel, fragmented and complex patterns of regulatory arrangements. Global food governance and regulation is increasingly the activity of not only national governmental actors, but also of a multitude and diversity of private actors and international organizations. Governmental food regulation has come under pressure. While on the one hand the limited capacity of state institutions in this policy sphere has become visible, there has on the other hand been a concomitant increase in the requirements of and expectations towards the state to regulate food safety and quality. Complex global food supply chains and the perception of insufficient governmental regulation point to the limitations of governmental food regulation. The growing public concern about food safety, new concerns about lifestyle risks, animal welfare, sustainability, and advances in scientific and technological capabilities have led to rising expectations of governmental food regulation. Responses of both public and private organizations to current challenges have resulted in a new landscape of food governance.

In this landscape we can observe a distinct shift from the national to the international governmental level and from public to private governance. The European Union has attempted to strengthen its food safety legislation with the establishment of the European Food Safety Authority. Furthermore, private actors took a leading role in global food safety regulation and the development of retail driven food safety regulation from the 1990s onwards. Both transitions resulted in fragmented and complex regulatory arrangements with a multiplicity of actors at multiple levels.

The new attention to food regulation provides an opportunity to investigate a number of broader issues that have concerned regulatory governance scholars. These issues include: (i) the legitimacy, effectiveness and consequences of public and private regulation; (ii) the interaction of both layers and networks of regulation; (iii) regulatory responses to crisis and contestation; and (iv) the distribution of power in regulatory arrangements. It is against this backdrop that this collection of chapters is set.

In this introduction we outline the major trends in the food supply chain and the expectations regarding adequate regulation and control of food. These developments constitute the background of changing regulatory arrangements in food governance. After that we provide a rough sketch of the responses of both governmental agencies and private parties to these developments. Finally the chapters in this volume are introduced.

1.2   DEVELOPMENTS RELATED TO THE FOOD SUPPLY CHAIN

Recent decades have seen new major developments, that have produced radically different challenges as well as opportunities for food quality and safety. These trends have on the one hand provided new hitherto unheard of opportunities for food adulteration and created new types of risks and uncertainties for food consumers, raising the expectations of citizens towards their governments to protect them from such risks. Such trends have also produced new opportunities for judging, monitoring, and improving quality and safety, both ex ante in production itself as well as ex post through new forms of regulation and oversight. These have raised the expectations of citizens further: whatever can technically be done to improve food safety, quality, and oversight, should be done. On the other hand there have been trends that have reduced the capacity of national governments to satisfy these raised expectations of their citizens. What are some of these major trends?

1.2.1   New Products and New Modes of Production

Each day new food products are launched on the market. In some cases it is merely a new package or a new name for an already existing product. In other cases new ingredients are added, new recipes are used or entirely new products are developed. Many food products are processed foods. Less than half of the food people in the US, Spain and France eat is unprocessed basic food such as vegetables, fruits and meat.[1] Even fresh vegetables, fruits, seafood and meat are increasingly bought ready-to-eat (washed, cut, spiced, pre-cooked, preserved, and mixed).

Consumers can value the freshness of fish or the looks of apples and tomatoes; but the quality and freshness of composed food products is more difficult to value. Consumers often do not know how their food is being produced. Which chemicals have been added and which conservation methods are used (radiation, pasteurization, heating), and what risks might be involved? Processed foods are also more vulnerable to fraud, in particular in cases where the fraud is not easily noticed by the consumer, for example when replacing an expensive ingredient with a cheap one (horsemeat in lasagna) or omitting costly process prescriptions (misrepresenting regular meat as halal or organic).

1.2.2 Complex Global Food Value Chains

The food supply chain has become more internationalized and much longer and the share of composed foods with ingredients from all over the world has increased. We can see the scale and geographies of commerce globalizing and expanding beyond the nation state. Like many other issue areas and systems of production, the past twenty years have witnessed the rapid 'globalization of the agri-food system' (Hatanaka et al. 2005). Products come to us from everywhere around the globe. This concerns not only processed food, but also fresh products. In response to consumer demand, improved techniques for transport and storage, and growing consumer incomes, European retailers increasingly obtain fresh products from all over the world enabling a year-round supply. The food chain encompasses places of production and trading around the globe. In a local supermarket in the Netherlands or the UK, you will find mangos from Mali, salmon from Scotland, avocados from South Africa, shrimps from Thailand and French beans from Kenya next to domestic produced foods.

Ingredients in processed foods are not just locally obtained, but are sourced from all over the world. The incident involving milk contaminated with melamine from China in 2008 illustrates the consequence of global sourcing of food ingredients. Melamine was found worldwide in various food products: in sweets, cookies, chocolate, baby food, pretzels, ice-cream, coffee and soya in countries such as Singapore, Indonesia, Canada, the United States, the Netherlands, the United Kingdom and Poland. These products were probably produced with an ingredient that contained contaminated Chinese milk.[2]

The global sourcing of food creates new types of risks within the supply chain 'as food is subject to greater transformation and transportation, and fragmented supply chains across multiple enterprises and food production systems with diverse producer characteristics, regulatory frameworks, environmental conditions and technical expertise are brought together' (Henson and Humphrey 2010). Such complex global food supply chains make things difficult for governmental agencies aiming at the production and marketing of safe food. This applies particularly to national governments without jurisdiction outside their national borders. They can only rely on inspections by foreign agencies (governmental or private) and import controls (see Constant Laforce in this volume).

1.2.3 Advances in Science and Technology

Scientific advances are important in food governance in several respects and give us more scientific knowledge about risks, food safety, and (un) healthiness of food ingredients and food habits. New technological knowledge results in new ways to produce, store, conserve, pack, transport and prepare food. New knowledge also results in more techniques to identify risks, substances and the authenticity of food, and new opportunities to manage and control identified risks. In food governance science plays an increasingly important role in risk assessment and risk management. International treaties from the WHO and the EU prescribe countries a science based food policy in order to avoid unfair competition, protectionism and trade barriers. Governments depend highly on external experts for scientific knowledge and risk assessment. Here, science has come to dictate in large part: (i) how food safety and quality standards are developed; (ii) who should develop them; (iii) what the contents of such rules should be; and (iv) how the standards should be enforced. Thus, there are important implications for not only the setting of standards, but also for the means of verification and implementation.

Monitoring and controlling food production processes and food products is highly dependent on technological devices and knowledge. Advances in scientific and technological capabilities to detect even small amounts of substances in food and the growing knowledge about diseases related to food add to the public perception of food safety risks. For example, the possibilities to connect information from different sources results in a higher level of detected food-borne diseases.

Modern information and communication technology provides many opportunities for worldwide easy and fast information exchange. This fosters the development of hypes: information or misinformation on the web can result in media coverage, consumer boycott or pressure on governments to take action.

Moreover, science is not only of instrumental value, but also of great normative value by providing constitutive and legitimating support to actors engaged in governance (Drori et al. 2002). Many commentators have observed the scientization of contemporary society through the expanded role played by science in many aspects of social, economic and political life. In particular, it has been noted that one of the most 'striking features of contemporary society is that science speaks with highly legitimate authority on the widest range of questions' (Drori and Meyer 2006a, 40). Importantly, the expanded authority of science is now also a central feature of contemporary governance. Indeed, the reliance upon science and scientific discourse as a base of legitimacy has taken a dominant role in the legitimating actions of actors engaged in governance to the extent that it has primacy over moral, political or pragmatic bases of legitimacy (Djelic and Sahlin-Anderson 2006, Drori and Meyer 2006). The expansion of scientific authority provides legitimating tools for actors as the knowledge assumed to be embedded in science provides justifications for political, economic, and social choices of actors. The reason for this lies in the perceived value neutrality of decisions and rules based upon science, and the fact that they emanate from experts. Political debates following the BSE crisis and the discussion around genetically modified foods have questioned the neutrality of scientific knowledge. However, while in many cases the perceived reliance on science and expert knowledge may only hold symbolic power, it still constitutes a significant institutional force (Jacobsson 2000, 40). Greater knowledge also brings new and extended responsibility of authorities. They cannot continue as if nothing has changed.

1.2.4 New Perceptions of Food Safety

What is regarded as safe food depends on available knowledge and hence changes over time. Due to the advances in science and technology we know more and more about food, risks, food-borne illness, allergens, and so on. Several risks may be connected to food: contamination with bacteria, prions or toxic material (animal pharmaceutical, herbicides, and dioxin), allergens and particular nutrients (sugar, fatty acids, unhealthy eating) (Van Kreyl and Knaap 2004, McCabe-Sellers and Beattie 2004). It is not always obvious which foods are safe for consumption. The same food may carry no risk at all for one consumer, and be quite dangerous for another consumer (due to allergic response, disease or eating habits). The ways food is stored and prepared can cause food disease or kill harmful microbes. Risks of using a particular production method or additives are not always known. There also might be a difference between subjective and objective risks.

Over time we see changes in what is considered to be the major food safety issue. Between 1970 and 1990 much attention was paid to harmful chemical substances in food. After 1990 healthy food became the most prominent issue. Recently the chemical safety of food is receiving attention once again, along with the health consequences of animal diseases and microbial contamination.

1.2.5   Public Concern about Food

Food scandals have regularly hit the media headlines. The 2013 horse-meat scandal concerned horsemeat being sold as beef or 'hidden' in meat products like hamburgers, sausages and lasagna. Around that time it was also discovered that some eggs were inaccurately claimed to be organically produced and in Germany frozen fish and seafood were made intentionally heavier by adding water. Some revelations were unfounded, such as the claim that Spanish firms had used the meat of abandoned cats and dogs in the production of animal feed and meatballs. Nevertheless they are reported in the media and result in consumer concern about adulteration and thus, the credibility of both the regulatory regime and food business operators.

More serious, however, are food incidents where human health is at risk. In 2011, a number of consumers became fatally ill as a result of the EHEC bacteria. It took some time before the source of the contamination was identified. Several raw vegetables notably cucumbers, tomatoes, lettuce, bean sprouts, and fenugreek from the Netherlands, Spain and Egypt were said to be the source of EHEC. This led several countries, including Russia, to close their borders to such products. In 2008, Chinese dairies added melamine to their milk in order to fraudulently increase the protein level of the milk (see Burns et al. in this volume). Six children died and 54 000 children were hospitalized as a result of consuming the adulterated milk. The scandal also had some unforeseen consequences, as the demand in China for foreign baby milk formula created a shortage of it in the Netherlands in 2013.

The best known of such incidents in recent decades has been the BSE crisis. In order to introduce a cheap means of protein into the animal feed system, animal protein such as bone meal was added to the feed chain. This introduction resulted in a new disease in animals that was subsequently passed through the food chain to consumers. Between 1986 and 2009, 168 people, mostly in the UK, died from the variant Creutzfeldt-Jakob disease, a deadly brain disorder.

The 20 March 1996 statement by the then Conservative British government that there was a probable link between Bovine Spongiform Encephalopathy (BSE) and variant Creutzfeldt-Jakob (vCJD) disease created unprecedented widespread concern among consumers about the safety of their food and a new heightened awareness of food safety issues.[3] This consumer concern permeated through Europe and has continued to do so in light of new manufactured risks such as genetically modified foodstuffs and pesticide residues. This transformation in the mind-set of European consumers has been linked by agricultural sociologist Hugh Campbell (2006: 126) to a broader shift in Western societies 'from politics of class (which has dominated modernity since the Industrial Revolution) to politics of risk' – a manifestation of Beck's 'risk society' (Beck 1992). As Moran (2002, 407) notes, '"risk society" in turn produces a regulatory society'.

Traditional public concerns regarding food were focused on the availability of enough food (food security) and the absence of dangerous or unhealthy food (food safety). However, public concern about food is not confined to issues of safety and health risks. Consumer expectations, preferences and attitudes have changed in relation to food quality and increased recognition of the external effects of their consumption. There has been increased emphasis and importance attached to non-traditional quality attributes of food associated with the environmental, social and animal welfare dimensions of food production processes and the corollary effects consumption can have on these issues (Kysar 2004). Increasingly, claims are being made that food has been responsibly produced (sustainable food production, fair trade, animal welfare and labour rights) and is healthy (with less sugar, salt, fat, additives, and fewer calories). These new concerns about sustainability, health, animal welfare and the social effects of the globalization of food production, add new requirements to the food production and distribution system.

1.3   DEVELOPMENTS RELATED TO GOVERNMENTAL REGULATION

The last decades have seen a growing public concern about food. Better informed, critical and assertive consumers expect their government to secure safe and healthy food and protection against all risks. We could speak of a revolution of rising expectations: as food becomes safer and as knowledge about food risks increases, we expect an increased level of food safety, or even better, 100 per cent safety.

1.3.1   Higher Expectations towards Public Authorities by their Public

The growing public concern about food contributed to the call for more transparency and accountability. This normative pressure takes the form of promoting a model of food safety and quality regulation that provides structures and procedures within the standard setting, monitoring and enforcement activities that seek to advance transparency, openness, representation, participation, deliberation and consensus. For example, the new UK food safety structure offers opportunities for participation and a high level of transparency. Many food safety authorities make documents, inspection reports and so on available to the interested public. Private parties are also faced with comparative demands to provide more transparency, openness, participation, deliberation and consensus.

Food safety developed from a mainly technical and apolitical issue into a politically debated and contested issue. Food safety got heightened issue saliency after several food related scares and disputes, such as mad cow disease, hormone-treated meat, dioxin contamination, genetically modified foods, EHEC and the horsemeat scandal. Food risks became more visible and recognized and are the subject of growing public concern. Food safety issues attract media attention and are debated by political groups. This puts pressure on public authorities and the food industry to take adequate measures to prevent future scandals and to secure the safety of food. Loeber et al (2011) show that framing incidents as 'food scares' (in contrast to framing them as environmental scandals or disasters in the past) goes hand in hand with institutional changes in the regulatory system in the European Union and in several EU member states.

1.3.2   With (Perceived) Limits to Government Regulation

Moreover, the BSE crisis and subsequent food scares have led to a decline in the perceived ability of state governance systems to effectively regulate and guarantee the safety of food (Caduff and Bernauer 2006). The identification of new risks has also changed consumers' attitudes towards food safety, and more importantly has damaged the trust consumers have in state regulation. The response of the British government to the BSE crisis has often been cited as a manifest illustration of the inability of the national government to deal with food risks. The BSE crisis also showed that the European Union failed to act adequately (Vos 2000). The Commission had followed a policy of disinformation that had prevented legislative activity and member states from restricting the import of British beef. The relevant committees had been influenced by British members and were under political pressure. The BSE crisis counts as a turning point in the European Union's food policy. This criticism on the effectiveness of governmental food regulation corresponds with the general perception that traditional command-and-control regulation is ineffective, inflexible and neglects the responsibilities of corporations and citizens. Enticott and Lee (in this volume) present an example of governmental regulation that is counterproductive. They show that the UK compensation policies for animal diseases such as bovine tuberculosis and foot and mouth disease provide no incentive to develop best practices and precautionary measures.

Paradoxically, governments are confronted with higher expectations and demands regarding the safety, quality, and reliability of food products on markets, while the past decades have seen an increasing dominance of the neo-liberal ideology favouring a limited role for the government in society in general and markets in particular. Neo-liberalism advocates economic liberalism, free trade, open markets, the reduction of government regulation, cutting of public expenditures and a small public sector. Moreover, national states are also constrained by international law from the WTO and the EU. In international relations the fear for protectionism and unfair competition is an important impediment for national food regulators.

1.4 THE RESULT: COMPLEX AND DIVERSE REGULATORY ARRANGEMENTS IN FOOD

Trends in the food industry pose new challenges to government regulation of food quality and safety. The globalization of food chains implies that production and distribution are increasingly beyond the territorial jurisdiction of national governments. The increased popularity of composed foods implies that it is more difficult to identify their composition, origin and the conditions of production. Advances in science and technology have increased our understanding about risks, but the counter side is that with more knowledge comes more responsibilities for the prevention, aversion or correction of risks. Knowledge cannot be undone. That has fueled public expectations towards governmental protection: through public regulation and of course instantaneous, effective, and efficient implementation and enforcement. Yet these same citizens are also wary of 'too big government'.

In the context of these developments new forms of food governance have emerged, notably new European Union food law, private food standards, corporate social responsibility initiatives, and transnational regulation. The current landscape of food governance contains a growing diversity of regulatory arrangements: public, private and hybrid, on national, transnational and global levels.

In response to food crises, the decline in consumer confidence and the threat of losing export markets, the European Union strengthened its food safety legislation and established the European Food Safety Authority. The European Commission responded to the accusation of lack of transparency and of manipulation during the BSE crisis with proposals for radical reform. It adopted an approach emphasizing food safety and consumer protection based on three general principles:

1. separation of the responsibility for legislation and for scientific advice;
2. separation of the responsibility for legislation and for inspection; and
3. greater transparency and information during decision-making and inspection.

The 2002 General Food Law lays down the general principles and covers the entire food supply chain, including not only food safety requirements but also issues of animal health, product quality, cattle feed and sustainability. European directives are replaced by regulations; regulations are a more immediate and hence stronger legal form because they are directly applicable, i.e. they do not need transposition by member states in national legislation to become effective.[4]

Several European member states have established new regulatory agencies or reformed existing agencies to oversee the food control activities (see Abels and Kobusch in this volume). Likewise, the Chinese governmental agencies responded to several food crises, and their negative effects on the reputation of Chinese export products with legal reforms and other measures (Collins and Gottwald; Burns et al. in this volume).

Producers and suppliers have become primarily responsible for food safety, while national governments have become responsible for controlling the adequacy of risk controlling mechanisms of companies in the food chain. Because of their legal responsibility and out of fear for potential reputation damage due to food scandals caused by claims of unsafe or unfair food products, the food industry and retailers have developed initiatives for decreasing food safety risks and increasing consumer confidence in food products. In the 1990s several large food manufacturers and supermarket chains developed their own quality control systems. In order to control the input, the companies want to make sure that the goods they purchase will meet particular standards and qualifications. A company quality control system often includes requirements for suppliers. For example, in the 1990s several British and Dutch supermarket chains contractually obliged suppliers to meet a comprehensive quality assurance standard, including unexpected inspections at farms, gardens and plants (e.g. Albert Heijn (AH) in the Netherlands, Tesco and Sainsbury's in the United Kingdom) (Havinga and Jettinghoff 1999, Havinga 2006). Since the 1990s private retail standards have expanded dramatically. Food retailers joined forces to harmonize supplier standards. Regulation of food safety by retailers using quasi-legislation as an instrument to force trade partners to take food safety measures evolved from regulation that originated from one supermarket chain to regulation of the united supermarkets. These standards are often monitored by independent certification and inspection organizations. National private certification schemes have crossed borders and became global or transnational (Fuchs et al. 2011; Fagotto in this volume).

Retailers use their purchasing power to impose food safety and quality requirements, as well as other specific product and process preferences, on farmers and food industry suppliers. Given the ever growing size of these food retail chains, suppliers are dependent on them and have to comply with their requirements if they want to sell (Boselie et al. 2003; Grabosky 1994, 429–432; Havinga 2006; Marsden et al. 2000, 2010).

Next to retail driven standards many other private food standards have emerged, initiated and promoted by the food industry, trading corporations, trade associations and non-profit civil society organizations or NGOs. Their objectives range from securing safe food to improving animal welfare, protecting the environment, labour rights, or ensuring fair trade. Examples include fair trade labels, sustainability, religious food standards (see Van Waarden and Van Dalen in this volume), organic food labels, food safety, vegetarian or biodynamic labels (Van der Meulen 2011).

In these new forms of regulation, private actors are assuming pivotal roles in rule-making, monitoring compliance, and enforcement. The food industry, and retail corporations in particular, have become key players in the governance of the global food system through the creation of governance institutions such as private standards, corporate social responsibility initiatives (CSR) and public-private or private-private partnerships. Kalfagianni and Fuchs (in this volume) and Oosterveer (in this volume) investigate the source of legitimacy and accountability of these private forms of governance.

Recently hybrid governance forms have also been developed involving both governmental and private actors. This hybridisation has consequences for the conceptualisation of regulatory roles and forms of governance (Havinga in this volume). Cooperation between government and industry in food governance challenges the existing distribution of power and responsibilities (Van der Voort in this volume).

1.5   AIM AND STRUCTURE OF THIS VOLUME

This volume examines the changing new governance of food. The introductory part sketches the developments and institutional challenges in food governance and the new forms of food regulation that have been developed. Tetty Havinga argues that new private and mixed forms of food regulation ask for a rethinking of the relevant distinctions between the actors involved and the roles they play in the regulatory process. A regulatory regime performs five functions: (1) rule making; (2) adoption of the rules; (3) implementation of the rules; (4) monitoring compliance; and (5) enforcement. Havinga contends that the traditional distinctions between public and private actors, and between state, market and civil society actors, masks interdependence, conflicts of interest and power, and advocates a more detailed analysis.

Part II investigates public policy responses to the challenges posed by food crises, in particular in the European Union and its Member States, and in China. Gabriele Abels and Alexander Kobusch analyze the national institutional choices concerning independent food safety agencies in 23 out of the 27 EU Member States. In so doing, they question whether these choices can be explained by path dependency or rather as a phenomenon of Europeanization. Abels and Kobush classify food risk governance regimes in three organizational models:

1. the bi-institutional model (risk assessment separated from risk management);
2. the integrated model (one food authority is responsible for both risk assessment and risk management); and
3. a fragmented model (during period of transition).

Both Europeanization and national historical tradition are shown to have been important in Austria, Sweden and Hungary – these three countries each represent a specific organizational model of food risk governance.

Drawing on case law and reforms of animal health legislation, Gareth Enticott and Robert Lee analyse the way the United Kingdom deals with animal diseases. For Enticott and Lee, compensation provided by the state when diseased animals are slaughtered should incentivise good practice, deter illegal or inappropriate practices and provide a fair system. They conclude that the current UK compensation system provides limited incentive for bio-security and has led to some perverse effects.

The next two chapters shift the focus from the European Union to China. The Chinese food safety system is important from a European perspective because of China's significance as a trading partner with the European Union, and recent food scares such as milk tainted with melamine. Neil Collins and Jörn-Carsten Gottwald analyze the impact of the new Chinese Food Safety Law 2009 on Chinese regulatory practice. They examine four dimensions: (1) organization; (2) guiding principles; (3) configuration of actors; and (4) specific reform capacity. The authors examine how the pressures of local interests have been accommodated to the demands of globalized capitalism. Furthermore, Collins and Gottwald illustrate the changing nature of the relationship of the state and its regulations to the citizens of China, again sometimes by conceding, sometimes by coercing.

John Burns, Jing Li and Xiaoqi Wang's comparative study of the Chinese mainland and Taiwan's reaction to adulterated milk powder highlights that politicians make institutional choices for the delivery of public services, including the regulation of food safety, based on the incentive systems through which they operate. On the mainland an incentive system that rewards officials for fulfilling a narrow range of targets has had the unintended consequence that they relatively ignore non-targeted policy goals. Pressure for food safety reform has probably come mostly from China's external trade partners. In Taiwan local officials are also looking up to their bureaucratic principals but the incentive system of competitive elections in a system with media freedom and a well developed civil society means that the public as principal is also important. Public disgust with the handling of a food safety crisis opened a window for administrative reform that could improve policy coordination through centralization.

Part III deals with new forms of private food governance. Peter Oosterveer investigates whether the theoretical frameworks of Sassen and Rosenau might enable us to better understand (environmental) authority in the global governance of food, and in particular, the balance that should be established between the public and the private sphere. Using the cases of two private food standards (GlobalG.A.P. and Marine Stewardship Council [MSC]), Oosterveer concludes that these standards do not derive their authority and legitimacy from formal procedures but from intended output. The case of MSC shows that a private standard is capable of including countervailing power within the regulatory arrangement. Developing upon Sassen and Rosenau, Oosterveer points to the role of science in food governance.

Effectiveness is a crucial criterion for the legitimacy of private forms of governance as it is frequently identified as private actors' claim to legitimacy. In their analysis of the effectiveness of GlobalG.A.P. in fostering sustainable development, Agni Kalfagianni and Doris Fuchs focus on the stringency of the GlobalG.A.P. standard. They argue that effectiveness is a function of external pressure, internal collaborative structures, and characteristics of available solutions, as well as the size and heterogeneity of the group of actors designing and implementing the governance institution. They expect that a 'larger degree of decision-making power of environmental and social NGOs in the GlobalG.A.P. governance mechanisms would likely have led to a different outcome (more stringency)'.

Federica Casarosa and Marco Gobbato analyze private quality standards operating in interfirm networks in the wine sector. Based on questionnaires answered by enterprises and institutional actors in five European countries, several models of networks, built by companies to achieve quality, are distinguished. While standard setting seems less costly in contractual networks compared to organizational networks, implementation may be more difficult in a contractual network.

Frans van Waarden and Robin van Dalen characterize the market for halal certificates in the Netherlands as a case of complex (proto)regulation in a liberalized market where increasingly a need for regulation is being felt. In the absence of any public regulation there have been multiple private initiatives for halal quality regulation in the form of organizations offering halal certification and halal hallmarks. However, consumers do not know how to value these halal certificates, the market is opaque, and a supreme authority seems to be required.

Part IV deals with situations of both public and private governance and investigates their interaction. Taking a law and economics approach, Elena Fagotto explores whether transnational private food safety arrangements complement or compete with public food safety regulation. She argues that private actors have significant incentives to achieve food safety, and that there is a strong alignment of public and private interests in providing safe food. As such, private food safety arrangements could offer a solution for known weaknesses of public regulation, namely institutional fragmentation, international dimension and insufficient enforcement capacity. Nevertheless, Fagotto warns not to replace public with private regulation given the shortcomings in the enforcement of private regulation by third party certification bodies.

Developing countries' exports are affected by food safety regulations and standards imposed by both EU governmental and non-governmental actors, such as those imposed by retailers. Vanessa Constant Laforce analyzes, from a legal perspective, the nexus between these two forms of food safety requirements, with a particular focus on pesticides. The export of tropical fruits from developing countries to the EU has largely increased during the last decade. SPS requirements and pesticide residues levels are the major trade obstacles for developing countries' opportunities to access the EU market. Private standards such as GlobalG.A.P. exceed official import requirements and are widely criticized by developing countries because they are significant barriers to their export.

The last chapter is a case study of a hybrid form of food governance. Haiko van der Voort analyzes an attempt of the Dutch government to incorporate private regulation. Van der Voort utilises the concept of 'metagovernance' to analyze change in a co-regulation regime on safeguarding the quality of Dutch eggs. Van der Voort sketches two perspectives on metagovernance: (i) metagovernance as design; and (ii) metagovernance as management. The Dutch Ministry of Agriculture has adopted an elaborate policy framework that describes institutional requirements for cooperation with industries and their self regulatory bodies, stressing the final responsibility of the government for the quality of the regulations and oversight. The egg quality system of the poultry sector was brought under this regime. Actors from the industry, the government and the certification industry were involved in this regulatory arrangement.

NOTES

1. New York Times, http://graphics8.nytimes.com/images/2010/04/04/business/04metrics_g/04metrics_g-popup-v2.jpg (last accessed 23 May 2012). In 2009, people in the US consumed 787 pounds per capita packaged food and 602 pounds fresh food; in Spain, 759 pounds packaged and 621 pounds fresh food; and in France, 739 pounds packaged and 462 pounds fresh food.
2. Kennisbank Voedselveiligheid VWA, Melamine, www.vwa.nl; David Bradley, Melamine contaminated food list, http://www.sciencebase.com/science-blog/melamine-contaminated-food-list.html; http://www.niernieuws.nl/?id=1747&cat=&loc=5#; http://evmi.nl/voedselveiligheid-kwaliteit/melamine-duikt-op-in-pindakoek/; http://evmi.nl/voedselveiligheid-kwaliteit/ah-waarschuwt-voor-melamine-zoutjes/ (all documents accessed 9 May 2012).
3. BBC, 'BSE and CJD: Crisis Chronology', http://news.bbc.co.uk/hi/english/static/in_depth/health/2000/bse/1996.stm, accessed 28 May 2012.
4. Regulation (EC) No 178/2002 of the European Parliament and of the Council laying down the general principles and requirements of food law, establishing the European Food Safety Authority and laying down procedures in matters of food safety (also referred to as the General Food Law). The three basic EU food hygiene regulations are: Regulation (EC) 852/2004 on the hygiene of foodstuffs, Regulation (EC) 853/2004 laying down specific hygiene rules for food of animal origin, and Regulation (EC) 854/2004 laying down specific rules for the organization of official controls on products of animal origin intended for human consumption.

REFERENCES

Beck, U. (1992), *Risk Society. Towards a New Modernity*, London: Sage Publications.

Beckert, J. and P. Aspers (eds) (2011), *The Worth of Goods. Valuation and Pricing in the Economy*, Oxford: Oxford University Press.

Boselie, D., S. Henson and D. Weatherspoon (2003), 'Supermarket Procurement Practices in Developing Countries: Redefining the Roles of the Public and Private Sectors', *American Journal of Agricultural Economics*, 85, 1155–1161.

Caduff, L. and T. Bernauer (2006), 'Managing Risk and Regulation in European Food Safety Governance', *Review of Policy Research*, 23, 153.

Campbell, H. (2006), 'Consultation, Commerce and Contemporary Agri-Food Systems: Ethical Engagement of New Systems of Governance under Reflexive Modernity', *The Integrated Assessment Journal*, 6, 117, 126.

Djelic, M-L. and K. Sahlin-Anderson (2006), 'Introduction: A World of

Governance: The Rise of Transnational Regulation', in M-L. Djelic and K. Sahlin-Anderson (eds), *Transnational Governance: Institutional Dynamics of Regulation*, Cambridge: Cambridge University Press, pp. 1–28.

Drori, G. et al. (2002), *Science in the Modern World Polity: Institutionalization and Globalization*, Redwood City: Stanford University Press.

Drori, G.S. and J.W. Meyer (2006), 'Scientization: Making a World Safe for Organizing', in M-L. Djelic and K. Sahlin-Anderson (eds), *Transnational Governance: Institutional Dynamics of Regulation*, Cambridge: Cambridge University Press, pp. 31–52.

Fuchs, D., A. Kalfagianni and T. Havinga (2011), 'Actors in Private Food Governance: The Legitimacy of Retail Standards and Multi-Stakeholder Initiatives with Civil Society Participation', *Agriculture and Human Values*, 28, 353–367.

Grabosky, P.N. (1994), 'Green Markets: Environmental Regulation by the Private Sector', *Law & Policy*, 16, 419–448.

Hatanaka, M., C. Bain and L. Busch (2005), 'Third-Party Certification in the Global Agri-food System', *Food Policy*, 30, 354.

Havinga, T. (2006), 'Private Regulation of Food Safety by Supermarkets', *Law & Policy*, 28, 515–533.

Havinga, T. and A. Jettinghoff (1999), 'Self-Regulation in Business: Beyond Associational Self-Regulation', in F. Van Loon and L. Van Aeken (eds), *60 maal recht en 1 maal wijn: Rechtssociologie, Sociale problemen en justitieel beleid, Liber Amicorum prof. dr. Jean Van Houtte*, Leuven: Acco, pp. 609–620.

Henson, S. and J. Humphrey (2010), 'Understanding the Complexities of Private Standards in the Global Agri-Food Chains as They Impact Developing Countries', *Journal of Development Studies*, 46, 1628.

Jacobsson, B. (2000), 'Standardization and Expert Knowledge', in N. Brunnson, B. Jacobsson and Associates (eds), *A World of Standards*, Oxford: Oxford University Press, p.40.

Kysar, D.A. (2004), 'Preferences for Processes', *Harvard Law Review*, 118, 525.

Loeber, A., M. Hajer and L. Levidow (2011), 'Agro-Food Crisis: Institutional and Discursive Changes in the Food Scares Era', *Science as Culture*, 20, 147–155.

Marsden, T., A. Flynn and M. Harrison (2000), *Consuming Interests. The Social Provision of Foods*, London: UCL Press.

Marsden, T., R. Lee, A. Flynn and S. Thankappan (2010), *The New Regulation and Governance of Food. Beyond the Food Crisis?*, New York/London: Routledge.

McCabe-Sellers, B.J. and S.E. Beattie (2004), 'Food Safety: Emerging Trends in Foodborne Illness Surveillance and Prevention', *Journal of the American Dietetic Association*, 104, 1708–1717.

Moran, M. (2002), 'Review Article: Understanding the Regulatory State', *British Journal of Political Science*, 32, 391.

Van der Meulen, B. (ed.) (2011), *Private Food Law. Governing Food Chains through Contract Law, Self-regulation, Private Standards, Audits and Certification Schemes*, Wageningen: Wageningen Academic Publishers.

Van Kreyl, C.F. and A.G.A.G. Knaap (eds) (2004), *Ons Eten Gemeten. Gezonde Voeding en Veilig Voedsel in Nederland.* Houten: Bohn Stafleu Van Loghum.

Vos, E. (2000), 'EU Food Safety Regulation in the Aftermath of the BSE Crisis', *Journal of Consumer Policy*, 23, 227–255.

2. Conceptualizing regulatory arrangements: Complex networks and regulatory roles[1]

Tetty Havinga

2.1 INTRODUCTION

Food regulation nowadays involves a broad variety of actors, including government agencies as well as other stakeholders. In this chapter I explore which actors are involved in private and mixed forms of food regulation. This question is important when considering such issues as the effectiveness, legitimacy and accountability of regulatory regimes. I argue that a dichotomous distinction between public (governmental) and private (non-governmental) regulation is not an adequate conceptualization for analyzing the reconfiguration of relationships between the actors involved in food regulation. We need more sophisticated distinctions linking the type of actor to the role they play in the regulatory process. I disentangle the regulatory process into multiple regulatory roles in order to analyze complex patterns of actor involvement in a regulatory regime.

The regulation and governance of food has changed dramatically in recent decades. Traditional food regulation consisted of national governments enacting food legislation and enforcing compliance with the laws. Several developments in society have contributed to the emergence of national and transnational private or mixed forms of food regulation.

Food supply chains are increasingly becoming international. Fresh products are sourced all over the world to assure Western consumers a continuous stream of fruits and vegetables throughout the year. Many processed food products are made up of a variety of ingredients, drawn from all over the world. Regulating complex global food supply chains is difficult for national governments since their jurisdiction is limited to their own national territory.

Food safety issues have been transformed from a predominantly neutral, technical issue that is the preserve of food experts into a contested political matter that is debated in parliament, on television and in the newspapers. Food scares and incidents such as mad cow disease (BSE), contaminated milk, and EHEC have received wide media attention. The risks connected with food have become increasingly visible.

Traditional government food regulation was perceived as no longer adequate, similarly to government regulation in other domains. Traditional regulation is believed to be ineffective and inflexible, while it disregards the responsibilities of citizens, businesses and social organizations. The way both the UK government and the EU handled the BSE crisis is often cited as a turning point, which demonstrated an urgent need to transform food regulation.

These social developments resulted in a shift towards private and mixed forms of regulation and a shift from national government regulation towards European Union regulation. In an attempt to restore consumer confidence and to retain export markets, governments in Brussels and the EU member states enacted stricter food safety regulations and reorganized the government food safety system. Food producers and suppliers expressly bore primary responsibility for food safety while national governments became responsible for controlling the adequacy of risk control mechanisms of companies in the food chain. As a result of their legal responsibility and from a fear of potential damage to their reputation in case unsafe food products should find their way to the market, the food industry and food retailers developed initiatives to decrease food safety risks and increase consumer confidence in safe food.

These reforms involved the emergence of new forms of food regulation, including transnational private food standards, corporate social responsibility initiatives, and codes of conduct. These transformations involve a new relationship and a changed distribution of responsibilities between government bodies on the one side and private actors on the other. New forms of food regulation are characterized by a less dominant role for the government and more responsibilities for private actors (Havinga 2006; Henson and Humphrey 2011; Marsden et al. 2010; Oosterveer 2005). These new forms of food regulation include not only public actors but also private actors, such as firms, NGOs and other organizations both inside and outside the food supply chain. Government regulation is moving from a prescriptive, command-and-control system towards an enforced self-regulatory approach (Braithwaite 1982; Hutter 2011; Martinez et al. 2007) in which the government lays down broad standards and leaves it to companies to develop, implement and monitor risk management systems. An example is the European General Food Law, which requires all food businesses to have controls that demonstrate how they manage food safety risks.

Recent trends are the emergence of retailer-led food governance and global coalitions for setting food safety standards, an increased use of global business-to-business standards and third party certification (Fulponi 2006; Harrison 1997; Hatanaki and Busch 2008; Havinga 2006; Marsden et al. 2000, 2010). Another trend is the increase of consumer hallmarks for 'new' issues, such as animal welfare, fair trade, sustainability, healthy food, and halal food.

Marsden et al. (2010) describe the new situation as the Public-Private Model of Food Regulation.

2.1.1 Various Forms of Food Regulation

Regulation is a means for controlling harm in the public interest in order to protect consumers, citizens and the environment (Hutter 2011, 10). Henson and Caswell (1999) distinguish between direct and indirect regulation of food safety (table 2.1). Direct regulation entails obligatory prescriptions and requirements for the production and handling of food to assure the production of safe food. Even though indirect regulation does not provide prescriptions for the production and the product, it is nevertheless expected to act as an incentive to implement food safety controls indirectly by shifting the cost-benefit balance or by imposing process requirements. For example, liability law is assumed to promote food safety by encouraging producers to do their best to produce safe products (Havinga 2010). A food company's consumer complaint procedure is an example of private, indirect regulation because the expectation is that learning from complaints will increase the product's quality. Direct regulation is intended to provide food safety whereas indirect regulation may aim at increasing food safety; however, a contribution to food safety may also be an unintended de facto effect.

Table 2.1   Types of food safety regulation

Source of the rules	Character of the rules	
	Direct	*Indirect*
Public	Dutch Commodities Act (Warenwet) UK 1990 Food Safety Act EU General Food Law	Product liability law TBT-GATT agreement
Hybrid Public-private	Industry guide to good hygienic practice	Liability insurance policy
Private	Private food safety certification scheme (GlobalG.A.P., MSC)	Food company complaints procedure

Until recently, most research on food safety has focused on direct forms of food safety regulation. Recently, however, not only public regulatory arrangements but also private forms of direct food safety regulation have started to attract attention (Fuchs et al. 2011; Fulponi 2006; Havinga 2006; Henson and Reardon 2005; Lytton and MacAllister 2014; Marsden et al. 2000, 2010; Martinez et al. 2007; Rothstein 2005; Van Waarden 2006; Verbruggen 2013).

This chapter deals with two questions in the context of the reconfiguration of the relationships between the various actors: which actors are involved in the new food regulatory arrangements? And which roles do these actors play?

2.2   PUBLIC AND PRIVATE ACTORS IN REGULATORY ARRANGEMENTS

Some authors only distinguish between public and private actors (e.g. Spruyt 2001; Josling, Roberts and Orden 2004, 156), state and non-state actors or government and non-government actors. Daniel Stewart (2010) implicitly distinguishes state actors from non-state actors in his analysis of the availability of judicial review to the actions of non-state actors. Bingen and Busch (2006, 246) observe 'a constantly evolving and changing global network of relationships among public and private, mandatory, voluntary, and national and international standards bodies instead of neatly delineated public and private responsibilities'.

Several authors on environmental regulation and sustainability have replaced this public-private dichotomy by the following threefold classification: state, market and civil society (table 2.2). In their analysis of non-state, market-driven governance systems, Bernstein and Cashore (2007, 356) and Abbott and Snidal (2009a, 2009b) distinguish between two types of non-state actors: firms and NGOs. A similar threefold classification is made by Levi-Faur (2011), who distinguishes between civil, market,

Table 2.2   Threefold classifications of actors involved in regulation

Abbott & Snidal 2009	Levi-Faur 2011	Marsden et al. 2010
States	State actors	Policy & regulatory interests
Firms	Market actors	Private interests
NGOs	Civil actors	Consumer & social interests

and state actors. For Levi-Faur, a non-governmental organization can be controlled by civil society actors (CiNGO), market actors (MaNGO), or state actors (GoNGO): 'This distinction between different types of NGOs which act as regulators will allow us to develop a clearer understanding of hybrid designs of regulatory institutions.' Because of the ambivalent definition of NGO I prefer to speak of civil actors (alongside government or state actors and firms or market actors).

2.2.1 The Governance Triangle

Abbott and Snidal (2009a) visualize the variety of regulatory standard-setting (RSS) in their Governance Triangle (figure 2.1). They distinguish three groups of actors directly involved in RSS: states, firms and NGOs. Abbott and Snidal consider RSS rules to be a form of regulation, even though they are voluntary (that is, not legally mandatory).

The seven zones in the triangle indicate the three forms of single-actor standards (1–3), three forms of dual-actor standards (4–6) and one form involving direct participation of all three groups of actors (7). Abbott and Snidal included only four food standards in their governance triangle;[2] in another publication they include another two food standards.[3] Further food standards could easily be included. Most food regulatory

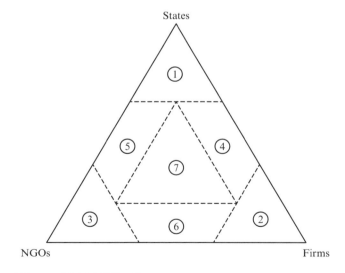

Source: Abbott and Snidal 2009a, 50.

Figure 2.1 The governance triangle

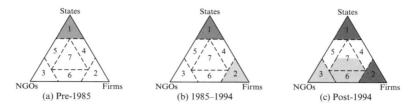

Source: Abbott and Snidal 2009a, 53.

Figure 2.2   *Evolution of the governance triangle over time*

arrangements are situated in zone 1 (state regulation) and zone 2 (industrial self-regulation).

Abbott and Snidal show the evolution of the governance triangle
(figure 2.2). In the pre-1985 period there are only a few RSS schemes,
mostly in zone 1 (state). The decade between 1985 and 1994 shows the
emergence of RSS schemes, especially firm schemes, as well as the first
multi-stakeholder and NGO schemes. The post-1994 period shows a continued proliferation of firm schemes and an increasing number of NGO
schemes, as well as the emergence of collaborative schemes (NGOs and
firms or tripartite, zones 6 and 7).

The governance triangle is useful for analyzing changes in regulatory
standards over time and for comparing regulatory arrangements between
different sectors or countries. Food regulatory schemes are dominated
by state regulation (zone 1) and by firm schemes (zone 2). This applies
particularly to food safety standards. The food standards that involve
civil actors are mainly concerned with other issues such as sustainability
or fair trade, but it is quite possible that civil actors will become more
important in food regulation in the future. We can already witness an
increase in the numbers of these actors in the regulatory domain, devoted
to social interests (e.g. fair trade), environmental interests (e.g. organic
food), or animal welfare (e.g. free-range meat).[4] It remains to be seen
whether future regulation in this field will develop in the way Abbott and
Snidal suggest.

However, an analysis focused on actor types also has its drawbacks.
Let us look at the example of GlobalG.A.P. (Global Partnership
for Good Agricultural Practices). GlobalG.A.P. is a private sector
body originally set up by European supermarket chains to set standards for the certification of agricultural products around the globe.
GlobalG.A.P. is classified as a single-actor standard in the Governance
triangle (Zone 2). In fact, however, GlobalG.A.P. is not a single-actor

standard, but a standard set by actors from one single category of actors (firms). Multiple actors are involved in GlobalG.A.P., all with very different positions and interests.

GlobalG.A.P. is a membership organization with three different types of members: retail and food service members, producer/supplier members and associate members such as certification bodies, consultancies; and the crop protection industry. Conflicts of interest exist within these member categories, for example between multinational supermarket corporations and small local retailers or between aquaculture industries in Norway and Thailand. Moreover, other stakeholders such as environmental NGOs, scientific experts and government officials are also involved in working groups and meetings of GlobalG.A.P.

The focus on actor types in the regulatory triangle neglects the possibility that a 'single-actor standard' might involve multiple actors with conflicting interests. Furthermore, retail food standards (e.g. the British Retail Consortium Global Standards), halal certification (e.g. the quality system of the Halal Correct Certification Foundation) and traditional industrial self-regulation (e.g. the South Africa Olive Commitment to Compliance scheme or the Unilever Supplier Qualification System) are zone 2 standards in the governance triangle, just like GlobalG.A.P., although they differ significantly in terms of the actors involved. We should therefore differentiate between various actors.

Authors on food regulation tend to focus less on NGOs or civil society than authors on environmental regulation, probably because civil society actors do not play a significant role in many food regulatory arrangements. Because of this, I neglected to include civil society organizations in an analysis of shifts in food safety regulation (Havinga 2006). However, in the field of food safety it is particularly important to distinguish between different types of private actors, so I distinguished three important institutional actors in this field: state (government agencies), industry (food industry and farmers) and third parties[5] (private auditing and certification organizations, retailers and consumer organizations) (Havinga 2006). Fuchs et al. (2011, 360) stress the importance of retailers in food regulation when they distinguish four types of stakeholders in private retail food standards: 1) retailers, 2) producers: food industry, growers, fishers, 3) certification bodies and 4) civil society and NGOs.

Dilling et al. (2008, 3–4) distinguish three actor constellations from which the para-legal systems of the business world emerge: single enterprises (corporate self-responsibility), transnational corporate networks and non-governmental organization-business partnerships.

2.2.2   Analyzing Networks and Production Chains

In another body of literature, authors do analyze the networks or production chains connected to a particularly food regulatory regime.

Marsden et al. (2010, 120) distinguish between three types of interest in
the new hybrid food policy-formation network:

1.   Policy and regulatory interests;
2.   Private interests; and
3.   Consumer and social interests.

These types of interest correspond to the three actor categories in the
regulatory triangle proposed by Abbott and Snidal (state, firms, NGOs,
see figure 2.1). Marsden et al. (2010, 283, italics in original, 290) argue that
'it is the *interactions* between public and private actors that are essential
to a fuller understanding of the food system' and the boundaries between
public, private and civil society interests become less clear with time.
Other authors also observe the blurring of the public-private distinction
and the rise of hybrid organizations and networks combining government
and non-governmental actors (e.g. Bingen and Busch 2006; Black 2002;
Havinga 2006; Hutter 2011; Levi-Faur 2011).

In their analysis of the new regulation and governance of food, Marsden
et al. pay attention to a variety of actors such as UK and EU government
bodies, corporate retailers, farmers, producers, manufacturers, global
standard-setting organizations, private certification bodies, logistic firms,
environmental and social NGOs. They paint a picture of various complex
networks involving many organizations and regulations (figure 2.3).

Bush and Oosterveer (2007, 391) describe export firms as key actors
in the shrimp trade, linking local producers in Thailand and Vietnam
with global trade networks. They conclude that certification bodies are
unable to audit the chain below the level of exporters, where capital
and information flow through informal, diffuse trade networks. This
governance arrangement involves a complex mix of state and non-state
actors: bureaucrats, retailers, wholesalers, importers and exporters,
local trade networks, producers, NGOs, processing companies and
consumers.

In a study of public-private protection of forests and fish (Forest
Stewardship Council and Marine Stewardship Council), Van Waarden
(2010) points to the involvement of a wide range of actors from all phases
in the value chain, with different interests, as one of the factors contributing to the success of these schemes: small and large scale fisheries, fishery
associations and cooperatives, suppliers, manufacturers, distribution,

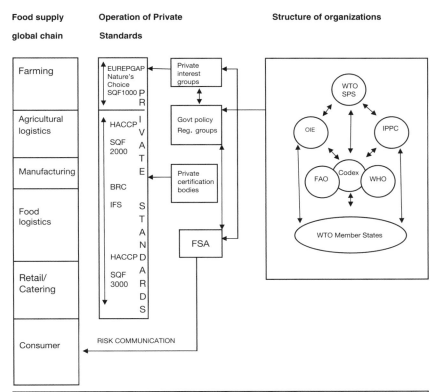

Food supply global chain

Operation of Private Standards

Structure of organizations

Abbreviations: BRC (British Retail Consortium), EurepGap (Euro-Retailer Produce Working Group Good Agricultural Practice), FAO (Food and Agriculture Organisation), FSA (Food Standards Agency), HACCP (Hazard Analysis and Critical Point), IFS (International Food Standards), IPPC (International Plant Protection Convention), OIE (Organisation Mondiale de la Santé Animale/ World Organisation for Animal Health), SPS (Sanitary and Phytosanitary Measures), SQF (Safe Quality Food), WHO (World Health Organisation), WTO (World Trade Organisation)

Source: Marsden et al. 2010, 280.

Figure 2.3 Regulation in the food supply chain and the role of different global organizations

retailers, scientists, indigenous people's organizations, fishery communities and environmental groups.

To conclude, the broad threefold categorization of actors involved in regulation (state actors, firms and civil society) is useful in analyzing the balance between these three actor types in comparative perspective, whether historical, as Abbot and Snidal do, or when comparing countries, industries or fields of regulation. However, a more sophisticated categorization of firms is needed for analyzing the involvement of actors in non-governmental and hybrid systems of food regulation. When analyzing the effectiveness and legitimacy of a regulatory regime it is important to distinguish between non-governmental actors which are regulated (regulatees), non-governmental actors which are part of the production chain but are not regulated themselves by the regulation under consideration (such as retailers), and non-governmental actors providing services to the regulated industry (such as certification and auditing organizations).[6] The increasing role of transnational and international government bodies in food regulation means it is inevitable also to distinguish between different levels of state actors. Following Marsden et al. (2010), civil society interests can be broken down into social interests (e.g. child labour, fair trade, occupational health, public health), environmental interests (e.g. biodiversity, sustainability, insecticides) and consumer interests (e.g. food safety, food security, choice and price).[7] Table 2.3 provides a survey of these distinctions.

2.3   REGULATORY ROLES

Traditional command-and-control regulation is conceptualised as state legislation. However, a regulatory regime comprises not only legislation and other rules. Picciotto (2002) conceptualised regulation as consisting of three elements: rule-making, monitoring compliance and enforcement.

Levi-Faur (2011) distinguishes further between three roles: regulator, regulatee and third party.[8] Combining these three roles with three actor types, he distinguishes 27 types of third party regulatory designs (table 2.4).

Mattli and Woods (2009) include implementation in their definition of regulation: 'the organisation and control of economic, political, and social activities by means of making, implementing, monitoring, and enforcing of rules'. Adding implementation implies that we should consider the regulatees as part of the regulatory regime.

For Abbott and Snidal (2009a, 63) the regulatory process comprises five main stages (or tasks):

1. Agenda-setting (placing an issue on the regulatory agenda);
2. Negotiation (negotiating, drafting and promulgating standards);
3. Implementation (implementing standards within the operations of targets of regulation such as firms);
4. Monitoring compliance; and

Table 2.3   Types of actors involved in regulation and their position in the supply chain

Type of actor		Position in regulation/supply chain	Actor role
State		– Transnational level – (Federal) level – State level – Local level	
Non-state/private	Market/firms	Inside regulated supply chain	– Regulatees – Associations of regulated industry – Firms up- or downstream in supply chain not target of regulation at hand
		Outside regulated supply chain	– Providing services (e.g. standard setting, auditing, certification, disinfectants, training, consultancy)
	Civil society (NGOs)		– Social interest groups – Environmental interest groups – Consumer interest groups

5. Enforcement (promoting compliance and responding to non-compliance).

Agenda-setting is added to rule-making. Abbott and Snidal use the abbreviation ANIME to refer to these five stages.

In my examination of private forms of food regulation such as GlobalG.A.P. and BRC, there seems to be one important phase missing in ANIME. In traditional command-and-control regulation, after making the rules, the next phase is implementing the rules. However, in private regulation drafting and promulgating, the rules are not enough. Rules from GlobalG.A.P. or BRC, for instance, are not just being implemented

Table 2.4   Types of third party regulatory designs

	State actors as regulators (e.g. regulatory agencies; GoNGOs)			Market actors as regulators (e.g. MaNGOs)			Civil actors as regulators (e.g. CiNGOs)		
	S	M	C	S	M	C	S	M	C
Type of third party enlisted									
State actor as regulatees	SSS	SMS	SCS	MSS	MMS	MCS	CSS	CMS	CCS
Market actors as regulatees	SSM	SMM	SCM	MSM	MMM	MCM	CSM	CMM	CCM
Civil actors as regulatees	SSC	SMC	SCC	MSC	MMC	MCC	CSC	CMC	CCC

Note: First letter means the regulator; second represents the enlisted third party; third letter the regulatee; S=State; M=Market; C=Civil.

Source: Levi-Faur 2011, 9.

in farms or the food industry. It seems to be crucial that these rules were first promoted and eventually made mandatory by dominant market parties such as big supermarket chains.

Regulatees have to adopt a regulation. Adopting a regulation means deciding to accept the rules and to aim at compliance. By and large, an organization may adopt a regulation because it is legally mandatory, because compliance with the regulation is an obligation imposed by a dominant actor in the market (such as the combined retailers) or because the regulatee considers adoption beneficial for some reason (e.g. improving reputation, quality, market share, price). Henson and Humphrey meet this objection by including adoption in the five functions involved in making a food standard operational: standard-setting, adoption, implementation, conformity assessment and enforcement (2011, 155–156). They are right to argue that the distinction between standard setting and adoption clarifies the issue of compulsion and obligation.[9]

3.   CONCLUSIONS

When I started working on this chapter, my purpose was just to add some distinctions of actors to the three main actor types (state, firm, NGO) and to include some regulatory activities among the three elements of regulation (rule making, monitoring and enforcement). However, my work on the chapter, which involved reading and rereading the literature, revealed the high level of complexity of regulation. Many distinctions are only important in the context of particular regulatory arrangements or a particular inquiry. Besides, it often is more important to know whether the different tasks or functions (e.g. drafting the rules, adopting the rules, implementing the rules, assessing conformity and enforcing compliance) are carried out by the same organization or by three or more different organizations, than to know that all tasks are carried out by market actors (making this a single-actor regulation in the governance triangle).

Black (2008) sees accountability problems because regulatory roles and responsibilities are distributed among several actors (deciding on goals, drafting standard, monitoring, enforcement). It is impossible to call a standard-setter to account for enforcement of the rules or to call the enforcer to account for rules he did not make. Black (2008) asks: 'How to call to account a constellation of regulators?'

To make it even more complex: the involvement of actors and the roles they perform develop over time. Bernstein and Cashore (2007) showed for non-state, market-driven governance systems that political legitimacy is constructed in a three-phase process with different relationships between the actors and participation of different actors. Bernstein and Cashore distinguish between the initiation phase, the phase of widespread support and the phase of political legitimacy. A picture of the actors and roles involved in Eurepgap in 1997 differs significantly from the picture of GlobalG.A.P. in 2010 (Van der Kloet and Havinga 2008, Van der Kloet 2011). The picture will be different again at some other moment in time.

Five main functions seem to apply to every regulatory arrangement (table 2.5). These functions are similar to the functions Henson and Humphrey (2011) distinguish for food standards, but are worded slightly differently to make them universally applicable. For a regulatory arrangement to be effective, rules have to be laid down and subsequently adopted and implemented, and compliance with the rules has to be monitored and enforced. All regulatory activities can be thought of as part of one of these functions.

1. Rule making (standard setting);
2. Adoption;
3. Implementation;
4. Monitoring compliance (assessing conformity); and
5. Enforcement.

Table 2.5   Catalogue of regulatory activities connected to five main functions

Actions	Sideline actions
I. Rule making	
1. First step (initiator) agenda setting	– Lobbying
2. Determining the goals of regulation	– Risk assessment
3. Negotiating the rules	– Mobilizing resistance or support
4. Drafting the rules	– Adapting the rules (to new
5. Laying down the rules (deciding on and promulgating the rules)	situations and acquired experience)
6. Further regulations and implementing the rules	
II. Adoption	
7. Adopting the rules	– Promoting and supporting the rules
8. Imposing the rules on suppliers or other actors in the supply chain (making the rules compulsory for other actors)	– Educating & coaching – Facilitating
III. Implementation	
9. Implementing the rules within firms (or other targets of regulation/ regulatees)	– Promoting and supporting the rules – Educating & coaching – Facilitating
IV. Monitoring	
10. Testing	– Accrediting certification bodies
11. Inspecting	– Trademark assurance
12. Auditing, verifying	– Evaluating and adapting the
13. Certifying	monitoring strategy
14. Documenting	
15. Tracing non-compliant and undesirable behaviour	
V. Enforcement	
16. Sanctioning non-compliance (warning, fine, withdrawal certificate)	– Accrediting certification bodies – Trademark assurance – Developing instruments
17. Legal enforcement (prosecution, civil law claim, appeal)	and strategy in response to non-compliance – Evaluating and adapting the monitoring strategy

The activities of these five functions begin in this order although they overlap and often have a cyclical character. The rule-making activities may repeat on another level (e.g. EU, Member States, agencies) and after some time in the future (revision of rules). Adoption activities may be repeated up- or downstream in the food supply chain in case requirements are passed on (e.g. supermarket-manufacturer, import firm-export firm-farmers). Monitoring is a continuing process.

We need to analyze particular regulatory regimes and establish which actors are involved, how they are interrelated and what role they play. A crude distinction between three parties – state, market and civil society – masks interdependence, conflicts of interest and power. Knowledge of which particular actors are involved and what their role is in the regulatory social field reveals power relations that may have an effect on the reliability of a certificate, the level of compliance with prescriptions, and the openness of decision making. These insights might trigger government agencies to interfere or to monitor more actively.

NOTES

1. The author thanks Frans van Waarden, Jaap van der Kloet and the participants in the Regulating Food Safety and Quality Stream at the Regulation in the Age of Crisis Third Biennial Conference of the Standing Group on Regulatory Governance of the European Consortium for Political Research (ECPR), 17–19 June, 2010, Dublin, for their comments on earlier drafts of this chapter.
2. Marine Stewardship Council (MSC) 1997, Max Havelaar (MH) 1988 (fair trade coffee) and International Federation of Organic Agriculture Movements (IFOAM) 1972 (organic food), all three in zone 6 (dual-actor standards with involvement of firms and NGOs) and WHO Code of Marketing for Breast-milk Substitutes (BM) 1981 in zone 1 (state standard).
3. GlobalG.A.P. 1997 and SQF 1994 (Safe QualityFood), Abbott and Snidal 2009b, 513, both in zone 2.
4. See footnote 2 for some examples of zone 6 standards.
5. This concept of 'third party' differs from the concept of Levi-Faur.
6. Havinga 2008.
7. Animal rights groups do not fit into this categorization very well.
8. Levi-Faur 2010 distinguishes three main strategies in regulation: 1. first party regulation: Regulator = regulatee (self-regulation); 2. second party regulation: regulator independent of regulatee (e.g. state regulation of business, or retailer imposing regulation on suppliers); and 3. third party regulation – relationship between regulator and regulatee is mediated by a third party as independent auditor (e.g. EurepG.A.P.).
   The meaning of the concepts 'first party', 'second party' and 'third party' is not consistently used in the literature. e.g. Van Waarden 2012: first party = self-regulation by actor, second party = actor involved in transaction imposing standards, third party = independent actor not involved in transaction; Bingen and Busch 2006: first party = supplier, second party = buyer, third party = independent third party assessing compliance, fourth party = state/regulatory agency. Havinga (2006) categorized retailers setting food safety standards for their suppliers as third party regulation.
9. Both Meidinger and Van Waarden distinguish different functions for certification

schemes. Van Waarden (2010) distinguishes three main functions for a certification standard organization such as FSC and MSC: standard setting, accreditation, and trademark assurance. Meidinger arrives at four functions: standard setting, certifying compliance, accrediting certifiers and labeling products (2008, 265).

REFERENCES

Abbott, K.W. and D. Snidal (2009a), 'The Governance Triangle: Regulatory Standards Institutions in the Shadow of the State', in W. Mattli and N. Woods (eds), *The Politics of Global Regulation*, Princeton: Princeton University Press, pp. 44–88.

Abbott, K.W. and D. Snidal (2009b), 'Strengthening international regulation through transnational new governance: overcoming the orchestration deficit', *Van der Bilt Journal of Transnational Law*, 42, 501–578.

Bernstein, S. and B. Cashore (2007), 'Can non-state global governance be legitimate? An analytical framework', *Regulation & Governance*, 1, 1–25.

Bingen, J. and L. Busch (eds) (2006), *Agricultural Standards. The Shape of the Global Food and Fiber System*, Dordrecht: Springer Netherlands.

Black, J. (2002), *Critical Reflections on Regulation*, London: CARR Discussion Paper Series.

Black, J. (2008), 'Constructing and contesting legitimacy and accountability in polycentric regulatory regimes', *Regulation & Governance*, 2, 137–164.

Braithwaite, J. (1982), 'Enforced self-regulation: a new strategy for corporate crime control', *Michigan Law Review*, 80, 1466–1507.

Bush, S.R. and P. Oosterveer (2007), 'The missing link: intersecting governance and trade in the space of place and the space of flows', *Sociologia Ruralis*, 47, 384–399.

Dilling, O., M. Herberg and G. Winter (2008), 'Introduction: Private Accountability in a Globalising World', in O. Dilling, M. Herberg and G. Winter (eds), *Responsible Business. Self-Governance and Law in Transnational Economic Interactions*, Oxford, UK and Portland, Oregon: Hart Publishing, pp. 1–13.

Fuchs, D., A. Kalfagianni and T. Havinga (2011), 'Actors in private food governance: the legitimacy of retail standards and multi-stakeholder initiatives with civil society participation', *Agriculture and Human Values*, 28, 353–367.

Fulponi, L. (2006), 'Private voluntary standards in the food system: the perspective of major food retailers in OECD countries', *Food Policy*, 31, 1–13.

Harrison, M., T. Marsden and A. Flynn (1997), 'Contested regulatory practice and the implementation of food policy: exploring the local and national interface', *Transactions of the Institute of British Geographers*, 22, 473–487.

Hatanaka, M., C. Bain and L. Busch (2005), 'Third-party certification in the global agrifood system', in S. Henson and T. Reardon (eds), 'Private Agri-food Standards: Implications for Food Policy and Agri-food Systems', *Food Policy*, 30, 354–369.

Hatanaka, M. and L. Busch (2008), 'Third-party certification in the global agrifood system: an objective or socially mediated governance mechanism?', *Sociologia Ruralis*, 48(1), 73–91.

Havinga, T. (2006), 'Private regulation of food safety by supermarkets', *Law & Policy*, 28, 515–533.

Havinga, T. (2008), *Actors in Private Food Regulation. Taking Responsibility or Passing the Buck to Someone Else?*, Nijmegen Sociology of Law Working Papers Series 2008/01, Nijmegen: Institute for Sociology of Law.

Havinga, T. (2010), *The Influence of Liability Law on Food Safety. On Preventive Effects of Liability Claims and Liability Insurance*, Nijmegen Sociology of Law Working Papers Series 2010/02, Nijmegen: Institute for Sociology of Law.

Henson, S. and J. Caswell (1999), 'Food safety regulation: an overview of contemporary issues', *Food Policy*, 24, 589–603.

Henson, S. and J. Humphrey (2011), 'Codex Alimentarius and Private Standards', in B. Van der Meulen (ed.), *Private Food Law. Governing Food Chains through Contract Law, Self-Regulation, Private Standards, Audits and Certification Schemes*, Wageningen: Wageningen Academic Publishers, pp. 149–174.

Henson, S. and T. Reardon (2005), 'Private agri-food standards: implications for food policy and agri-food systems', *Food Policy*, 30, 241–253.

Hutter, B.M. (2011), *Managing Food Safety and Hygiene. Governance and Regulation as Risk Management*, Cheltenham/Northampton: Edward Elgar Publishing.

Josling, T., D. Roberts and D. Orden (2004), *Food Regulation and Trade. Towards a Safe and Open Global System*, Washington DC: Institute for International Economics.

Levi-Faur, D. (2011), 'Regulation and Regulatory Governance', in D. Levi-Faur (ed.), *Handbook on the Politics of Regulation*, Cheltenham: Edward Elgar Publishing, pp. 3–21.

Lytton, T.D. and L.K. MacAllister (2014), 'Oversight in private food safety auditing: Addressing auditor conflict of interest', *Wisconsin Law Review*, 2014(2), 289–335.

Marsden, T., A. Flynn and M. Harrison (2000), *Consuming Interests. The Social Provision of Foods*, London: UCL Press.

Marsden, T., R. Lee, A. Flynn and S. Thankappan (2010), *The New Regulation and Governance of Food. Beyond the Food Crisis?*, New York/London: Routledge.

Martinez, M.G., A. Fearne, J.A. Caswell and S. Henson (2007), 'Co-regulation as a possible model for food safety governance: Opportunities for public-private partnerships', *Food Policy*, 32, 299–314.

Mattli, W. and N. Woods (eds) (2009), *The Politics of Global Regulation*, Princeton: Princeton University Press.

Meidinger, E. (2008), 'Multi-Interest Self-Governance Through Global Product Certification Programmes', in O. Dilling, M. Herberg and G. Winter (eds), *Responsible Business. Self-Governance and Law in Transnational Economic Transactions*, Oxford, UK and Portland, Oregon: Hart Publishing, pp. 259–292.

Oosterveer, P. (2005), *Global Food Governance*, Wageningen: Wageningen University.

Picciotto, S. (2002), 'Introduction: reconceptualizing regulation in the era of globalization', *Journal of Law and Society*, 29, 1–11.

Rothstein, H. (2005), 'Escaping the regulatory net: why regulatory reform can fail consumers', *Law & Policy*, 27, 520–548.

Spruyt, H. (2001), 'The supply and demand of governance in standard-setting: insights from the past', *Journal of European Public Policy*, 8, 371–391.

Stewart, D. (2010), 'Excluding judicial review from the decisions of non-state actors', paper presented at the Regulation in the Age of Crisis Third Biennial

Conference of the Standing Group on Regulatory Governance of the European Consortium for Political Research (ECPR), Dublin, June 2010.

Van der Kloet, J. and T. Havinga (2008), *Private regulation of food safety from a regulatee's perspective*, Nijmegen Sociology of Law Working Papers Series 2008/07, Nijmegen: Institute for Sociology of Law.

Van der Kloet, J. (2011), 'Transnational Supermarket Standards in Global Supply Chains. The Emergence and Evolution of GlobalGAP', in J. Van der Kloet, B. De Hart and T. Havinga (eds), *Socio-Legal Studies in a Transnational World*, Special Issue *Recht der Werkelijkheid*, 3(32), 200–219.

Van Waarden, F. (2006), 'Taste, Tradition, Transactions, and Trust: The Public and Private Regulation of Food', in C. Ansell and D. Vogel (eds), *What's the Beef? The Contested Governance of European Food Safety*, Cambridge, MA: MIT Press, pp. 35–59.

Van Waarden, F. (2010), 'Governing Global Commons: Public-Private Protection of Fish and Forests', in J. Swinnen, J. Wouters, M. Maertens and A. Marx (eds), *Private Standards and Global Governance. Legal and Economic Perspectives*, Cheltenham: Edgar Elgar Publishing.

Van Waarden, F. (2011), 'Varieties of Private Market Regulation: Problems and Prospects', in D. Levi-Faur (ed.), *Handbook on the Politics of Regulation*, Cheltenham: Edward Elgar Publishing, pp. 469–485.

Verbruggen, P. (2013), 'Gorillas in the closet? Public and private actors in the enforcement of transnational private regulation', *Regulation & Governance*, 7(4), 512–532.

PART II

Public policy responses to food safety challenges

3. Regulation of food safety in the EU: Explaining organizational diversity among Member States

Gabriele Abels and Alexander Kobusch

3.1 INTRODUCTION

Triggered by major food scandals since the 1990s, European and national food safety policies and regulatory structures have been subject to profound reforms. In particular, the BSE crisis 'created a window of opportunity for the development of a more internally integrated food safety policy' (Ugland and Veggeland 2006, 618). Until then, food safety regulation had developed 'in a piecemeal fashion' (Alemanno 2006, 237). Scholars criticized a lack of relevant expertise in committees, the systematic exclusion of critical scientists, lack of timely release of information to the public, and the blending of science and politics (Buonanno 2006, 262–263). Accordingly, the organization of science and expertise was a major issue of the General European Food Law (GFL) adopted in early 2002. The GFL lays down principles on food safety regulation and specified rules for the newly founded European Food Safety Authority (EFSA), yet not for the institutional design of agencies at the *national* level. Most EU Member States set up agencies with different organizational features sometimes modelled after EFSA, and in other cases following national administrative traditions. How can we explain these institutional choices?

Based on a survey of all EU Member States and the EU level,[1] this chapter aims to identify patterns of risk regulation regimes and the forces that shaped them. Inspired by regulation theory and our empirical analysis, we employ two ideal types of regimes (Vos and Wendler 2006): those strictly separating risk assessment and risk management, and those taking an integrative approach. We then argue that a combination of European influences and domestic factors explains the institutional design. After introducing the separated model of EFSA, we focus on Austria (also taking Germany into account), Sweden, and Hungary. These countries each represent a specific organizational model and allow identifying explanations for different organizational choices.

3.2   IDEAL TYPES OF FOOD SAFETY REGIMES

The most important lesson learnt from the BSE crisis was that mingling scientific and policy responsibilities opens the door to intruding political and private interests, thus jeopardizing the independence and credibility of scientific expertise. The 'scientification of politics' and the concurrent 'politicisation of science' are interrelated and impinge on the role of science in policy-making (Weingart 1999: 160). While scientification is crucial for the legitimacy and accountability of non-elected experts in policy-making, politicisation puts the credibility of scientific expertise at risk. Thus, the separation of the regulatory process in risk assessment carried out by independent experts and risk management by elected and accountable officials shall solve the inherent dilemma. Consequently, the strong call for an 'agency solution' (Alemanno 2006, 238) and a crosscutting, integrated policy approach was the dominant political response to the food crises.

The last two decades witnessed a boom of agencies. 'Agencification' (Christensen and Lægreid 2006) has major implications for governance. Independent agencies – that is free from political interference – acting at 'arm's-length' from ministries are believed to perform more efficiently than hierarchical bureaucracies do and to solve the elected policy-makers' time-consistency problem by fostering credible commitment (Gilardi 2008; Majone 2001). Agencies are today the backbone of regulatory regimes, especially in the EU (Wonka and Rittberger 2010). Selznick conceptualizes regulation as 'sustained and focused control exercised by a public agency over activities that are socially valued' (Selznick 1985, cited in Scott 2006, 653). Regulation as bureaucratic and administrative rule-making – separated from legislative or judicial rule-making – is restricted to the stage of implementing policies. Legislative acts and goals formulated by *legislative* bodies are transposed into rules and enforcements established by *administrative* bodies, i.e. regulatory agencies as 'non-departmental organizations' (Levi-Faur 2011, 11). Accordingly, the regulatory process encompasses fact-finding in the preparatory stage, rule-making, monitoring during implementation, enforcement, and adjudication[2] (ibid.). This differentiation allows characterising agencies according to their scope of functions and their role in the regulatory process. Taking the separation of risk assessment and risk management into account, fact-finding is a component of risk assessment while the remaining tasks are classical risk management responsibilities.

Vos and Wendler (2006) edited a study that compares food safety regulation in five EU Member States and at EU level. The study identifies three different models based on the relation between risk assessment and risk management:

1. *the bi-institutional or separate model*, which draws a clear-cut line between risk assessment and risk management with responsibilities being separated between institutions and a high degree of scientific independence;
2. *the structurally more integrated model* with responsibilities being functionally divided within a strong regulatory agency (or ministerial department) endowed with both risk assessment and management tasks; and
3. *the fragmented model* with partly integrated and partly overlapping responsibilities (cf. Dreyer et al. 2006).

3.3   THE DEVELOPMENT OF FOOD SAFETY REGIMES: PATH DEPENDENCY VS. EUROPEANIZATION

Theoretically, the development of various regimes into three models poses questions both on differentiation and isomorphism: what kind of differences and commonalities do we observe between the regimes? How can we account for them? Path-dependency and Europeanization are two prominent possible theoretical explanations, which are not inevitably mutually exclusive.

Historical institutionalism provides a powerful explanation for the institutional design of regulatory regimes. The rational choice version claims that actors' rational preferences explain the initial design of institutions based on maximising their utility. These initial decisions have temporal causal consequences, establishing a certain development path that is costly to reverse. However, short-term considerations may affect initial preferences whereas, over time, lags between decisions and long-term consequences occur. Due to lock-in effects and attempts to immunize new institutions from potential changes by opponents (i.e. changes in government parties), institutions are not under full supervision from governments but enjoy some autonomy, which they may use to develop a life of their own (Pierson 1996, 132–136).

'Critical junctures' as key events may allow actors to leave a given path and to adapt to new functional demands. The BSE crisis was such a seismic event. It challenged existing organizational routines and shed light on performance failures. Yet, 'risk assessment has traditionally been an area of policy in which national sentiments are strong' (Ugland and Veggeland 2006, 618). Hence, different national legacies and bureaucratic cultures affect if and in which way regulatory regimes change at the national level. Given the European nature of the BSE crisis and the development of a specific regime at the supranational level, Member States had to take the latter into account and to engage in the developing transnational network. In order to participate in such regulatory network structures, there is a need to create a sense of identification and organizational routines. In food safety, a dense network between the European and national agencies developed (Abels et al. 2014). This is particularly the case if institutional change is induced by a performance crisis as Olsen (2009, 24) claims: in such cases 'institutional developments are more likely to be influenced by the interaction, collisions, conflicts, meta-rules, and power struggles between several institutional spheres, adapting to each other'. We argue that European networks provide for such environmental feedback; to gain professional reputation and 'mutual recognition' as competent authorities is an important consideration in design processes (Majone 1996, 273; Abels et al. 2014). Consequently, there are rational incentives to incorporate designs allowing agencies to engage actively in transnational networks and to cooperate with European partner organizations. Aiming at isomorphism may be a strategy to allow for the smooth functioning of cooperation.

Europeanization is a highly contested phenomenon. A point 'most definitions have in common is the identification of Europeanization with the domestic impact of European integration' (Radaelli and Exadaktylos 2010, 192); it refers to the '*central penetration of national systems of governance*' (Bulmer 2007, 47; emphasis in original). The key supposition holds: being a member of the EU involves fundamental domestic changes of political and economic institutions, intergovernmental relations, judicial structures, public administration, state traditions and collective identities (Börzel and Risse 2000a, 60).

Europeanization works via different mechanisms. 'Europe as pressure' is a perspective very strong in studies on regulatory policies emphasizing vertical mechanisms. This is the case with the specific content of European Food Law becoming effective at national level. Yet, for studying the impact on the polity dimension, it is more useful to employ the 'Europe as usage' perspective (Ladrech 1994), since we only deal with *soft* pressure, as the EU Food Law does not prescribe a mandatory model for national food safety authorities. In this sense, EFSA might serve as a role model for national institutional choices, but the EU has no power to impose this model on the Member States. Furthermore, it is fruitful for analysing regulatory multi-level networks to integrate the horizontal concept of policy transfer and diffusion of national institutional models. We assume that is it most fruitful to include a combination of both *horizontal* as well as *vertical* Europeanization. The EU may only provide 'the architectures and the procedures for horizontal transfer' (Radaelli and Exadaktylos 2010, 193) between Member States and serve as an 'arena' for interaction among agencies (i.e. information gathering and sharing, joint project management, benchmarking and best-practice learning). According to this perspective, 'what is necessary for Europeanization to occur [. . .] is the presence at the EU level of a forum of discussion, an arena for negotiation, or a political architecture for interaction and discourse' (*ibid.*, 194).

The evolution of a transnational food safety network provides for such an EU-induced arena, a forum where EFSA works as a facilitator for policy transfer fostering the willingness to cooperate, advancing professional standards and emphasizing the notion of 'common ownership' of knowledge as done in recent strategic documents (Abels et al. 2014). A high density of communication is most likely a favourable condition for both vertical and horizontal effects of Europeanization. Eberlein and Grande (2005) have advanced the core of this argument: although focusing on less formalized and institutionalized networks, they argue that transnational regulatory networks have become important forums for European coordination and for an informal, soft harmonization of Member States' regulatory activities. Professional information and knowledge become key resources for soft governance with the EU institutions working as information broker. Crisis-induced reform pressure often increases the willingness to experiment with new institutional designs and best practices tested in other countries. This does not imply that we expect full convergence but only a substantial set of commonalities or at least a trend towards enforcing commonalities.

The advanced theoretical explanations are not necessarily rival claims, yet they can be complementary to each other, since Europeanization effects are always domestically framed 'when Europe hits home' (Börzel and Risse 2000a). We further highlight this aspect in the next section, where we briefly introduce EFSA followed by an analysis of three countries, Austria, Sweden and Hungary, representing the introduced regulatory models. We focus on the identification of domestic and European factors in the design and transformation of food safety regimes.

3.4   EFSA AND NATIONAL AGENCIES

At EU-level, the separation of risk assessment from risk management is mainly due to the balance of power among EU institutions and is prescribed in the GFL (Regulation (EC) 178/2002: Art. 3(10)-(13)). Neither Member States nor European institutions themselves were interested in a full-blown regulatory agency like 'an oracle of Delphi spelling out the "truth" in all scientific matters. Rather they wanted to preserve the right of their national food agencies to carry out scientific studies, thus expressing their specific perception of a certain risk' (Alemanno 2008, 24). While EFSA is the exclusive body responsible for risk assessment, the democratically accountable institutions (Council, Commission and European Parliament) reserve all risk management decisions. Accordingly, the Union's own definition of agencies is very limited with regard to the tasks assigned to them 'in order to accomplish a very specific technical, scientific or managerial task' (European Commission 2010). Building up a transnational network of competent authorities is a key element of EFSA's mandate; EFSA Focal Points, i.e. national contact points in all Member States, are important network partners (Abels et al. 2014). The development of shared standards of risk assessment by the network is a central goal. Experts of national authorities are often involved in risk assessments conducted by EFSA as they may also serve as independent experts selected into EFSA's Scientific Panels, though they are selected solely for their professional merits and not based on their affiliation with national authorities.

3.5   AUSTRIA: AN EFSA-INSPIRED DESIGN WITH A DOMESTIC FLAVOUR

In Austria, risk assessment is clearly separated from risk management. The Austrian Agency for Health and Food Safety (AGES) was established in 2002 as a private limited liability company (GmbH) owned by the Republic of Austria. It is a merger of eighteen federal agencies and offices active in different food-related fields. Due to the merger, AGES today has more than 1400 employees and is one of the largest food agencies in the EU. It is supervised by the Ministry of Health (BMG) as well as the Federal Ministry of Agriculture, Forestry, Environment and Water Management (BMLFUW), which act as risk managers (table 3.1). AGES was set up simultaneously with EFSA. The division of risk regulation tasks is very similar to the division at the supranational level.

Austria is the only Member State in the EU where federal responsibilities affecting the food supply chain 'from farm to fork' are concentrated in one public body. Yet, the AGES' mandate is restricted: it is only involved in risk assessment and in risk communication, whereas the Federal Office for Food Safety (BAES) enjoys the enforcement authority. While its

Table 3.1   Current risk regulation regime in Austria

Public body	Fact-finding	Rule-making	Monitoring	Enforcement
AGES	RA	–	–	–
BAES	–	–	RM	RM
BMLFUW/ BMG	–	–	RM	RM

Notes: RA = Risk assessment; RM = Risk management; – = no competence

Source: Compiled by the authors.

administration is part of the AGES structure, it acts politically indepen-dently following its own rules of procedure established by its own director.

The Austrian case resembles the German case of the establishment of the Federal Institute for Risk Assessment (BfR).[3] Unlike in the Austrian case, the German *Länder* inhibited more far-reaching innovations such as a re-structuring and centralisation of enforcement capacities at federal level, as in the case of BAES. Austria and Germany are both, yet to dif-ferent degrees, 'unitary' federal systems with a joint-decision making structure between national and sub-national level. Federalism impedes on the extent and the specific ways in which European impulses affect the domestic level (Börzel and Risse 2000b, Bursens 2007, Schmidt 1999). The authority of the *Länder* is weaker in Austria than in Germany. While they are involved in monitoring and enforcement of food legislation 'on the ground', with BAES a strong federal risk manager is established.

The public pressure for reforming the food safety regime following the BSE scandal opened a window of opportunity to introduce a com-prehensive new concept and a new, encompassing public administration. Considerations to integrate the whole food chain into a single public administration follow efficiency and transparency concerns. Thus, the reform process in Austria is a deliberate attempt to copy the structure found at the European level (isomorphism). The Austrian case is a strong example of the impact of Europeanization, even though the extent and path of reform is clearly also shaped by domestic factors.

3.6   SWEDEN: A SEPARATED SYSTEM WITH A HIGH DEGREE OF STABILITY

As early as 1972, Sweden set up the Swedish National Food Administration (SLV) as an independent food safety agency (Ferreira et al. 2006). SLV's

Table 3.2   Current risk regulation regime in Sweden

Public body	Fact-finding	Rule-making	Monitoring	Enforcement
SLV / JV	RA	RM	RM	RM
SVA	RA	–	–	–
LD	–	RM	–	RM

Notes: RA = Risk assessment; RM = Risk management; – = no competence

Source: Compiled by the authors.

mandate encompasses independent risk assessment and food research, food monitoring, and rule-making (decrees). All activities are open to public scrutiny. The SLV reports directly to the government and especially to the Ministry of Rural Affairs (LD), which has the main responsibility for food safety regulation. Nevertheless, the ministry's influence in the agency's day-to-day work is rather limited, and SLV 'enjoys important independent powers, following the Swedish tradition of division of responsibility between smaller ministries and independent (and powerful) agencies' (Elvbakken et al. 2008, 138). Further risk assessment institutions are the Swedish Board of Agriculture (JV; feed safety only) and the Swedish National Veterinary Institute (SVA) (table 3.2).

Designed as a structure with no separation between risk assessment and management, minor reforms in 2000 resulted in stricter *intra*-departmental division of authority. Ferreira et al. (2006, 333–334) regard these as a response, firstly, to transnational trends towards new public management in the 1990s, and secondly, to debates in the World Health Organization (WHO) and the Food and Agriculture Organization (FAO) concerning functional separations in the Codex Alimentarius system. The 2005 food law transposed EU regulations into national law but 'does not mark a turning point in national food safety policy' (Dreyer et al. 2006, 22, cf. Elvbakken et al. 2008, 137–138). In contrast to most EU Member States, the BSE crisis did not affect reforms in Sweden.

Institutional and cultural factors are crucial to explain the design and high degree of stability of the Swedish system. Key principles of Swedish public administration are, firstly, 'a distinction between a dualist system of government that rests on constitutional separation of policy and administration' (Yesilkagit and Christensen 2010, 59); and secondly, the public administration is perceived to be 'a professional elite of regulators sharing an ideal of rational planning based on scientific expertise' (Ferreira et al. 2006, 331). Finally, the publicity principle guides public administration meaning that 'all citizens have the right of access to governmental documents' (*ibid.*). Centralized 'expert-based professional organizations exercising their assigned tasks fully independent of political institutions' are a vital component of Swedish government (*ibid.*, 332). Public authorities not only implement policies, but also enforce regulations and initiate rule-making, of which SLV is a typical example.

While Europeanization scholars often argue that the impact of the EU usually tends to be more profound in unitary Member States (as opposed to federal systems with a more dispersed power system; Schmidt 1999), this was clearly not the case in Sweden, which is a plain case of a unitary country (Bursens 2007, 123). The Swedish model deviates from the separation model that EFSA represents. Following the EFSA model was not possible due to a deeply rooted institutional misfit. Because there was only soft Europeanization pressure, there was no strong urge to reduce the misfit; in addition, there were strong national traditions affecting the design (professional and independent public authorities), yet compatible with EFSA's professional standards. In Germany and Austria, the need for efficiency and transparency resulted in isomorphism between the EU and national organizations, whereas in Sweden the choice for a completely independent, solely expert-based professional agency was affirmed. In summary, the Swedish case is an example of a strong influence of domestic factors with a very limited impact from Europeanization.

3.7   HUNGARY: FROM A FRAGMENTED TO A BI-INSTITUTIONAL TO AN INTEGRATED MODEL

Dreyer et al. (2006, 23–24) classify Hungary as a *fragmented model* because of a structure with partly overlapping activities and an indistinct separation of responsibilities. In 2007, the Hungarian system has undergone a tremendous change towards a bi-institutional system (Träsch 2011) resulting from the impact of Europeanization in the course of EU accession. A further institutional reform took place in March 2012 merging the risk assessment and the risk management branch into a single authority. Hence, today Hungary largely follows the integrated model.[4] Yet Europeanization evolved in different steps shaped by domestic factors.

With the democratic transformation after 1989 and subsequent EU accession, the pressure for building up a national food safety regime increased, leading to substantial changes towards a separation between politics and administration (Ferencz et al. 2006). We observe a legal harmonisation in food safety regulation between 1993 and 2003 and, eventually, in 2003 the establishment of the Hungarian Food Safety Office (MÉBIH).

Accession required the transposition of the *food-related acquis* into

Table 3.3   Risk regulation regime in Hungary (2000–2012)

Public body	Fact-finding	Rule-making	Monitoring	Enforcement
VM / EÜM	–	RM	–	RM
MÉBIH	RA	–	–	–
MGSZH	–	–	RM	RM

Notes: RA = Risk assessment; RM = Risk management; – = no competence

Source: Compiled by the authors.

national law, establishing a clear case of top-down Europeanization. While the *acquis* prescribes neither a separation of tasks nor a certain institutional model, the creation of EFSA was perceived as a demand for the creation of a domestic regulator. Hitherto, the Hungarian system was highly fragmented, in particular regarding monitoring and enforcement. European and national food crises led to domestic calls for a more coordinated structure. MÉBIH should foster domestic and external coordination. Since its inception, several – mainly crisis-induced – reforms were undertaken. In the 2004 'Aflatoxin scandal', contaminated ground paprika was detected in Hungarian spice-producing companies (Ferencz et al. 2006, 422). Deficits in crisis management led authorities to transfer supervision over MÉBIH from the Ministry of Agriculture and Rural Development (VM) to the Ministry of Health (EÜM). Three years later, oversight was transferred back to VM where it remains until today (table 3.3).

MÉBIH's key task was the scientific assessment of risks in food and feed. With only 18 employees, it lacked the capacity for in-house research, hence it had to rely on risk research conducted either by other Hungarian organizations (such as universities) or in other European countries. MÉBIH's strong coordinating role of the early days had become less important since 2007, when a single risk management and enforcement unit – the Central Agricultural Office (MGSZH; subordinate to VM) – was set up. Thus, reforms resulted in a major regime restructuring. While MÉBIH lost its coordinating functions, it could now concentrate on risk assessment. Given the small size of the agency, this was a major challenge. MÉBIH's key principles resembled the ones adopted by EFSA: credibility, reliability, excellence, openness, and integrity. We find several indicators (e.g. principles, advisory forum, scientific panels) that EFSA has been a role model for MÉBIH, triggered by the idea of improving smooth cooperation between the Hungarian and European agencies (Träsch 2011). These are soft, yet nevertheless powerful effects of Europeanization, based on the perceived demand for efficient networking and the need for external scientific data. The 2012 reforms centralized all tasks in a single body, the National Food Chain Safety Office (NÉHIB) consisting of MÉBIH and MGSZH.

In summary, the Hungarian system shifted from the fragmented to the bi-institutional model. A transformation slowly occurred in several steps against the background of, firstly, EU accession and, secondly, the domestic 'Aflatoxin scandal' as triggers. Between 2007 and 2012, there was hardly any functional overlap; responsibilities were separated. The concurrence of Europeanization factors and domestic factors had been a particularly strong driver for change. Among the Central and Eastern European Countries, Hungary was an exception in terms of creating a clear structure with identifiable responsibilities. In Poland and Slovakia, which also follow the bi-institutional model, separation of responsibilities is less clear. Aside from the effects of the vertical, we also see signs of horizontal Europeanization between Member States via pre-accession Twinning Projects. Germany has been the partner of Hungary in food safety regulation, therefore the German choice for a separated system may have additionally contributed to these developments in Hungary. The 2012 reforms shifted the institutional arrangements towards an integrated model; this might be seen as part of the general trend of centralisation in Hungary. Hungary serves thus as an example for still ongoing transformations in food safety regimes.

3.8   COMPARING REGULATORY REGIMES

The previous section describes changes in European food safety regulation. If we include information about all 28 Member States (table 3.4), we can outline some general patterns before we come back to our theoretical hypotheses.

The existence of two basic models provides against functionalist arguments claiming that the same problems would increase the likelihood for single or at least very similar solutions. The third, fragmented, model will most likely be a transitional one. Most Member States have chosen the integrated system. However, there is some diversity regarding the exact role of agencies in risk management. Moreover, some countries (Cyprus, the Czech Republic and Slovenia) have not set up an independent agency until now. Almost all agencies are subordinate to one or several ministries. In nine Member States, food agencies work under the aegis of the ministries of agriculture,[5] whereas the ministry of health[6] supervises them in only three cases and in five cases both ministries are responsible.[7] The struggle for control over food safety between the administrations of health and of agriculture indicates tensions between producer interests,

Table 3.4   Classification of risk governance regimes

Bi-institutional, separate model		Structurally more integrated model		Fragmented model
EU	*Austria*	Belgium	Cyprus**	Bulgaria*
Croatia	Denmark	Czech Rep.**	Estonia*	*Hungary*
Finland	France	Greece	*Hungary*	*(until 2007)*
Germany	*Hungary*	Ireland	*(since 2012)*	Luxembourg
Netherlands	*(until 2012)*	Latvia	Italy	Malta
Slovakia	Poland	Portugal	Lithuania*	
		Slovenia**	Romania	
		Sweden	Spain	
			UK	

Notes: * = first signs of separation; ** = countries with no agency, department of ministry is responsible

Source: Compiled by the authors.

promoted by agricultural ministries, and consumer interests, advocated by health ministries (Elvbakken et al. 2008). In seven cases, the agency is fully independent from ministries. In general, bigger Member States have, as a rule, larger agencies employing more staff, including research staff. Small Member States (e.g. Luxembourg, Malta) often lack the capacity for conducting in-house risk research and therefore have to rely on studies conducted elsewhere. Particularly for these countries, shared norms and procedural standards in risk research are crucial for confidence-building between agencies since they have to trust in foreign expertise. In addition, there is some evidence that the larger Member States (Germany, France, the UK, but also the Netherlands, Sweden and Austria) are more actively involved in EFSA's scientific panels (Kobusch 2010).

We have introduced the *path-dependency* hypothesis and the *Europeanization* hypothesis to explain similarities and differences in institutional design. Actually, both factors complement each other. In response to crises in most Member States and at the EU level, food safety regimes have been reformed – often dramatically. In many cases, we can find diffusion, transfer and emulation of models. Reforms were especially radical when Europeanization effects and domestic pressure coincided. This was the case in Hungary, but also in Belgium, France, Germany and the UK. Improving transparency and effectiveness were prominent rationales for change. EFSA often served as an explicit design model when Member States opted for the bi-institutional model and introduced organizational reforms at about the same time as at the European level. By institutional isomorphism policy makers try to avoid a misfit between agencies at different levels.

Domestic factors have also been prominent in the design of agencies and national regulatory regimes. We find radical change in both models (e.g. Austria, the UK). National legacies and traditions of public admin-istrations are decisive for institutional development paths; this has been obvious in all cases discussed – yet to different degrees. Yesilkagit and Christensen (2010, 71) conclude that '[i]t is striking to what extent solu-tions with deep roots in the administrative tradition of each country are preferred'. This is obvious in Sweden, but also in Hungary. In general, Central and East European countries are stragglers. Their institutional systems are still somewhat in the making; this is also true for Malta and Cyprus. Several of these countries have so far not established food agen-cies independent from political interference. Furthermore, we observe that all southern Member States fit the model of integrated systems, and hitherto there has been little change. These form a stable regional pattern.

Federalism is another domestic factor, which in general impedes on Europeanization effects. This is not so obvious in our study. Profound restructuring involving institutional innovations was possible in federal countries such as Germany and Austria (less so in Belgium). However, in the German case there is evidence that the *Länder* vetoed an even more far-reaching reform also of the enforcement regime. In all Member States, regional and/or local authorities are involved in enforcement on the ground (e.g. food inspection). Policy- and rule-making are located at the national level.

We have argued that the presence of a 'forum of discussion, an arena for negotiation, or a political architecture for interaction and discourse' on the European level (Radaelli and Exadaktylos 2010, 193) fosters the Europeanization impact on the Member States. Twinning projects (e.g. Germany-Hungary, Germany-Croatia) and the search for models in response to crisis increased horizontal policy transfer between Member States. Furthermore, creating a transnational regulatory food safety network is one of the key objectives of EU reforms. EFSA is supposed to serve as a node in the evolving network. In twenty Member States, national agencies are designated EFSA Focal Point, acting as national interfaces with the EFSA network.[8] EFSA was built on a 'separatist' model adjusted to a delicate power-sharing system in the EU and based on current thinking on politics and science and became a model for creating competent authorities in many Member States.[9] The underlying assump-tion is that co-operation of national authorities with one another and with EFSA works more smoothly if there is something of an 'institutional fit'. This was the case in Hungary and, to some extent, in Austria and Germany. This finding fits the neo-institutionalist proposition that structural similarities help improve the effectiveness of cooperation between network actors. This is not to say that all agencies have to be alike. Yet, common methods, procedures, and substantive rules are an essential part of rather informal, bottom-up harmonisation in European regulatory networks. They are crucial for building trust and reputation as important assets of risk assessors and a requirement for efficient regulation.

3.9   CONCLUSIONS

Governance structures in food safety regulation have shifted considerably in the last decade mainly in response to numerous food scandals. This is obvious at the EU level as well as in all 28 Member States. Firstly, 'agencification' (Christensen and Lægreid 2006) is *the* prominent reaction to these often crisis-induced modifications. Either new agencies have been set up or an already existing system of competent authorities has been subject to sometimes minor, yet often significant change. These competent authorities are interlinked. The development of a multi-level regulatory network involving EFSA and national competent authorities – mostly specialized food safety agencies – provides important enabling structures for Europeanization, i.e. for the diffusion of designs, standards and practices both in a vertical and horizontal dimension. Yet, 'when Europe hits home' (Börzel and Risse 2000b), the impact differs – even more so when we deal with changes of the polity structure itself and when Europeanization effects are soft. Domestic factors, including historical traditions of public administration, come into play; this is obvious in all our cases.

Secondly, a major aspect regarding the agencification of food safety governance was restructuring the relationship between science/expertise and politics. This is important with regards to the organization of different tasks in risk regulation. Our findings suggest the development of two basic models – we call these a 'separatist' and an 'integrationist' model based on the key criterion of how risk assessment and management are interrelated. Real types of both models are of course more diverse and non-static; also, hybrid forms with overlapping responsibilities exist. In the separatist model risk assessment and management are tasks assigned to different bodies: while the scientific assessment of risk is left to independent agencies that are to deliver neutral expertise, drawing conclusions and implementing risk management is left to administrations and policy-makers. This model shall improve the credibility of risk assessment by 'liberating' experts from political interference. In turn, management decisions shall become more open to societal and political considerations, thereby increasing the democratic legitimacy of risk regulation. In the integrated model, in contrast, risk assessment and management are incorporated in one organization, yet often functionally divided within such a competent authority. This model pays tribute to the practically difficult strict separation between scientific assessment and its political implications. The effectiveness of risk regulation shall be improved by considering policy alternatives within the risk assessment process, in an area where evidence-based decisions of experts usually dominate. Both models, however, still adhere to the dominant notion of 'sound', i.e. neutral science. We do not claim that one model is superior; but we observe that the separate model evolved after the integrated one and its introduction was backed up by arguments derived from science policy (cf. Jasanoff 2005, Millstone et al. 2008).

Our results indicate that the separatist model has spread most across countries that aimed at isomorphism between their national competent authority and EFSA. We classify this development as a form of soft Europeanization. However, whether or not organizational isomorphism improves the interaction between national agencies and EFSA; whether one model will be more effective than another in terms of providing protection of consumers from food-borne diseases and in preventing/handling future food crises; and whether some agencies will be more influential in the multi-level regulatory network – all these questions remain open. Based on a survey of all 28 Member States (see footnote 1) we present preliminary results regarding typical cases for the proposed models. Future research can clearly draw on the ever growing body of literature focusing on agencies' formal and de-facto independence (Gilardi 2008, Maggetti 2007, Wonka and Rittberger 2010), their autonomy and control (Groenleer 2009, Lægreid and Verhoest 2010, Verhoest 2010) and their accountability and legitimacy (Maggetti 2009). According to our results such research needs to address the question whether and how institutional design in risk regulation, differing levels of independence and autonomy and varying scopes of action affect the day-to-day policy performance of agencies in an evolving multi-level food safety regime.

NOTES

1. Our overview of the national agencies stems from a study conducted for the German Federal Institute for Risk Assessment (BfR) in 2008/09. It includes the evaluation of the online presentations of national agencies supplemented by a BfR survey of all national agencies to verify online information (Federal Institute for Risk Assessment 2009). In early 2014, a third revised version was published by BfR and translations into Chinese,

French and Spanish are underway. We are grateful to the participants of the panel 'Changing patterns of food safety regulation in the EU and China' at the ECPR conference 'Regulation in the age of crisis' in Dublin and to the editors and reviewers of this volume for helpful comments.

2. We do not address *adjudication*; to our knowledge, none of the food safety agencies in the EU has responsibilities in this area.

3. Fischer (2007) persuasively illustrates that the German BfR, also established in 2002, is a clear case of policy transfer from the European to the national level, claiming a convergence between the BfR and EFSA regarding agencies' objectives, organizational principles and outcome of reform processes. Indicators are timing and mandate. Moreover, several actors were simultaneously involved at both national and EU level.

4. Our original case selection and assessment base on the situation in 2011 when Hungary was still an example for the bi-institutional model. In order to exemplify this model we refer mainly to the period 2007–2012.

5. Estonia, Finland, Germany, Greece, Hungary, Latvia, Lithuania, Slovak Republic and Sweden.

6. Italy, Malta and Spain.

7. Austria, Bulgaria, Luxembourg, Poland with the exception of the Netherlands, where the Food and Consumer Product Safety Authority (NVWA) is supervised by the Ministry for Health and the Ministry for Economic Affairs. Only in Portugal is the Economy and Food Safety Standards Authority (ASAE) solely supervised by the Ministry of Economy and Employment.

8. In Belgium, Cyprus, the Czech Republic, Estonia, Poland, the Slovak Republic and Slovenia ministries serve as Focal Point, in Lithuania a subordinated administration is liaison office.

9. At the same time, the establishment of EFSA itself was influenced by ideas on institutional design in other Member States, especially the forerunners UK and Ireland.

REFERENCES

Abels, G., A. Kobusch and J. Träsch (2014), 'Scientific Regulatory Cooperation within the EU: On the Relationship between EFSA and National Food Authorities', in A. Alemanno, S. Gabbi (eds), *Foundations of EU Food Law & Policy: 10 Years of European Food Safety Authority*, London: Ashgate.

Alemanno, A. (2006), 'Food Safety and the Single European Market', in C. Ansell, and D. Vogel (eds), *What's the Beef? The Contested Governance of European Food Safety*, Cambridge, MA/London: MIT Press.

Alemanno, A. (2008), 'The European Food Safety Authority at Five', *European Food and Feed Law Review*, 1, 2–29.

Alemanno, A. and S. Gabbi (eds) (2014), *Foundations of EU Food Law & Policy: 10 Years of European Food Safety Authority*, London: Ashgate.

Börzel, T.A. and T. Risse (2000a), 'Conceptualizing the Domestic Impact of Europe', in K. Featherstone and C.M. Radaelli (eds), *The Politics of Europeanization*, Oxford: Oxford University Press.

Börzel, T.A. and T. Risse (2000b), 'When Europe Hits Home: Europeanization and Domestic Change', *European Integration online Papers (EIoP)*, 4. Online. Available at http://eiop.or.at/eiop/texte/2000-015a.htm (accessed 13 May 2011).

Bulmer, S.J. (2007), 'Theorizing Europeanization', in P. Graziano and M.P. Vink (eds), *Europeanization: New Research Agendas*, New York: Palgrave Macmillan.

Buonanno, L. (2006), 'The Creation of the European Food Safety Authority', in

C. Ansell and D. Vogel (eds), *What's the Beef? The Contested Governance of European Food Safety*, Cambridge, MA/London: MIT Press.

Bursens, P. (2007), 'State Structures', in P. Graziano and M.P. Vink (eds), *Europeanization: New Research Agendas*, New York: Palgrave Macmillan.

Christensen, T. and P. Lægreid (2006), 'Agencification and Regulatory Reforms', in T. Christensen and P. Lægreid (eds), *Autonomy and Regulation: Coping with Agencies in the Modern State*, Cheltenham, UK and Northhampton, MA: Edward Elgar Publishing.

Dreyer, M., O. Renn, K. Borkhart and O. Julia (2006), 'Institutional Re-arrangements in European Food Safety Governance: A Comparative Analysis', in E. Vos and F. Wendler (eds), *Food Safety Regulation in Europe. A Comparative Analysis*, Antwerpen/Oxford: Intersentia.

Eberlein, B. and E. Grande (2005), 'Beyond Delegation: Transnational Regulatory Regimes and the EU Regulatory State', *Journal of European Public Policy*, 12, 89–112.

Elvbakken, K.T., P. Lægreid and L. Hellebø Rykkja (2008), 'Regulation for Safe Food: A Comparison of Five European Countries', *Scandinavian Political Studies*, 31, 125–148.

European Commission (2010), *Agencies and decentralized bodies. Regulatory agencies and bodies: Policy agencies*, Brussels: European Union. Online. Available at http://europa.eu/agencies/index_en.htm (accessed 16 May 2011).

Federal Institute for Risk Assessment (2009), *EU Food Safety Almanach*, Berlin: Federal Institute for Risk Assessment. Online. Available at www.bfr.bund.de/cm/364/eu_food_safety_almanac.pdf (accessed 13 May 2011).

Ferencz, Z., M. Hajdu and A. Vári (2006), 'Food Safety Regulation in Hungary', in E. Vos and F. Wendler (eds), *Food Safety Regulation in Europe. A Comparative Analysis*, Antwerpen/Oxford: Intersentia.

Ferreira, C., Å. Boholm and K. Borkhart (2006), 'Food Safety Regulation in Sweden', in E. Vos and F. Wendler (eds), *Food Safety Regulation in Europe. A Comparative Analysis*, Antwerpen/Oxford: Intersentia.

Fischer, R. (2007), 'Unabhängige Bewertungsagenturen im gesundheitlichen Verbraucherschutz: Ein Beispiel für gelungenen Politiktransfer in der Europäischen Union?', in K. Holzinger, H. Jörgens and C. Knill (eds), *Transfer, Diffusion und Konvergenz von Politiken, PVS-Sonderheft 38*, Wiesbaden: VS Verlag für Sozialwissenschaften.

Gilardi, F. (2008), *Delegation in the Regulatory State. Independent Regulatory Agencies in Western Europe*, Cheltenham: Edward Elgar Publishing.

Groenleer, M. (2009), *The Autonomy of European Union Agencies. A Comparative Study of Institutional Developments*, Delft: Eburon.

Jasanoff, S. (2005), *Designs on Nature. Science and Democracy in Europe and the United States*, Princeton, NJ: Princeton University Press.

Kobusch, A. (2010), 'Linking the Levels: Independence and Influence in the European Two Tiered Network of Food Safety Agencies', paper presented at the Third Biennial Conference 'Regulation in the Age of Crises' of the ECPR Standing Group on Regulatory Governance, Dublin, 17–19 June 2010. Online. Available at http://regulation.upf.edu/dublin-10-papers/3D2.pdf (accessed 28 October 2011).

Ladrech, R. (1994), 'Europeanization of Domestic Politics and Institutions: The Case of France', *Journal of Common Market Studies*, 32, 69–88.

Lægreid, P. and K. Verhoest (eds) (2010), *Governance of Public Sector Organizations.*

Proliferation, Autonomy and Performance, Houndsmills, Basingstoke: Palgrave MacMillan.

Levi-Faur, D. (2011), 'Regulation and Regulatory Governance', in D. Levi-Faur (ed.), *Handbook on the Politics of Regulation*, Cheltenham: Edward Elgar, pp. 3–21.

Maggetti, M. (2007), 'De Facto Independence after Delegation: A Fuzzy-Set Analysis', *Regulation & Governance*, 1, 271–94.

Maggetti, M. (2009), 'Delegated Authority. Legitimizing Independent Regulatory Agencies', in I. Blühdorn (ed.), *In Search of Legitimacy: Policy Making in Europe and the Challenge of Complexity*, Opladen: Barbara Budrich Publishers.

Majone, G. (1996), *Regulating Europe*, London: Routledge.

Majone, G. (2001), 'Two Logics of Delegation. Agency and Fiduciary Relations in EU Governance', *European Union Politics*, 2, 103–122.

Millstone, E., P. Van Zwanenberg, L. Levidow et al. (2008), *Risk-Assessment Policies: Difference across Jurisdictions*, Luxembourg: JRC Scientific and Technical Reports.

Olsen, J.P. (2009), 'Change and Continuity: An Institutional Approach to Institutions of Democratic Government', *European Political Science Review*, 1, 3–32.

Pierson, P. (1996), 'The Path to European Integration: A Historical Institutionalist Analysis', *Comparative Political Studies*, 29, 123–163.

Radaelli, C.M. and T. Exadaktylos (2010), 'New Directions in Europeanization Research', in M.P. Egan, N. Nugent and W.E. Paterson (eds), *Research Agendas in EU Studies: Stalking the Elephant*, New York: Palgrave Macmillan.

Schmidt, V.A. (1999), 'The EU and Its Member-States: Institutional Contrasts and Their Consequences', Cologne. MPIfG Working Paper 99/7. Online. Available at http://www.mpifg.de/pu/workpap/wp99-7/wp99-7.html (accessed 13 May 2011).

Scott, C. (2006), 'Privatization and Regulatory Regimes', in M. Moran, M. Rein and R.E. Goodin (eds), *The Oxford Handbook of Public Policy*, Oxford: Oxford University Press.

Träsch, J. (2011), 'From Chaos to Separation – An Update of the Hungarian Food Safety Regulation System', *European Journal of Risk Regulation*, 2(4), 560–566.

Ugland, T. and F. Veggeland (2006), 'Experiments in Food Safety Policy Integration in the European Union', *Journal of Common Market Studies*, 44, 607–624.

Verhoest, K. (2010), *Autonomy and Control of State Agencies: Comparing States and Agencies*, Houndsmills, Basingstoke: Palgrave Macmillan.

Vos, E. and F. Wendler (eds) (2006), *Food Safety Regulation in Europe. A Comparative Analysis*, Antwerpen: Intersentia.

Weingart, P. (1999), 'Scientific Expertise and Political Accountability: Paradoxes of Science in Politics', *Science and Public Policy*, 26, 151–161.

Wonka, A. and B. Rittberger (2010), 'Credibility, Complexity and Uncertainty: Explaining the Institutional Independence of 29 EU Agencies', *West European Politics*, 33, 730–752.

Yesilkagit, K. and J.G. Christensen (2010), 'Institutional Design and Formal Autonomy: Political versus Historical and Cultural Explanations', *Journal of Public Administration Research and Theory*, 20, 53–74.

4. Buying biosecurity: UK compensation for animal diseases

Gareth Enticott and Robert Lee

4.1 INTRODUCTION

Where there is a failure in market provision, one might well anticipate state intervention (Ogus 2004). In relation to biosecurity, it is not uncommon to find compensation provided by the state where diseased animals are slaughtered. For centuries this approach has formed the basis of veterinary epidemiology and state intervention in animal disease: in 1713 Thomas Bates, the surgeon to King George I, managed to eradicate cattle plague in England by slaughtering animals suspected of carrying the disease and compensating their owners. That such a system continues to support animal disease policy long after its first use is surprising. One might expect that such losses would be borne by the producer and the risks internalized by insurance or pricing mechanisms lest the ready payment of public compensation creates a moral hazard. In the UK, section 32 of the Animal Health Act 1981 embeds this approach allowing the Minister to arrange the slaughter of any animal which is affected, suspected of being affected or which has been exposed to the infection, in line with a number of European Commission directives.[1]

There would appear to be two possible reasons for the provision of compensation by the state in cases where diseased animals are slaughtered. The first is a strong public interest in maintaining food production (Mol and Bulkeley 2002), the promotion of uninterrupted supplies of food and regeneration of production following disease. A second explanation is that the compensation buys intervention rights on the part of the State, and, in order to encourage producers to behave in certain ways, compensation acts as a mechanism to influence behaviour. Compensation incentivises producers to report disease and it may be dependent on the producer following a mandated course of action.

While various types of payments and subsidies are employed in the agricultural industry to promote environmental management and to address failings in public policy (Burton et al. 2007; Brauer et al. 2006), if the rationale for compensation policies is to buy 'intervention rights', then compensation ought to shape regulatory policy. Drawing on case law and animal health legislation, this chapter suggests that policy goals are poorly attained, with confused regulatory objectives, because compensation is not applied consistently to secure intervention. The chapter also shows that compensation policies have introduced a series of perverse effects in the management of animal disease and have lagged behind wider socio-economic changes within agriculture and the countryside. As the basis of compensation involves drawing distinctions between endemic and epidemic diseases of animals, the chapter reviews one example of each type of disease: bovine tuberculosis (bTB) and foot and mouth disease (FMD) respectively. It then draws upon adjudications of disputes under English law concerning the cull of diseased farm animals and the awards of compensation following slaughter.

4.2   BOVINE TUBERCULOSIS

Bovine tuberculosis (bTB), described as the most difficult animal health problem in the United Kingdom (Parry 2010), is a zoonosis caused by the bacterium *Mycobacterium bovis* that is commonly found in cattle and wildlife, particularly badgers. At its height, approximately 50 000 human cases of bTB were recorded annually, killing 5 per cent of those infected (Waddington 2006). Since then, a range of public and animal health measures have been progressively implemented – including milk pasteurization and meat inspection – such that the risk to humans is judged to be negligible (HPA 2009). In 1925, bTB was made a notifiable disease, requiring farmers to report cases. However, the failure of voluntary campaigns to eradicate the disease from the national herd led to the government intervention following the Second World War. All cattle were injected with tuberculin using a 'skin test'. If cattle 'reacted' to the tuberculin (a 'breakdown') they were slaughtered and farmers financially compensated. Farms were then restocked from bTB-free areas.

The use of the skin test to detect bTB infected cattle was later recognised at the European level by Council Directive 64/432/EEC. More specifically, Council Directive 78/52/EEC is aimed at the eradication of bTB by the investigation and surveillance of suspect cattle leading to their slaughter where tests are positive (Articles 14, 15). These directives also govern international trading status as set out in the Animal Health Code of the Office des Epizooties (OIE 2010) with the most favourable 'officially free status' set at 99.8 per cent of a nation's herd being free from bTB over the immediate three year period.

In the UK, by 1960, using skin tests followed by slaughter, the number of bTB cases was estimated at 28 (Proud 2006). Since then the disease has risen steadily: in 2013, over 26 000 cattle were slaughtered because of bTB (Defra 2014). This reversal of fortunes has been attributed to the endemic nature of the disease, particularly in the badger. As bTB is thought to maintain itself in the badger population, it is difficult to eradicate the disease in nearby cattle. Culling badgers is promoted on the basis that fewer badgers would mean less bTB (ISG 2007). Ironically, the link between bTB in badgers and in cattle was established just as the Badgers Act 1973 gave badgers statutory protection as an endangered species (Enticott 2001; Muirhead et al. 1974). By the end of the 1970s, the Bern Convention listed the badger as a protected species. As badger numbers are low in many European countries the maintenance of a British badger population is crucial. The Protection of Badgers Act 1992 now consolidates the law and it allows the government to issue licences to cull badgers on the grounds of animal health. This is highly contentious because, while there is acceptance of epidemiological links between bTB in the two animal populations (VEERU 2009), there is little agreement on methods for appropriate and humane control of the disease.

Extensive field trials suggest that culling badgers makes little contribution to the protection of cattle, meaning that efforts might be better directed at more effective biosecurity and diagnostics (ISG 2007). Badgers as territorial animals may migrate, as areas are culled out, creating a 'perturbation effect', spreading rather than containing the disease (Woodroffe et al. 2006). Notwithstanding these independent scientific findings, governments in both England and Wales have turned towards badger culling. In England, the Coalition Government announced an affordable option for a 'carefully-managed and science-led policy' of badger control in areas with high, persistent levels of bTB in cattle (Hansard 2010). Currently under two pilot schemes, first run in 2013 and continued in 2014, badgers may be shot by licensed farmers. In Wales, having voted in an earlier Coalition Government for a cull of badgers, in majority Government, the Labour Party is now claiming significant reductions in the incidence of bTB following increased cattle testing and a pilot study using badger vaccination.

Tension is high; farmers have become dissatisfied with bTB control mechanisms in the absence of a national cull. Decisions not to issue licences for badger culling following the ISG report (ISG 2007) appear contrary to the 1992 Act, which accords farmers that opportunity. Meanwhile, badger conservation groups overturned a proposed Welsh badger culling policy in the courts (see *R (the Badger Trust) v Welsh Ministers* [2010] EWHC 768) in part prompting the use of vaccines in Wales. As we shall show, legal challenges have highlighted wider issues relating to the effectiveness of test and slaughter policies, diagnostics and the role of compensation in regulating bTB.

4.2.1   Challenges to the Test and Slaughter Policy in bTB Policy

There are two cases challenging the blanket nature of the test and slaughter policy in terms of human rights compliance. The first, *R (Swami Suryanda) v the Welsh Ministers* [2007], invoked Article 9 of the European Convention on the Protection of Human Rights (ECHR). The judgment ruled that in applying its surveillance and slaughter policy to a sacred bullock (named 'Shambo'), the National Assembly for Wales failed to consider the rights of the religious community when pursuing public benefits of the bTB control policy.

Shambo was central to the life of a Hindu community as a temple bullock. The monks saw their duty to care for and preserve the rights of animals as akin to that owed to human beings. Shambo tested positive for bTB and an 'intention to slaughter notice' was issued. The practice of the Welsh Government (WG) is to slaughter in all cases where tested animals show a reaction to the skin tests. The powers under the Animal Health Act 1981 allow discretionary slaughter as the Minister thinks fit.[2] The monks sought exceptional treatment of Shambo given its religious significance, and had isolated Shambo and were prepared to expend all necessary resources on antibiotic treatment of the bTB. The WG's insistence on the slaughter notice led to an application for an injunction on the basis that it had closed its mind to all but its surveillance and slaughter policy. The argument was that, although the WG had taken expert biosecurity advice, it had failed to address questions of religious belief. Therefore, it was argued that the WG breached Article 9 of the ECHR as the freedom to manifest religious beliefs can be restricted only for certain legitimate State aims, and only by means of justified and proportionate measures (Nason 2008; Leigh 2009). Public health is a potential public interest that might justify the interference with religious freedom.

Experts stated in court that the biosecurity risk (given the isolation and treatment of Shambo) was 'negligible'. The monks argued that in such circumstances there would be a disproportionate violation of rights under Article 9 ECHR bringing into question the WG's insistence on slaughter, its failure to consider alternatives and its refusal to assess the health risks attaching to the plans for Shambo. The WG argued at the hearing that because of the impact of the spread of bTB, it was right to follow the veterinary experts and the policy of precautionary slaughter based on skin tests.

By the time the case came to court there were thousands of signatures to an online petition to save Shambo and a webcam depicting Shambo ('Moo-Tube'). The Judge quashed the slaughter notice and ordered that the WG reconsider its decision, portraying the treatment of the Community's religious beliefs as 'grudging' and 'unfortunate'. The WG's policy, based on zero risk, mandated slaughter, but this failed to adequately deal with human rights issues once Article 9 ECHR was engaged. The WG had failed to consider the necessity and proportionality of its slaughter policy given the possible infringement of Article 9 ECHR.

This ruling was successfully appealed. The Court of Appeal (at [2007] EWCA Civ. 893) ruled that the WG had acted lawfully as the Minister had analyzed and balanced both sides of the argument and there was no requirement for the WG to consider risks associated with the 'speculative alternatives' given the biosecurity issues attaching to bTB. This was so even allowing for 'a very grave and serious interference with their religious rights'. The Court found the policy on culling to be proportionate and Shambo was slaughtered; post-mortem testing did disclose that he suffered from bTB. Yet, while bTB can affect humans, the risks are considered to be low and eating meat from an animal with bTB (unlikely to happen to Shambo) carries little risk. Although public health is invoked as a reason for action, what was at stake in this case was largely an economic policy, designed to protect trading status in animal products so that economic considerations were given primacy over religious rights.

In a second case from Northern Ireland, *Crawford v Department of Agriculture and Rural Development* [2012] NICA 53, eleven pedigree Limousin cattle were slaughtered after they falsely tested positive for bTB a few days after the cattle had been vaccinated against another disease, Blackleg. The farmer was later acquitted in criminal proceedings when charged with interfering with the administration of the test. However, the Department sought to withhold compensation for the slaughter relying on art. 18(6)(a) of the Diseases of Animals (Northern Ireland) Order 1981 which would allow this where the farmer had prejudiced the control of the disease. When the Department sought to convene a panel to determine if such prejudice had occurred, this action was restrained by the courts as unlawful and contrary to the right to a fair trial under Article 6 of the ECHR. The criminal courts having determined the matter, Article 6(2) ECHR applied in the circumstances to prevent what was effectively a retrial of the farmer's conduct. It might be observed that this is one of a number of cases in which the payment of compensation, ordinarily readily offered, becomes an issue where the behaviour of farmers, sometimes in resisting culling, is not seen as compliant.

4.2.2   Challenges to Diagnosing Bovine TB

A second line of cases involve challenges to the clinical method of detecting bTB as required by the EU Directive 78/52/EEC. In *Suryanda* (2007), evidence was presented suggesting that the skin test was flawed, although this was not key to the case. However, two other incidents in 2006 and 2007 prior to the *Suryanda* case had raised concerns over the legitimacy of the skin test within any animal health surveillance policy. Although these never reached court, the Department for Environment Food and Rural Affairs (Defra) was forced to re-test two herds following complaints of malpractice by private vets. In the first case Devon farmer, Sheilagh Kremers, asked for a re-test when a nine month old Dexter bull (called 'Fern') tested positive for bTB. When Defra refused, Kremers would not release the bull to be slaughtered. During subsequent legal proceedings it became clear that the test procedure had not been conducted according to Defra's protocols. The case was dropped; Kremers was granted a re-test and an apology by the Minister for Animal Health in Parliament. While Fern failed his re-test and was subsequently slaughtered, the case prompted a review of skin testing by veterinary inspectors (DNV Consulting 2006). A year later, farmer Richard Bown's pedigree Holstein dairy cow ('Ecstasy Journalist Roxie') was deemed to have failed the skin test. Bown was due to show the cow at an international agricultural show, with valuations ranging from £40 000 (Long 2007) to between £95 000 and £115 000 (Driver 2007). Litigation commenced when Bown was offered £800 compensation for the slaughter of the cow, but the case was settled out of court with Bown granted a re-test, which the cow successfully passed.

There is a considerable reluctance to re-test in this manner as the view of the Department seems to be that testing is precautionary, so that even though there may be errors in testing this ought not of itself trigger a re-test. This line of argument was defeated, however, in *Jackson v Defra* [2011] EWHC 956, a case involving a pedigree bull ('Hallmark Boxter') whose blood samples were wrongly mixed post testing. The farmer challenged the slaughter order offering to settle the matter by a re-test. Defra pressed on to court, however, on the basis of the argument laid out above, only to be told by the Court that a failure to re-test defeated a legitimate expectation on the part of farmers that, particularly because the slaughter policy was precautionary, testing would be conducted under the requirement of good administration, by which public bodies ought to deal straightforwardly and consistently with the farming community.

These cases in part reflect Defra's policy to identify and remove infected cattle at the earliest opportunity (Defra 2009). This policy formed the basis of a more recent case involving a different clinical tool to assess bTB infection. In 2005, Defra began using a Gamma Interferon blood test, said to detect bTB at different periods of infectivity when compared to the skin test. The two tests have different sensitivities and specificities. In short, one may prove positive, but the other negative. The test is approved as an auxiliary test to the skin test under EU Regulation 1226/2002. However, because it can often detect large numbers of bTB infections where the skin test has found none, there are concerns that the test may be prone to identifying false positives. In April 2008, the use of the test was challenged in *R (High Burrow Organic Farming) v Secretary of State for the Department of the Environment, Food and Rural Affairs* [2008] EWHC 953 (Admin). The claimant argued that 'where blood and skin tests, taken together, produce statistically surprising results, then some further step . . . (such) as re-testing by blood and skin tests, should be undertaken to check the result'. Presiding, Mr Justice Mitting stated that 'there is simply no empirical evidence to show that blood tests which have proved positive may, if retaken, prove negative', suggesting that the discrepancy in test results was likely to be because of early detection of an 'explosive outbreak' rather than any of the other potential sources of error within the test. As a result, he stated that:

> [T]he policy adopted by Defra of using blood tests on herds in areas previously free from tuberculosis is lawful, and that its decision to proceed to slaughter animals which test positive on such tests is not only lawful but mandatory, save in the case identified by it in its policy where there is reason to doubt that the test has been properly performed.

Despite the Judge's statement that 'there is simply no empirical evidence to show that blood tests which have proved positive may, if retaken, prove negative', soon afterwards another farmer, Tom Maidment, sought a re-test of cattle after the gamma interferon test had identified thirty-one positive cattle. His local Animal Health Office, unaware of a refusal from London to do so, ordered re-tests using the skin test. None of the animals were identified as positive though none were spared slaughter (Booker 2008). Whilst this was not a re-test using the blood test, for many farmers the apparent unreliability of the screening tests for bTB is a cause of constant complaint, generating a loss of trust in government and declining compliance with Animal Health surveillance systems (see Enticott 2008b).

4.2.3 Challenging Compensation in Bovine TB Policy

A third line of cases involves compensation values offered by Defra for cattle testing positive for bTB. In July 2008, the values were challenged in *R (on the Application of Partridge Farms Limited) v The Secretary of*

State for the Department of Environment, Food and Rural Affairs (Defra) [2008] EWHC 1645 (Admin). Compensation values were reduced in 2006 as part of a 'cost-sharing' approach to animal health, prompted largely by the financial costs of the 2001 Foot and Mouth Disease (FMD) outbreak (see below) because compensation values were proving consistently higher than market values. At the time of FMD, in spite of the wish to cull quickly to stamp out the disease, the valuers had incentives to press for higher values as their remuneration was based on a percentage of payments made (Campbell and Lee 2003b). Even with endemic disease, valuers may have a stake in higher compensation values as they may be selling new cattle to bTB affected farmers. Yet financial disincentives for a bTB breakdown would better incentivize biosecurity. Whilst bTB breakdowns do have economic and social effects, the phrase 'farming TB' is often used to describe those farmers who deliberately seek remuneration through compensation.

Compensation is assessed through a table of valuation from the date of a bTB skin test leading to slaughter. The table contains 51 categories of cattle to reflect differences in age, type of animal (beef/dairy), sex and pedigree or non-pedigree status. The calculation is based on the average market price of cattle over the last month, for non-pedigree cattle, or the last six months, for pedigree cattle. The values in the tables are re-calculated each month according to market prices. The six month period to establish the market valuation of pedigree stock is telling. Animals of truly high value are much less frequently traded at market but sold by breed 'showcase' and private sale; these transactions are excluded from the calculation method. The average market value formula produces a broad brush approach and the Court heard evidence that in establishing average market value of the different categories of livestock, there were significant variations between the table value and the actual value.

The claimant, Partridge, argued that he was discriminated against by the tabular valuation as his total compensation of £8726 for eight high yielding, prize cows did not reflect their true value of (on average) more than £3000 each, so that his compensation should have been more than £24000. The failure of the table to reflect high-value animals such as elite breeding stock, high-value pedigree and organic cattle was said to have a discriminatory effect. The employment of a rigid average-value system discriminated against certain owners of high-value animals and the Order was said to be irrational, unfair, discriminatory, unlawful under English Law and contrary to the general principle of equality under EU law, contravening Article 3.2 of Council Directive 77/52/EEC, which requires that 'breeders are appropriately compensated'.

Defra denied that the claimant had been treated differently, but even if this were so, such a distinction was capable of objective justification applying a wide margin of appreciation to which the Secretary of State was entitled. Defra argued that it would be impossible to produce a table under which 'high value' animals could be readily and objectively ascertained. Finally it was disputed that the EU Directive requires the UK to pay appropriate compensation; or, alternatively, the compensation payable was appropriate.

The case was supported by the National Farmers' Union (NFU), which had opposed the table throughout, saying in a consultation response:

> The industry remains totally opposed to a table based system of valuation, on the grounds that the median price this gives will under compensate some animals and in some instances over compensate others. Such a system is unacceptable to our members who see it as unjust and not within the spirit of partnership and co-operation that Defra are so keen to promote (Lee 2008).

In the High Court, Stanley Burnton LJ held that EU law demands that any element of discriminatory unfairness be struck down unless objectively justified as a proportionate response. The claimants argued, on the basis of the ECJ judgment in *Royal Scholten-Honig (Holdings) Limited v Intervention Board for Agricultural Produce; Tunnel Refineries Limited v Intervention Board for Agricultural Produce* (joined cases 103 and 145/77, [1979] 1 CMLR 675), that differential treatment could not be justified by administrative convenience. The judge held that the greater the differential treatment then the greater the requirement for justification. Here the difference was described as 'enormous'. The Order attempted to locate a market value for a healthy animal, but this level of compensation was not provided to the claimant, entailing discriminatory treatment that the Secretary of State needed to justify by reference to objective criteria. Although the Court expressed sympathy with the difficulty of devising a fair scheme, it was not the job of the courts to devise such a scheme, but to rule on the legality of the present one.

On appeal by Defra, in the Court of Appeal (at [2009] EWCA Civ, 284) Lawrence Collins LJ found there was no discrimination as the true value of any animal, once it had tested positive to bTB, was simply the salvage value of its carcass. On this analysis, the true value of the Partridge cattle was not 'materially different' to any other cattle diagnosed with bTB and the table already compensated farmers in excess of the salvage value:

> All owners of pedigree cattle receive sums in excess of the salvage value of the cattle. It is true that, as a result of the table valuation scheme, some farmers such as the claimant suffer greater losses from TB than others. But that is not the result of discrimination against them.

The compensation tables were neither disproportionate nor discriminatory under EU law, as they provided a 'comprehensive solution to a problem of general public importance'.[3]

4.2.4   Summary of Challenges to Bovine TB Policy

There are some very clear messages concerning priorities within biosecurity policies relating to bTB arising out of the cases. The first is the preference given to precautionary slaughter. The perceived need to eliminate animals suspected as diseased overrides other competing claims, as the *Suryanda* case demonstrates. The stance is unashamedly precautionary. Notwithstanding the doubts attaching to screening tests, the Government persists in relying on such tests, defending the policy in the courts when necessary. The second is the pursuit of a 'one-size fits all' policy. *Suryanda* highlights how changing uses of the countryside are bringing new challenges to traditional agricultural policy. Test and slaughter policies reflect an era of agricultural paternalism (Marsden et al. 1993) in which farmers relied on the state for subsidies and were prepared to contribute to national needs. The decline of this productivist era of agriculture has led to the fragmentation of this relationship and the emergence of new forms of countryside use and ownership, exhibiting different values. *Suryanda* spotlights the difficulty of the state investing considerable time and resources into conducting tests as livestock owners refuse to test. Such owners do not see themselves as part of the agricultural system. Some stock animals fall victim to bTB but without compensation (e.g. Alpacas and Llamas); other stock animals are 'wild' and very difficult to test. Not only does this threaten the blanket test and slaughter policy, but it also highlights the limits of the compensation system as a means of securing tests. Thirdly, the cases emphasize the difficulties of a compensation system. Farmers will not generally challenge a slaughter policy where compensation is offered at a market rate. However, this is less true of farmers with specialist or elite breeds. Here, changes in compensation policy have produced resistance and the outcome of *Partridge* might have put at risk the compensation policy itself. If the value of an animal is no more than that of the carcass, then this changes the entire indemnity policy. Breeders are no longer indemnified against risk to high value stock. This, in turn, raises perplexing questions as to the purpose of compensation. Some of these issues of indemnification can now be explored further in relation to the epidemic disease of FMD.

4.3 FOOT AND MOUTH DISEASE

Foot and Mouth Disease (FMD) is a viral infection affecting cloven-footed animals. Known for at least four centuries (Grubman 2004), the FMD virus is a member of the aphthovirus genus within the family *Picornaviridae* (Sutmoller 2003). Though extremely contagious, it is very rarely fatal to a healthy animal contracting it. There are even less consequences for human health than with bTB. As with bTB, there are no human health implications of eating meat from FMD infected animals (FSA 2001, Prempeh et al. 2001), as happened through much of the 19th century in the UK (Woods 2004). Direct contact with infected or carrier animals will spread the disease, which can survive for considerable periods of time in animal wastes. It may spread by being physically carried by humans, or other creatures which cannot themselves contract the disease, by vehicles and by air. The disease has been described as 'probably the most contagious virus known in mammals' (Donaldson and Alexandersen 2002).

In 2001, after FMD was discovered at an abattoir, at least six million animals were slaughtered across the UK in order to 'stamp out' the disease. Such was the virulence of the virus that by the time it was discovered it had already spread throughout the country (Davies 2002). The race was on to outstrip the disease by culling not only animals suspected of being infected but also stock on surrounding, contiguous farms. In the event fewer than one in four animals slaughtered were infected (Vincent 2006; Campbell and Lee 2003b, Select Committee on Public Accounts 2003).

The costs of the 2001 outbreak have been estimated at around £9 billion (Defra/DCMS 2002), including £3 billion in direct costs to the public sector and £5 billion in costs to tourism and the rural economy. Compensation payments to farmers for the slaughter of their animals were said to amount to £1.34 billion. The lasting impact on the farming and wider rural community of this has scarred not only those farmers whose animals were culled, but also those unaffected by the disease that were unable to move stock to market, and received no compensation under the Animal Health Act 1981.

As with bTB, the events of FMD also found their way to the courts, highlighting the limits to, and confused objectives of, animal disease management policies. The legal challenges concerning FMD focussed on the legality of precautionary culling and compensation.

4.3.1 Challenges to Precautionary Culling

The tactic of stamping out disease, rather than using vaccination, depends upon effective tracing of diseased stock. However, in 2001, before the first case of FMD was diagnosed, more than 50 (Anderson 2002, 51) or 100 (King 2002) sites of infection existed. This being the case, stamping out was destined to failure and five weeks into the outbreak a contiguous cull policy was introduced. This policy required the destruction on a 'precautionary' basis of 'animals within . . . 3 kilometre zones' established around premises believed to be infected (Anderson 2002, 89), in order to create a firewall around suspected infection (Ferguson et al. 2001). The creation of these firewalls led to such significant numbers of slaughtered animals.

The legality of such a policy was open to considerable doubt (Campbell and Lee 2003a; Tromans 2002). Under the Animal Health Act 1981, Schedule 3 para 3(1) deals with slaughter for disease control purposes and provides:

> The Minister may, if he thinks fit, in any case cause to be slaughtered
> (a) any animals affected with foot and mouth disease, or suspected of being so affected; and
> (b) any animals which are or have been in the same field, shed, or other place, or in the same herd or flock, or otherwise in contact with animals affected with foot and mouth disease, or which appears to the Minister to have been in any way exposed to the infection of foot and mouth disease.

The problem for the contiguous cull was that, in its design, it extended to the slaughter of animals with no known contact with the disease or exposure to the infection. Zoning for the cull was mapped from London. As such, the geographical and physical barriers to the spread of disease were ignored. The misdiagnoses of suspected infections meant that not only was any farm under suspicion culled out, but so too were farms in the immediate vicinity.

Unsurprisingly there were court challenges to this seemingly *ultra vires* action. Not all such actions were well conceived. For example in Wales, Janet Hughes acquired ten sheep on the Brecon Beacons in order to gain standing to bring an unsuccessful judicial review of the culling of around 20 000 sheep (Hughes 2004). However, since these hefted sheep were unfenced, it was open to the Welsh Government to argue the possibility of exposure to infection. In England, there was only one case which succeeded in defending the contiguous cull, but this case has been roundly criticised in not providing the court with evidence from the Government's own research establishment that infected sheep could not spread wind borne infection over more than 100 metres (Hansard 2002). When this evidence was produced in a later case, the Court had little hesitation in prohibiting an injunction to prevent the killing of 'Grunty' – a pig that had starred in the film 'Babe'. The pig, it later transpired, was not infected by FMD.

According to a west country solicitor who gave evidence to the EU Temporary Committee on Foot and Mouth, the Department brought just fourteen cases to challenge resistance to the cull in England and Wales (Addey 2002), withdrawing from eleven and losing two of the three it took into court. Nonetheless, the Animal Health Act 2002 now remedies matters, allowing the Minister to slaughter '*any* animals the Secretary of State thinks should be slaughtered with a view to preventing the spread of foot and mouth disease'; seemingly faith is still placed in culling notwithstanding its spectacular failure.

4.3.2 Challenges to Compensation

Although there were pockets of resistance to the culling policy, the majority of farmers acknowledged that their stock would be culled and accepted the compensation. As valuations seemed to rise throughout the epidemic (HM Comptroller and Auditor General 2002), there were few incentives to resist. Farmers not affected by the disease, but unable to bring stock to market because of movement restrictions, received no compensation. This became clear at the time of a later outbreak, in 2007, which was caused by the escape of the FMD virus from the Government's laboratory at Pirbright. FMD broke out within three miles of the research establishment and the strain of the disease was one found only in the laboratory.

As with previous FMD outbreaks, herds were culled within a protection zone. Following the culling of this zone and a surveillance zone, restrictions were lifted over a five week period because the Chief Vet was 'satisfied that foot and mouth has been eradicated from the UK in 2007' (Woods and Montague 2007). This turned out to be mistaken, for only four days later a further episode of FMD was confirmed. Coming more than a month after the initial outbreak and outside the maximum 14-day incubation period for the virus, this later outbreak was a significant blow to the farming community. As the NFU pointed out, this outbreak came just as stock was due to be moving from upland to lowland areas. In addition the European Commission immediately revoked its earlier decision to allow the UK to resume meat and livestock exports. National restrictions on animal movements were progressively lifted but some remained until the end of 2007.

Following the settlement of claims with farmers whose animals were culled as diseased, other claimants brought proceedings to recover income lost as a result of inability to sell or export healthy animals during movement restrictions (Lee 2009). In *Pride v. Institute for Animal Health* [2009] EWHC 685, the claimants sued the Institute of Animal Health, Merial (a vaccine manufacturer) and Defra, as the licensing authority, in negligence and private nuisance under the rule in *Rylands v. Fletcher* (1868), LR 3 HL 330. It was assumed in court that the outbreak was caused by the negligent escape of the FMD virus through faulty drains. Nevertheless, the defendants argued that the claims should be struck out on the basis that the losses claimed fell outside the scope of any duty owed because the losses were purely economic and/or indirect, as the losses were caused by the imposition of government measures rather than any physical damage caused by the escaped virus.

Tugendhat J. struck out these claims and awarded summary judgment. The judge found pure economic losses, rejecting the notion of an intermediate category of damage which, while not physical damage, could be treated as such on the basis of interference with or effect upon physical property 'analogous to physical damage'. Economic losses were irrecoverable in negligence and nuisance because of the 'exclusionary rule', which removes such losses from the scope of any duty of care, as supported by long standing authority. The exclusionary rule prevented opening the floodgates to unlimited liability to an indefinite number of persons, as all British livestock owners were potentially affected by the ban on movements. The exclusionary rule had been applied so as to exclude liability for losses at auction in the case of an earlier outbreak of FMD (*Weller v. Foot and Mouth Disease Research Institute* [1966] 1 QB 569). In *Pride*, it was held that the claimants were in no greater proximity than the auctioneers in *Weller*. There was no 'connecting link' between the livestock infected by the virus and any consequential losses suffered by the claimants, which were outside the scope of any duty owed by the defendants. The judge did allow that the claimants might prove physical losses arising out of the condition and welfare status of the animals as a result of the movement ban. This would depend on further exploration of such losses. However, in respect of such damage, any losses fell outside of the scope of any duty of care owed by the defendants because of the indirect nature of the damage.

4.3.3   Summary

The FMD cases demonstrate the commitment to slaughter as the sole response to disease control. During the 2001 FMD outbreak, the Government was prepared to stretch its powers beyond the boundaries of legality in pursuit of such a policy and to avoid vaccination. In 2007, vaccination was again rejected notwithstanding an earlier review of policy which suggested greater willingness to use vaccines in the future (Scudamore 2001). The reluctance to vaccinate may seem mysterious unless one takes into account trade policy. The WTO adopts OIE classifications to govern permitted import restrictions under the SPS agreement. Countries without

FMD, and without resort to vaccination, will achieve disease free status where there has been no outbreak within a twelve-month period. Where FMD occurs thereafter, if the outbreak can be restricted by stamping out, then disease free status will be regained within a three-month period of the last slaughter where this is followed by serological surveillance. This classification offers more favourable treatment to the one-third of countries without FMD which, by choosing not to vaccinate, control the conditions of trade with countries that need to resort to vaccination. The desire to protect this trade status governed the choice of a cull in 2001; yet at that time the gross value of the relevant meat exports amounted to around £500m compared to the estimated £9bn cost of the outbreak.

Where animals were slaughtered, compensation was paid at a generous level but only to those whose farms were culled out. There were many other farming losses but these went uncompensated. Most farmers were uninsured against FMD, unsurprisingly given the availability of state compensation. Yet those few who were insured received both state and private insurance payments. The presence of rare but significant events of epidemic disease would seem to be suited to an insurance market. However, state compensation deters the development of an insurance solution. State compensation provides little incentive to biosecurity since farmers will not bear the losses, whereas, perversely, losses occasioned by farmers whose stock is not diseased go uncompensated. This would seem to suggest that compensation is not paid empathetically out of concern for the farming community so why compensate?

4.4 CONCLUSION: WHAT IS COMPENSATION FOR?

Two, perhaps competing, logics emerge from the cases as to why compensation should be paid for both endemic and epidemic animal diseases. The first is to address events of market failure, a common reason for regulatory intervention. Here the failure would be that of the market to provide adequate indemnity against inherent risk; thus, rendering it necessary for the state to make provision by investing in a centralized system of disease prevention to achieve efficiencies unattainable without intervention. Given the prevalence of persistent endemic or catastrophic epidemic disease in the UK in recent years, one may question the effectiveness of the centralized systems. Nonetheless, under centralized systems, the state may be minded to compensate where there is no conviction that the risk can be internalized by insurance or through pricing mechanisms, and where there is a strong public interest in maintaining production. The latter point is significant. In effect, by readily paying compensation we are treating biosecurity (and arguably farm production of meat) as a public good. A second reason for compensation might be to 'buy' intervention rights, employing compensation as a mechanism to influence behaviour. Compensation can be made dependent on the person following a desirable course of action. This may include both the reporting of disease and the rendering up of stock for slaughter. In the light of the epidemiology of the two diseases and the analysis of regulation viewed through cases of opposition to intervention, these two explanations for the payment of compensation are explored.

The market failure argument must be met with scepticism as there seems to be little reason why an insurance market could not provide cover. In the case of epidemic disease, the sporadic nature of outbreaks makes insurance a ready option since there would be many years in which there would be no claims made. Endemic disease is more problematic since there may be geographical locations which are much more prone to risk. Nevertheless, such risk might be managed by premium weighting with premium levels tied to effective biosecurity measures. There is no obvious reason why the private insurance policing of biosecurity, through usual mechanisms of disclosure, would be less effective than public controls. Indeed, compensation payments from the State distort the true cost of the disease that might otherwise be conveyed by the market pricing of cattle losses (Bicknell et al. 1999). This may be particularly so if, as the case law suggests, links between the amount of compensation paid and the value of the infected cattle become disconnected.

While it is commonly asserted that the role of compensation for bTB is to address failings in public policy, it is submitted that the true purpose of compensation is to buy intervention rights. Historically, compensation for bTB was introduced because of the failure of voluntary tuberculin testing schemes before the Second World War (Defra 2010, Annex A). Simply, farmers did not want to present their animals for testing because the resulting losses might outweigh appeals to the wider public good by reducing the incidence of TB. The failure of these voluntary schemes prompted the government to introduce compensation as support for a bTB eradication strategy. In the case of FMD, the chosen mechanism of stamping out the disease depends on rapid tracing of seats of infection and this is most likely to come through farm reporting. Without the promise of compensation, there might be great reluctance to make a speedy report. Compensation backs the chosen method of intervention, namely the culling of livestock.

Compensation is a price paid to retain biosecurity policies that are contentious. In either case, the policy hinges on international trade status, as governed by OIE criteria. Whether the protection of that status justifies the cost compensation is a complex question, but the answer is assumed

rather than assessed. In the FMD outbreak of 2001, the spending to preserve trade status by resisting vaccination hardly made economic sense.
If compensation is not there to rescue livestock production from events
of market failure, but to buy intervention rights, then meat and dairy
production are promoted as a public good. Yet such produce is a classic
private consumption good, the costs of production of which should be
internalised into the market price. That this is not done discloses much
about the condition of modern agriculture in which margins have been
squeezed in food supply chains to the point that state subsidy (through
compensation) maintains the profits available largely to those at the end
of food supply chains

In the case of *Partridge*, attempts to drive down the amounts of compensation, which had risen because of events of regulatory failure, meant
that only the carcass value of livestock was offered to the farmer, reducing incentives for farmers of high-value breeds to trigger intervention by
reporting. In 2001, the court challenges came from elite breeders resisting
the contiguous cull policy. Moreover, not all losses are compensated as
movement restrictions cause considerable losses, which go unmet, offering little justice to farmers successfully protecting their herds from the
spread of disease. Yet, as in *Pride*, even in the most deserving of cases
(given that the Government sponsored laboratory caused the outbreak)
losses go uncompensated. A policy that compensates those falling victim
to disease but not those resisting it, in the name of a biosecurity policy,
seems perverse. Moreover, the general policy is to pay compensation for
slaughter on suspected infection without bothering to wait for evidence to
confirm the initial, tentative diagnosis and this resulted in many healthy
animals being slaughtered. The need for speed, given the presence of
infection, is invoked. Despite this, the FMD cull only succeeded because
it culled a very large proportion of the UK stock. Similarly, in the case
of bTB, the disease persists and is proving intractable in spite of present
policies.

Compensation is only loosely dependent on the quality of biosecurity
measures and largely there to provide a financial incentive to present
animals for testing. Where this objective has already failed, then there
seems little logic to compensation. In England, it is only since 2012 that
compensation has taken into account farmers' refusal to conduct bTB
tests on time.[4] Defra's most recent bTB strategy (Defra, 2014) also proposes reducing farmers' Single Farm Payment where bTB testing regulations have been ignored. Compensation, if employed, should incentivise
good practice, deter illegal or inappropriate practices and provide a fair
system for taxpayers and farmers. The current compensation system may
generate contrary behaviours given the complicated social, economic

and natural factors that constitute the problem of bTB. Evidence from England suggests that attempts to reduce compensation are more likely to promote illegal behaviour (such as badger culling) rather than best practice in disease management (Enticott 2011).

Eliminating perverse incentives will require a bTB policy that addresses not just levels of compensation, but aspects of the management of the disease in a manner trusted by the relevant stakeholders. It is instructive that in those countries that have successfully eradicated or reduced bTB – namely Australia and New Zealand – decisions over compensation have been driven by the farming industry itself. In both countries, disease control is funded through a farmer levy from which compensation is drawn. Collectively, farmers agree to deliberately set compensation at lower than market rates to encourage disease prevention behaviours (Enticott 2014). It should be recognised that farmers' motivations are not solely financial but rely on other socio-cultural values (Garforth et al. 2006). Increasingly, farmers' values will divert from those implicitly suggested by the logic of compensation. Cases such as *Suryanda* show how socio-economic changes within the countryside are leading to new types of countryside with their own ethical and moral values.

Creating some link between compensation and biosecurity might seem an obvious idea, yet research shows that farmers in higher risk areas have become fatalistic towards bTB outbreaks, viewing precautionary measures as a waste of time and money (Enticott 2008a). The link between compensation and biosecurity is difficult precisely for this reason. Any approach of withdrawing compensation needs to promote biosecurity standards, the absence of which can be causally linked to infection. In the case of bTB, however, no such standards exist; there is an absence of research on the effectiveness of biosecurity interventions, and the evidence that exists acknowledges that such interventions play only a small role (ISG 2007, NAO 2009). In the case of FMD, the virus spreads rapidly once an outbreak occurs and there are limited steps to resist transmission. Other than seeking to combat illegal activities, there appears to be little farm-based activity that might reasonably reduce infections so as to justify reductions in compensation payments. This may suggest that it would be better to jettison the compensation regime rather than to argue about the fairness of valuations. But one should not underestimate the difficulties in so doing. It is a persistent feature of subsidies that, once introduced into the market, they make restoration of market behaviours a matter of considerable hardship (Lee 2014).

NOTES

1. EC Council Directives 77/391/EEC on Community measures for the eradication of brucellosis, tuberculosis and leucosis in cattle; 78/52/EC establishing the Community criteria for national plans for the accelerated eradication of brucellosis, tuberculosis and enzootic leucosis in cattle; and Council Directive on Community measures for the control of foot-and-mouth disease (repealing Directive 85/511/EEC and amending Directive 92/46/EEC (2003/85/EC)).
2. Section 32 Animal Health Act 1981 and Article 4 of the Tuberculosis (Wales) Order 2006 (now repealed by Tuberculosis (Wales) Order 2010).
3. Following the case, the Individual Ascertainment of Value (England) Regulations allow the Secretary of State in the absence of current sales data to offer the most recently ascertained value for an animal in the same category or the current agreed market value of the animal itself.
4. The Cattle Compensation (England) Order 2012 now allows a schedule of reductions in compensation for slaughtered cattle whose tests are significantly overdue.

REFERENCES

Addey, A. (2002), 'Notes for Presentation to the EU Temporary Committee on Foot and Mouth Disease', 26 March 2002, para. 17, available at www. warmwell.com.

Anderson, I. (2002), *Foot and Mouth 2001: Lessons to be Learned Inquiry*, London: Stationery Office.

Bicknell, K.B., J.E. Wilen and R.E. Howitt (1999), 'Public Policy and Private Incentives for Livestock Disease Control', *Australian Journal of Agricultural and Resource Economics*, 43, 501–521.

Bräuer, I., R. Müssner, K. Marsden, F. Oosterhuis, M. Rayment, C. Miller and A. Dodoková (2006), *The Use of Market Incentives to Preserve Biodiversity*, Brussels: Ecologic, available at http://earthmind.net/teebforbusiness/docs/The_Use_of_Market_Incentives_to_Preserve_Biodiversity.pdf.

Booker, C. (2008), 'TB Blood Test has Bloody Results', *Daily Telegraph*, 18 May 2008.

Burton, R.J.F., J. Dwyer, K. Blackstock, J. Ingram, K. Brown, J. Mills, G. Schwarz, K. Mathews, B. Slee (2007), *Influencing positive environmental behaviour among farmers and landowners – a literature review*, London: DEFRA, available at http://randd.defra.gov.uk/Default.aspx?Menu=Menu&Module=More&Location=None&Completed=0&ProjectID=14518.

Campbell, I.D. and R.G. Lee (2003a), 'The Power to Panic: The Animal Health Act 2002', *Public Law*, 17, 372–386.

Campbell, I.D. and R.G. Lee (2003b), 'Carnage by Computer: The Blackboard Economics of the 2001 Foot and Mouth Outbreak', *Social and Legal Studies*, 12(4), 425–459.

Davies, G. (2002), 'The Foot and Mouth Disease (FMD) Epidemic in the United Kingdom', *Comparative Immunology Microbiology and Infectious Diseases*, 25, 331–343.

Department for Environment, Food and Rural Affairs (Defra)/Department of Culture, Media and Sport (DCMS) (2002), *Economic Cost of Foot and Mouth Disease in the UK*, London: Defra.

Department for Environment, Food and Rural Affairs (Defra) (2009), *Gamma Interferon Diagnostic Blood Test for Bovine Tuberculosis: A Review of the GB Gamma Interferon Testing Policy for Tuberculosis in Cattle*, London: Defra.

Department for Environment, Food and Rural Affairs (Defra) (2010), *Bovine Tuberculosis: The Government's Approach to Tackling the Disease and Consultation on a Badger Control Policy*, London: Defra.

Department for Environment, Food and Rural Affairs (Defra) (2014), *The Strategy for Achieving Officially Bovine Tuberculosis Free Status for England*, London: Defra.

DNV Consulting (2006), *Review of TB Testing Procedures Report for Defra and the Welsh Assembly Government*, London: DNV, available at http://www.defra.gov.uk/foodfarm/farmanimal/diseases/atoz/tb/documents/dnv-report.pdf.

Donaldson, A.I. and S. Alexandersen (2002), 'Predicting the Spread of Foot and Mouth Disease by Airborne Virus', *Science and Technical Review*, 21(3), 569.

Driver, A. (2007), 'Credibility of TB Tests is Called into Question', *Farmer's Guardian*, 10 May 2007.

Enticott, G. (2001), 'Calculating Nature: The case of badgers, bovine tuberculosis and cattle', *Journal of Rural Studies*, 17, 149–164.

Enticott, G. (2008a), 'The Spaces of Biosecurity: Prescribing and negotiating solutions to bovine tuberculosis', *Environment and Planning A*, 40, 1568–1582.

Enticott, G. (2008b), 'The Ecological Paradox: Social and natural consequences of the geographies of animal health promotion', *Transactions of the Institute of British Geographers*, 33(4), 433–446.

Enticott, G. (2011), 'Techniques of Neutralising Wildlife Crime in England and Wales', *Journal of Rural Studies*, 27, 200–208.

Enticott, G. (2014), 'Biosecurity and the Bioeconomy: The Case of Disease Regulation in the UK & New Zealand', in T. Marsden, A. Morley (eds), *Researching Sustainable Food: Building The New Sustainability Paradigm*, London: Earthscan.

Ferguson, N.M., C.A. Donnelly and R.M. Anderson (2001), 'Transmission Intensity and Impact of Control Policies on the Foot and Mouth Epidemic in Great Britain', *Nature*, 413, 542–548.

Food Standards Agency (FSA) (2001), *Statement on Food and Mouth Disease*, 22 February, London: FSA.

Garforth, C., T. Rehman, K. McKemey, C.M. Yates, R.B. Rana, K. Green, M. Wilkinson, S. Beechener, K. Hollis and L. McIntosh (2006), *Research to Understand and Model the Behaviour and Motivations of Farmers in Responding to Policy Changes*, London: Defra.

Grubman, M.J. and B. Baxt (2004), 'Foot-and-Mouth Disease', *Clinical Microbiology Review*, 17, 465–493.

Hansard (2002), Lord Willoughby de Broke, House of Lords, 25 June 2002, Volume 636, Column 1275.

Hansard (2010), Mr Jim Paice, House of Commons, 30 June 2010, Volume 560, Column 4744.

Health Protection Agency (2009), *Tuberculosis in the UK*, London: HPA.

Hughes, J. (2004), *The Killing Pens*, Montgomery: Laurels Publications.

HM Comptroller and Auditor General (2002), *The 2001 Outbreak of Foot and Mouth Disease*, HC 939 Session 2001–2002.

The Independent Scientific Group on Cattle TB (ISG) (2007), *Bovine TB: The Scientific Evidence*, London: Defra.

Lee, R.G. (2008), 'Compensation for Bovine TB', *Environmental Law Monthly*, 17(7), 1–5.

Lee, R.G. (2009), 'The (Not So) Great Escape: The legal and moral responsibility for the Foot and Mouth outbreak in 2007', in J. Gunning, S. Holm and I. Kenway (eds), *Ethics, Law and Society*, 4, 377–388.

Lee, R.G. (2014), 'European Food Governance: The contrary influences of agricultural exceptionalism and market liberalisation', in T.K. Marsden and A. Morley (eds) (2013), *Sustainable Food Systems: Building a New Paradigm*, London: Routledge.

Leigh, I. (2009), 'Recent Developments in Religious Liberty', *Ecclesiastical Law Journal*, 11(1), 66–72.

Long, J. (2007), 'Farmer Devastated as TB Reactor Ends his Dream of Showing at SIMA', *Farmers Weekly*, 22 February.

Marsden, T., J. Murdoch, P. Lowe, R. Munton, A. Flynn (1993), *Constructing the Countryside*, London: UCL Press.

Muirhead, R.H., J. Gallagher and K.J. Birn (1974), 'Tuberculosis in Wild Badgers in Gloucestershire: Epidemiology', *Veterinary Record*, 95, 522–555.

Mol, A. and H. Bulkeley (2002), 'Food Risks and the Environment: Changing perspectives in a changing social order', *Journal of Environmental Policy and Planning*, 4(3), 185–195.

Nason, S. (2008), 'Multiculturalism, Human Rights, and Proportionality', *King's Law Journal*, 19(2), 391–401.

National Audit Office (2009), *The Performance of the Department for the Environment, Food and Rural Affairs*, London: NAO.

Ogus, A. (2004), *Regulation: Legal Form and Economic Theory*, Oxford: Hart Publishing.

Office International des Epizooties (OIE) (2010), *Terrestrial Animal Health Code 2010*, Paris, OIE, available at http://www.oie.int/eng/normes/mcode/en_som maire.htm.

Parry, J. (2010), 'Mycobacterium Bovis in Cattle: Here today, where tomorrow?', *Culture*, 31(1), 5–8.

Pendell, D.L., J. Leatherman, T.C. Schroeder, G.S. Alward (2007), 'The Economic Impacts of a Foot-and-Mouth Disease Outbreak: A regional analysis', *Journal of Agricultural and Applied Economics*, 39, 19–33.

Prempeh, H., R. Smith, B. Muller (2001), 'Foot and Mouth Disease: The human consequences. The health consequences are slight, the economic ones huge', *British Medical Journal*, 322, 565–566.

Proud, A. (2006), 'Some Lessons from the History of the Eradication of Bovine Tuberculosis in Great Britain', *Government Veterinary Journal*, 16(1), 11–18.

Scudamore, J. (2001), *Memorandum for Anderson Inquiry: Foot and Mouth Disease Contingency Planning*, London: CVO.

Select Committee on Public Accounts (2003), *The 2001 Outbreak of Foot and Mouth Disease* (Fifth Report 2002/03), London: House of Commons.

Sutmoller, P., S.S. Barteling, R.C. Olascoaga and K.J. Sumption (2003), 'Control and Eradication of Foot-and-Mouth Disease', *Virus Research*, 91, 101–144.

Tromans, S. (2002), 'Silence of the Lambs: The Foot-and-Mouth Crisis, its Litigation and its Environmental Implications', *Environmental Law and Management*, 14(4), 197–207.

Veterinary Epidemiology and Economics Research Unit (VEERU), Reading University (2009), *Descriptive Epidemiology of the bTB Outbreak in England*

since 1980, London: DEFRA, available at http://randd.defra.gov.uk/Default.
aspx?Menu=Menu&Module=More&Location=None&ProjectID=16382&Fr
omSearch=Y&Publisher=1&SearchText=se3253&SortString=ProjectCode&
SortOrder=Asc&Paging=10#Description.

Vincent, R. (2006), 'Silence of the Lambs, Calves, Sheep, Cattle and
Mathematicians', *Veterinary Times*, 6 March, 2.

Waddington, K. (2006), *The Bovine Scourge: Meat, Tuberculosis and the Public's
Health, 1860s–1914*, Woodbridge, Suffolk: Boydell.

Warrier, M. (2009), 'The Temple Bull Controversy at Skanda Vale and the
Construction of Hindu Identity in Britain', *International Journal of Hindu
Studies*, 13(3), 261–278.

Willis, J.W. (1950), 'A Short History of Rent Control Laws', *Cornell Law
Quarterly*, 36, 54–76.

Weller v. Foot and Mouth Disease Research Institute [1966] 1 QB 569.

Woodroffe, R., C. Donnelly, R. Cox, J. Bourne, R. Delahay, G. Gettinby,
J. McInerney, W. Morrison (2006), 'Effects of Culling on Badger *Meles Meles*
Spatial Organization: Implications for the control of bovine tuberculosis',
Journal of Applied Ecology, 43, 1–10.

Woods, A. (2004), 'The Construction of an Animal Plague: Foot and Mouth
Disease in Nineteenth-Century Britain', *Social History of Medicine*, 17 (1),
23–39.

Woods, R. and B. Montague (2007), 'EU Scorns British Foot and Mouth Errors',
Times, 16 September.

5. Being well fed: Food safety regimes in China

Neil Collins and Jörn-Carsten Gottwald

5.1 INTRODUCTION

The integrity of the food supply has always been high on the implied contract between governments and their citizens, but in China the issue also has deep cultural and historical significance. Chinese cuisine is famous for its variety of ingredients, most of them supposed to improve the consumers' health. In recent years, however, substances like 'ink, dye, bleach, wax and toxic chemicals' have all been found in the food Chinese people consume (Burkitt 2011a). The discovery of fake wine, fake tofu and fake eggs made of cheap chemicals marked a new peak in a series of scandals (Huei 2011).

Food safety is an ongoing serious political issue in the People's Republic of China (PRC). It challenges the Communist Party's (CCP) assertion that its monopoly of power is in the interests of the people. Regular promises by the party leaders to secure food safety remain unfulfilled (LaFraniere 2011b). Food scandals question the Party's claim to the traditional Chinese ideal of the benevolent leader and, to this extent, damage the CCP's legitimacy (Shue 2010). Selling dangerous food, adding illegal substances and avoiding public scrutiny undermine the ethical foundations of the modern Chinese society at a time when the Chinese leadership is re-inventing itself as provider of a harmonious and just society. Food scandals complicate the task of securing food for a population of more than 1.3 billion inhabitants.

While China is unique in its size and culture, it nevertheless offers significant insights from a comparative perspective (see Burns, Li and Wang in this volume). In developing an efficient structure for the supervision and control of food and food supplies, China shares many of the same difficulties as other states. Conflicts of interest between local authorities and the globalised capitalism supported by the central leadership are a constant obstacle to efficient policy-making. The PRC has been undergoing a fundamental transformation of its economic and social order with wide ranging implication for the way policies are made and implemented. Under the CCP's leadership, China has experimented with a broad range of regulatory structures over the last decades (Gottwald and Collins 2011).

When the Chinese leadership embarked on its bold policies of economic reform in the late 1970s, parts of the agricultural production system were among the first and most successful innovators. Food availability increased very significantly and consumer-buying patterns altered markedly as a result (Zhou 2010).

The impact of this ongoing socio-economic change on the political order remains disputed: some observers still anticipate a transformation of China's political system (Pei 2007; Yang 2007), while others claim, somewhat paradoxically, that the deepening and broadening of market oriented economic reforms has overall improved the party-state's capacity to survive (Brady 2007). The CCP's grip on power appears in no immediate danger but, whatever the longer term outlook, its core message remains that its monopoly is in the people's interests. For this reason, the regime is attentive to public disquiet (Veeck, Yu and Burns 2010) and has introduced mechanisms to improve accountability and participation. It follows global models of regulation in order to address, like other states, internal and external pressures within the context of a competitive world economy. To attract foreign capital, technology and know-how, the PRC has to reconcile its political dominance with a regulatory regime modelled on global standards and best practices. This has proven to be a huge incentive to depoliticise policies and, in some sectors at least, to promote technical expertise over the involvement of market participants.

5.2   REGULATION AND FOOD PRODUCTION IN CHINA'S TRANSITION

The importance of sound decision-making and successful political management of regulatory reform is nowhere clearer than in countries that embark on a course of radical modernisation. A reputation for good governance is a comparative advantage (Porter 1985). This might be offset, however, if the regulatory regime chosen imposes higher compliance costs compared to those in rival jurisdictions (Parker et al. 2004). Crucially, the demands for protection of the local *modus operandi* have to be set against the need to meet the criteria set by outsiders for foreign direct investment (FDI).

Many multinational food companies have responded to China's policy of opening to the world. Among the foreign food companies to take advantage of the continuing economic reforms were the big five chocolate manufacturers – Ferrero, Mars, Cadbury, Hershey and Nestlé. They arrived in the last decade but found themselves managing 'by the seat of their pants when dealing with China's mercurial economic and regulatory environment' (Allen 2010, 38). The attraction of China for the food sector has been changing, however, even as the regulatory environment has become more comprehensible.

Despite substantial growth, the food producing industry itself is extremely diverse and based on small-scale operations. Both the supply and demand sides of food have changed markedly in recent years adding to the complexity for regulators. There are nearly half a million food processing factories, of which 80 per cent are food workshops employing less than ten people (Engardio et al. 2007). For the authorities, these small producers represent a major safety problem (Johnson 2008). The food distribution network is also very disparate (Zhang et al. 2008). Further, the retail sector has been particularly influenced by the opening up of China to FDI (Skallerud and Grønhaug 2010).

In some food sectors, small enterprises have transformed into large corporations, like the dairy producer Mengniu, 'a miracle of Chinese enterprises' (Xie and Zhang 2009). The owners and managers of such large enterprises are often closely associated with the Party (McGregor 2010). This makes the CCP's task of distancing itself from public ire at safety breaches more difficult. In 2011, a survey in the *People's Daily* (23 May 2011) found that 93.7 per cent of 'the respondents said they cannot trust supervision departments any more'. Food safety is, therefore, both topical and provides useful insights into the Chinese approach to regulation and to the preservation of legitimacy by the party-state.

Following earlier studies of regulatory regimes (Gottwald 2011; Gottwald and Collins 2011), the analysis here will examine four interrelated dimensions of regulation in relation to food safety: organisation, guiding principles, configuration of actors and the specific reform capacity.

5.3 ORGANISATION

The challenge to provide food safety for China is enormous. According to official newspaper reports, in 2010 the authorities dealt with '130 000 cases of regulation violations or improper practices and detained 248 people suspected of criminal charges'.[1] They have to deal with more than 400 000 production sites for food and food related produce. China's first comprehensive Food Safety Law (FSL) came into effect in June 2009. The law had been expected for several years. Various food scandals caused a delay as the latest lessons were absorbed. With each deferral, public expectations rose. The FSL addresses the need for specialist agencies in an area of increasing technological sophistication with the level of coordination that critics suggested was lacking previously. Under the new arrangements, the State Council was called on to establish a national food safety commission which it did in early 2010. In a sign of the importance of food safety to the CCP, the commission was headed by Li Keqiang, Wen Jiabao's successor as premier. Below this top level, however, responsibility for oversight and supervision remains divided among several competing agencies and ministerial level organizations such as the Ministries of Health (MOH); Industry and Information Technology (MIIT) and Agriculture (MOA); the State Administration for Industry and Commerce (SAIC); the General Administration of Quality Supervision, Inspection and Quarantine (GAQSIQ); and the State Food and Drug Administration (SFDA).

The FSL mandates local government at or above the county level to supervise food safety regulations in the manufacture and trading of food. Overarching powers in the area of food safety are given to the MOH, which will take control of future food safety incidents. Medical institutions are also now obliged to notify local authorities of any patient with food-borne diseases, food poisoning or similar conditions in a timely manner. Similarly, food companies must put in place recall procedures, safety training, etc.

The new set-up is meant to address the uneven enforcement, patchwork of standards and overlapping mandates that typified the former arrangements. Nevertheless, food safety regulations will be the shared responsibility of a large number of government entities at several levels. The FSL is dealing with a diverse and dispersed sector and the organisational structure reflects this. It still relies, however, on local officials to enforce national food standards that include:

- limitations on hazardous ingredients;
- controls on food additives;
- nutritional specifications for foods for vulnerable groups such as infants;
- labelling and instruction requirements; and
- hygiene levels for food production and distribution.

In 2013, in response to continuing scandals and criticism of the fragmentation of the food safety framework, the China Food and Drug Administration (CFDA) was finally established. It has full ministerial status and works to support the State Council. The CFDA brief is very broad although little will change in the way it regulates healthcare products. For food safety, the new body still shares responsibilities with another new body, the National Population and Family Planning Commission (NHFPC), and MOA. The SFDA is no longer involved. The food production safety functions of AQSIQ and the food distribution safety functions of SAIC are now with CFDA. The agency has the responsibility to draft and promulgate food regulations although the more important ones require the central government to pass them.

As is common in Chinese legislation, the penalties for breaches are draconian but the enforcement of previous regulations has been markedly uneven. On 30 May 2011, for example, the Xinhua news agency reported the Supreme People's Court as suggesting that in cases 'where people die from food safety violations, convicted suspects should be given the death sentence, while criminals involved in non-lethal cases should face longer prison terms and larger fines'.

5.4   GUIDING PRINCIPLES

> We feel great sorrow about this milk incident. I once again solemnly emphasise that it is absolutely impermissible to sacrifice people's lives and health in exchange for temporary economic development. (. . .) All foods must meet international standards, and in particular, exported foods must meet the standards of importing countries (. . .).[2]

Both President Hu Jintao and Premier Wen Jiabao have signalled unmistakably the central government's concerns with the various food scandals. As per the standard operating procedure following disasters, the leadership 'feel' the people's pain and hound local officials. In the case of food, however, there was also an important foreign audience in countries that invoked safety concerns to end trade with China. Even Hong Kong, which relies very heavily on mainland sources, has imposed increasingly strict controls on trade. As Song and Chen show, for Chinese food exporters that bear the cost of compliance with foreign food safety standards, there was:

> (. . .) a significantly negative impact on China's short run export but a significantly positive effect on (. . .) long run export. Overall, it was found that the impact of increased food safety regulations (. . .) on China's exports was positive (Song and Chen 2010, 436).

Doubts remain, however, regarding the guiding principles for China's socialist market economy. The general idea of promoting economic efficiency through the introduction of market mechanisms into China's economy has only too often come into conflict with the desire of the CCP leadership to preserve their monopoly of power including privileged access to profitable assets. The rise of the 'princelings', an elite offspring from revolutionary elders, has triggered a debate on how much more concerned China's economic policies are with the interest of powerful clans than the overall economic development.[3] The conflicts between interests within the regulation framework are less prevalent in food safety however. The decentralized structure of the food industry prevents it from being controlled by only a few groups at the central level. At the local and provincial level, however, food processing only too often forms part of cadre-capitalist networks hindering efficient implementation of central policies.

> In truth, a local party fiefdom might be just down the road from the capital and still be able to keep the central government in the dark about what is happening in their bailiwick. So self-contained and opaque are party bodies that they have the power to contrive to keep secrets not just from the public, but from each other as well (McGregor 2010, 173).

As McGregor points out, the *Sanlu* case, the major milk adulteration scandal in 2008 (see Burns, Li and Wang in this volume), was initially hidden from Beijing by local officials in Shijiazhuang to protect 'the city's most valuable company':

> (. . .) disobedient localities have (. . .) been one of communist China's greatest strengths. The central leadership is invariably portrayed as a force for good in the narrative of China's rise, dragging the recalcitrant, corrupt and backward localities along behind it. It is true that many local leaders will ignore Beijing's edicts if they can get away with it (McGregor 2010, 173).

Therefore, attempts of centralizing and strengthening the national bodies are also part of a broader move of the party leadership to secure their control of developments in the lower echelons of the state. The decision on how to reform food safety regulation reflects the ongoing turf-wars between different central organizations as much as the never-ending conflicts between the central state and its local branches. To overcome the resistance of various organizations and local branches, the central leadership even tolerates ongoing public criticism of the newly reformed supervisory structure.

The central objectives of the new food safety regime, therefore, are regaining public confidence in China, assuring foreign markets by clarifying lines of responsibility. The government's analysis appears to be that the food safety problem arises from a combination of insufficient central control and unclear standards and procedures. So the guiding principle, to use May's term, is 'traditional regulation that emphasizes enforcement of rules by governmental agencies and penalties for noncompliance with the rules' (May 2007, 8). The PRC largely eschews voluntary approaches, self-auditing, management-based systems or performance-based models, all of which have informed food safety regulation elsewhere.

Multinational companies operating in China trumpet the role of supra-national institutions, which produce standards about product quality, quality assurance and risk management, and they may exert normative background pressure on the authors of Chinese regulations. The FSL, however, assigns no role to external bodies or to civil society, national or international. The rules are set to be highly prescriptive and top-down. They are also highly particularistic, specifying actions, such as product recall, forms of notification and transportation, and standards, in areas such as testing, training and food handling. The assumption is that stick-ing to the rules will ensure acceptable outcomes.

Unlike its predecessor, the FSL does not exempt 'trusted' companies, which had been left largely unsupervised. For example, many large dairy companies were given inspection-free status by the AQSIQ. Nevertheless, the food safety incidents that triggered the new regulations were not the result of a lack of law but a failure of enforcement. Under the FSL, it is not surprising to note that an early target of improved enforcement is the dairy industry. The pressure for action is relentless.

> China's baby milk powder [market] can (. . .) be divided into high, middle and low grades. After the Melamine Incident, China's middle and high-end infant milk powder market is mainly occupied by (. . .) foreign brands. China's middle and low-end infant milk powder market is mainly occupied by (. . .) local brands (. . .) [D]ue to their seriously descending confidence [among consumers] in milk powder produced by China's local enterprises (. . .) [i]n 2010, China imported over 400,000 tons of milk powder, increasing by over 60 per cent over 2009 (China Research 2010).

Mainland buying of milk powder at the end of 2010 and the beginning of 2011 caused shortages in Hong Kong and Macao. In February, after another adulterated milk incident, the AQSIQ warned that it will 'harshly crack down on and punish companies that illegally process or produce milk using leather protein'. From 1 March 2011, SAIC required new licences for the distribution of infant formula milk powder, which some industry commentators estimate will effectively close a third of producers.[4] Nevertheless, as with environmental and other regulatory areas based on local implementation:

> (. . .) local officials are often in cahoots with [errant] factory managers (. . .) either because the officials have a financial stake in the enterprise or because

they are afraid that closing a factory, or making it more expensive to operate, will diminish local employment and lead to social unrest (. . .) In other cases, local officials want to do the right thing but are too weak in the face of powerful enterprise managers (Economy 2007, 29).

Further, the supply chain of law from the NPC to local food producer is very long and, in practice, locally generated regulations issued by individual departments and local authorities are often poorly formulated and indifferently implemented. In some localities, substantial parts of the budgets of the supervisory bodies are covered by fines imposed on the industry. While this sets an important incentive to control the regulated scrupulously, it is a strong disincentive to put into practice efficient structures for the prevention of scandals.

5.5   CONFIGURATION OF ACTORS

The FSL has ensured the publication of new regulatory standards but the configuration of actors has hardly changed. Wishnick draws an instructive parallel between the PRC's capacity in space exploration with its food safety record as illustrated by the 2008 tainted milk scandal:

> Producing a glass of milk that meets health and safety standards . . . showcases all of the weaknesses of the Chinese political and economic system: poor enforcement of national standards at the local level, inadequate regulation, and a lack of accountability and transparency (. . .) (Wishnick 2009, 219).

The supply chain for food in China can be very long. In the case of milk, millions of farmers sell to middlemen who, in the past at least, have been largely unregulated.

For most commodities, China's food industry was highly fragmented and most suppliers were small local companies supervised by provincial and lower levels of government. In almost all cases, the major policy imperative for local officials has been economic development and there is considerable evidence that they are loath to hamper local production. For example:

> (. . .) the widespread implementation of regulations designed to improve food safety may force the general level of beef prices up in the mass market thus reducing the demand for beef and retarding industry growth and development (Brown, Longworth and Waldron 2002, 270).

As one ethnic group, the Hui, dominates the beef sector, the livelihoods of these 10 million people would be compromised. The political and social implications would be significant, particularly for officials in Ningxia Autonomous Region, and, as the production, processing and marketing is highly decentralized, enforcement matches local contingencies. A complicating factor in the beef industry is that many of the most economically vulnerable processing facilities are state-owned enterprises. Interestingly, good quality beef with a reputation for safety does command a premium in export markets as well as the top end of the premium domestic market. Nevertheless, the mass market is dominated by low quality produce which, due to Chinese consumer preference, is neither chilled nor frozen, often contains injected water and may be sold at early morning ad hoc markets that:

> (. . .) operate outside the practical control of local government health and hygiene authorities (. . .) [M]ajor municipalities have sought at various times to ban morning markets from selling wet beef but often without success (Brown, Longworth and Waldron 2002, 277).

The implementation of food safety suffers enormously from the fact that 'oversight remains utterly haphazard, in the hands of ill-trained, ill-equipped and outnumbered enforcers whose quick fixes are even more quickly undone' (LeFraniere 2011a). Apparently, 'a weak point of the Chinese food safety system resides in the lack of trained personnel' (Pei et al. 2011, 414).

In April 2011, AQSIQ was pointing to local government weaknesses in deploying quality control systems to 'crack down' on illegal food additives and abusing food additives. The local enforcers seemed to lack fairly basic data. AQSIQ director Zhi Shuping urged that:

> (. . .) quality inspection departments should first grasp and understand the overall situation of the food industry, especially in the number of local food manufacturers, the number of food additive manufacturers, the situation of illegal food additives and food additive abuse, as well as the hidden rules of the food industry.[5]

AQSIQ also called for its field quality inspection departments to urge local governments to establish public reporting mechanisms.

The FSL's heavy penalties are designed to reassure the domestic and foreign consumers of the quality of Chinese food. As were, for example, the death penalties that followed the milk scandal and the execution in 2007 of Zheng Xiaoyu, the former head of the State Food and Drug Administration, who accepted almost €600 000 in bribes from drug companies.

As discussed in Burns, Li and Wang in this volume, news of the milk tainting scandal was suppressed for wider political reasons associated with the Olympic Games of 2008.

> Although early warnings of a problem in the milk industry went unheeded and then were downplayed in the interest of the Olympics, immediately after the scandal broke in September, the Chinese leadership took action. President Hu Jintao visited a dairy production center in Anhui province and called for diligence about food safety, while Prime Minister Wen Jiabao apologized for the scandal on national television and claimed that the government would do everything possible to resolve food safety issues within the next two years (Wishnick 2009, 214).

Nevertheless, the CCP quickly sought to ensure that media coverage was not prolonged.

Multinational companies operating in China may, as their publicity material declares, go beyond the regulatory standards applying there. They too, however, share an interest in protecting the 'made in China' label. Such companies may apply different standards, for example on genetically engineered ingredients, in particular markets so they too do not welcome negative publicity.

Associated with the constraints on media coverage of food safety irregularities and other negative news is the problem of corruption in the Chinese bureaucracy. Even after widespread discontent, the central government finds it nearly impossible to implement changes to the supervision and enforcement on the ground. The complexities of central-provincial relations and the pervasive corruption among local and provincial party members impose severe restrictions on the ability of the central leaders to deal with a magnitude of smaller cases. The only viable option seems to be the involvement of the Central Discipline Inspection Commission (CDIC). But sending in the very powerful inner-party watchdogs is an option that cannot be used on a daily basis. Besides, rumours are ripe in China regarding the increasing corruption of members of the CDIC, which is also used as a weapon in inner-party conflicts.

In the configuration of actors, the role of individual companies in ensuring food safety regulation is crucial. Self-regulation, an important element in other jurisdictions because of the reputational damage and potential exposure to legal suits, is dampened in the PRC. Roth *et al* suggest that Chinese food producers:

> (. . .) [face] cut-throat competition (. . .) Any profitable company must regularly fend off hordes of copycats that will undercut its price (. . .) in China's ultracompetitive business environment, company survival is simply impossible without breaking some rules (. . .) [L]ow cost dominates supply managers' outsourcing decisions (. . .) (Roth et al. 2008, 26).

They also speculate that:

Some suppliers might justify their own questionable behaviours because of perceived inequities in the way that profits are shared among the parties in the supply chain.

In this business environment, individual companies take a very short-term perspective, in which process integrity concepts like traceability and transparency play no part. Many sell into a partially price-controlled market where margins are tight and survival is precarious. Exports are also very price sensitive and the temptation to make substitutions of cheaper ingredients ever present. In addition, in China's rapidly changing business environment, new norms are being established but buying organisations are still able to keep their suppliers' identity hidden – a practice reinforced by the custom of collecting full payment from buyers up front. The middleman's goodwill is more significant than that of the end consumer way down in the supply chain.

Chinese workers in the food industry are poorly paid and often migrant rural workers. For many the 'excessive' demands of a regulatory environment increasingly informed by globalised standards may seem almost ridiculous and faddish. Food production methods, such as deliveries and storage, often reflect the patterns of domestic Chinese life. Training, which the FSL now requires, could modify this outlook but the staff turnover is very rapid indeed. Taking a further step on the supply chain, China has about 300 million farmers tending farms often less than one hectare and earning less than €140 a year. Paper records, let alone computer databases, are impractical and not routinely collected. Roth et al. also identify 'smuggling, double record-keeping and the coaching of workers to give untruthful responses during inspections' as 'management practices that lower transparency' in the Chinese food supply chain (Roth et al. 2008, 26).

Another aspect of the food supply chain that suffers from a transparency gap is the exact reserve level of China's grain stock. This should, in broad terms, be an issue of food security rather than food safety but the data is not published. It is very unlikely that the PRC falls below the FAO approved limits, although yields have been growing relatively slowly in recent years due to drought and input prices. The problem for regulators, however, is that, because of price controls on grain aimed at addressing the needs of low-income families, there can be a temptingly high differential between Chinese and world prices. Thus, some officials are thought to smuggle grain out of China, thus compromising the system of regulation. As in other areas of food production and processing, competition is fierce with at least 5000 local grain-processing enterprises in China as well as the international players. In this environment, reliable information on the storage and related standards is hard to verify.

> (. . .) the domestic consumer market is changing with breathtaking speed: every month around a million or more Chinese enter the hallowed ranks of the middle class. The proliferation of consumerism in China is impressive and the transformation that the ongoing consumer revolution brings is of unprecedented historic proportions (Zhang et al. 2008, 38).

Regulation, such as the FSL, is only part of the food safety picture. Perhaps a more important element is consumer awareness.

Chinese consumers have a reputation for being highly price-sensitive in food purchase decisions, but consumers' willingness to pay for safer food is still uncertain and evolving (Wang, Mao and Gale 2008, 27).

In the larger cities and among the more affluent, a willingness to pay a price premium, knowledge of logos denoting quality standards and concern for quality is increasing but from a low base. Some supermarket chains, especially foreign ones such as Carrefour, are seeking to position themselves in the market as attentive to food safety.

> China, a country where supermarkets were almost unknown prior to 1990, has seen a migration of consumers from traditional wet market shopping into supermarkets for fresh foods. The modern food chain comprises around one-quarter of the country's food retail sales (Fox and Vorley 2004, 13).

By emphasizing their own food safety standards and marketing on the basis of trust and quality, supermarkets can benefit from food scares. Some food brands are adopting similar marketing strategies. In addition, the increasingly affluent upper middle-class of urban China has started to turn to organic foods hoping that the enforcement of the specific standards is somewhat better.

5.6   SPECIFIC REFORM CAPACITY

The FSL is designed to increase the PRC's regulatory capacity in the area of food safety. China has few trained and deployed regulatory personnel relative to the scale of the task. The new legal framework has done little to incentivize those charged with inspection and enforcement to change their current modus operandi. The FSL is seeking consistency but is still reliant on local bureaucrats to ensure compliance with prescribed actions. It is unclear that over-reliance on poorly trained third-party inspectors, in conjunction with exemplary punishments for serious transgressions, will be sufficient to change behaviours in such a diverse sector as food. The FSL has reinforced the role of traditional regulators rather than increased the reform capacity through the use of professional expertise from within the industry together with personnel and third-party experts.

A further shortcoming in the FSL reforms is the limited capacity that the Chinese system allows for citizens to use the court system to obtain damages for food safety violations. Regulators strongly discourage private legal action in safety and health related matters. As Dickinson suggests:

> One of the most important reforms would be to allow the effective operation of the existing system of private civil litigation and bankruptcy that would allow injured parties to take action independent of the government (. . .) Without these effective private sanctions, the standards imposed by the new food-safety law are unlikely to have any real effect (Dickinson 2009).

The FSL's capacity for reform is still governed by the huge, fractured and largely small scale of the food sector and an environment where evading or ignoring regulation has been widespread. The political mandate from the top for change in the area of food safety is clear but the local resistance in many cases remains robust. Thus, for example, on the generally tightly controlled border between the PRC and Hong Kong, where the enforcement of quotas and collection of duties is generally quite strict, customs officials are simply looking the other way. According to the blog of a Hong Kong law firm:

> (. . .) you will see many, many people bringing back (. . .) massive quantities of baby formula and (. . .) all sorts of other packaged foods (. . .) These people (. . .) simply do not trust China's food supply (. . .) [Locally] it would be politically unpalatable to crack down on this sort of thing.[6]

One way the Chinese authorities are tackling the problem is with public campaigns to create awareness and educate the people (Burkitt 2011b). With its vast network of cadres in organizations, enterprises and administrations plus its significant funds, the party-state can easily afford and order advertising in mass media or it can call for special meetings to discuss food safety policies. In this context, reports and speeches by Chinese leaders[7] have a dual role: to announce the latest policy initiatives and to prepare the basis for follow-up meetings and studies. While Chinese media generally operate within well-guarded limits of formal and self-censorship, the authorities are usually accepting of investigative journalism dealing with issues in food safety. Nevertheless, the risks for journalists, lawyers and NGOs dealing with these issues remain significant. Some Chinese experts propose to offer awards to the public for reporting on the food industry, a step the Chinese authorities have not yet taken. But the public is invited to report – even anonymously and using online access – on the misbehaviour of party-cadres through the website of CDIC.

In this regard, the ongoing series of scandals and the reports in the Chinese media might even constitute a positive sign. A more efficient supervisory regime, slightly better trained and equipped staff and party-state backing for investigative journalism in this area should raise the number of cases detected.

5.7   CONCLUSION

> The central position that food occupies in people's lives extends well beyond the necessity of food for basic survival or even its position as the foundation of most economies. Food serves a vital function in organizing the rhythm of people's days and facilitates the delineation of roles and rituals in a society. Given the prominent role that food serves to define and interpret cultures, rapid transformations in food systems can have profound reverberations in virtually all aspects of people's lives (. . .) (Veeck, Yu and Burn 2010, 225).

The politics of food safety are important in all political systems. Governments cannot neglect the citizen as food consumer even under authoritarian regimes. It is not just food scandals that hit the headlines that are important. Citizens will also count the income lost through sick days, medical expenses incurred and the cost of imported foreign substitutes linked to poor domestic food standards. Similarly, food producers, distributors and other commercial interests look to politics to provide a business environment that protects them from unfair competition, legal uncertainty and market shocks. Further, although food was once overwhelmingly a matter of domestic political concern, it is now a globalised commodity and subject to international trade agreements and understandings. The Chinese regulatory system operates within these realities.

China shares with other developing countries problems associated with rapidly changing eating habits and the associated health dangers. In the PRC, the issues are rarely about insufficient food, although shortages of particular products can occur and price fluctuations occasionally lead to political pressure. Much more important, however, are concerns about the safety of food because the effects of these can undermine trust in the political system. This is particularly serious if, as in China, the stream of negative news about food seems inexorable and broad-ranging. In food safety, the good work of many diligent and honest contributors to the supply chain counts for little compared to the malfeasance of a few. As Peter K. Ben Embarek, a World Health Organisation's food safety official based in Beijing, said of such incidents: 'It's clear that the credibility of the system will suffer' (*People's Daily* 23 May 2011). The sole custodian of that system is the CCP and the party's leadership are keenly conscious of the political challenges recurrent food safety breaches pose for them.

The trend in the West is for the increasing concentration of food producers and distributors into larger and larger units (Fox and Vorley 2004). In China, such developments are mitigated by political considerations and local protectionism but they remain significant. Nestle suggests that such concentration elsewhere leads to:

1. The relentless pressures exerted by food companies on government agencies to make favourable regulatory decisions; and
2. The invocation of science by food companies as a means to achieve commercial goals (Nestle 2003, x).

It is likely that the PRC will need to accommodate such trends although its system will obscure the political mechanics. At the moment, farmers and processors are too numerous and dispersed to have much negotiating power, although some larger and well-connected players may be influential. In any event, the CCP is unlikely to allow organized independent pressure groups representing their interests to form. Similarly, despite the FLA and central government's propensity for reform, power in the regulatory framework is dispersed.

The new regulatory framework for food safety, with its reliance on local enforcement, is likely to mean that changes will be very much dependent on local political circumstances and this remains a danger for the wider political system.

NOTES

1. 'Supervisory agencies blamed for food scandals', *China Daily Online*, 19 April 2001, at http://www.chinadaily.com.cn/china/2011-04/19/content_12358296.htm [accessed 3 May 2011].
2. Jiabao Wen speaking to the editor of *Science* quoted at http://www.aaas.org/news/releases/2008/1016chinese_premier.shtml.
3. See 'China's crackdown: Repression and the new ruling class', *The Economist*, 16 April 2011, pp. 11, 51–52.
4. See Food Safety Net report at http://foodsafety.suencs.com/archives/15719 (accessed 4 June 2011).
5. *People's Daily*, 29 April 2011.
6. http://www.chinalawblog.com/2011/08/china_food_safety_hong_kong_as_safety_valve.html.
7. See 'Chinese Premier Wen Slams Food Scandal', *Caijing online*, 18 April 2011, at http://english.caijing.com.cn/2011-04-18/110695434.html (accessed 10 May 2011).

REFERENCES

Allen, Lawrence (2010), *Chocolate Fortunes: The Battle for the Hearts, Minds, and Wallets of China's Consumers*, New York: Amacom.

Brady, Anne-Marie (2007), *Marketing Dictatorship: Propaganda and Thought Work in Contemporary China*, Lanham, MD: Rowman and Littlefield.

Brown, Colin G., John W. Longworth and Scott Waldron (2002), 'Food Safety and Development of the Beef Industry in China', *Food Policy*, 27, 269–284.

Burkitt, Laura (2011a), 'Why China Struggles with Food Safety', *China Real Time Report*, 25 April 2011, at http://blogs.wsj.com/chinarealtime/2011/04/25/why-china-struggles-with-food-safety/ [accessed 10 May 2011].

Burkitt, Laura (2011b), 'A Positive Take on China's Food Scandals', *China Real Time Report*, 29 April 2011, at http://blogs.wsj.com/chinarealtime/2011/04/29/a--positive-take-on-chinas-food-safety-scandals/ [accessed 7 May 2011].

China Research and Intelligence (2010), 'Research Report on China's Dairy Industry, 2011–2012', at http://www.cri-report.com/251-research-report-on-china-s-dairy-industry-2011-2012.html [accessed 4 June 2011].

Dickinson, Steven (2009), 'Food Fumble: China can't regulate away its safety problems', *Wall Street Journal*, 3 March.

Economy, Elizabeth C. (2007), 'China vs. Earth', *The Nation*, 7 May, 284(18), 28–30.

Engardio, Pete, Dexter Roberts, Frederik Balfour and Bruce Einhorn (2007), 'Broken China', *Business Week*, 12 July.

Fox, Tom and Bill Vorley (2004), *Concentration in Food Supply and Retail Chains*, London: Department for International Development.

Gottwald, Jörn-Carsten (2011), *Die Regulierung des Europaeischen Finanzmarktes*, Baden-Baden: Nomos.

Gottwald, Jörn-Carsten and Neil Collins (2011), 'The Chinese Model of Regulatory State', in David Levi-Faur (ed.), *The Handbook of the Politics of Regulation*, Cheltenham: Edward Elgar Publishing.

Huei, Peh Shing (2011), 'China has Fake Wine, Tofu . . . and Now Eggs', *The Straits Times*, 5 January.

Johnson, Toni (2008), 'China's Troubled Food and Drug Trade', background paper for Council on Foreign Relations, Washington, at http://www.cfr.org/publication/17545/.

LaFraniere, Sharon (2011a), 'The Invisible Poison Corroding China', *International Herald Tribune*, 16 June.

LaFraniere, Sharon (2011b), 'In China, Fear of Fake Eggs and "Recycled" Buns', *New York Times*, 8 May.

May, Peter J. (2007), 'Regulatory Regimes and Accountability', *Regulation & Governance*, 1(1), 8–26.

McGregor, Richard (2010), *The Party: The Secret World of China's Communist Party*, London: Harper.

Nestle, Marion (2003), *Safe Food: Bacteria, Biotechnology, and Bioterrorism*, Berkeley: University of California Press.

Parker, Christine, Colin Scott, Nicola Lacey and John Braithwaite (2004), *Regulating Law*, Oxford: Oxford University Press.

Pei, Xiaofang, Annuradha Tandon, Anton Alldrick, Liana Giorgi, Wei Huang and Ruijia Yang (2011), 'The China Melamine Milk Scandal and its Implications for Food Safety Regulation', *Food Policy*, 36(3), 412–420.

Pei, Minxin (2007), 'How Will China Democratize', *Journal of Democracy*, 18(3), 53–57.

Porter, Michael (1985), *Competitive Advantage*, New York: Free Press.

Ramzy, Austin (2009), 'Will China's New Food-Safety Laws Work?', *Time Magazine online*, 3 March, at http://www.time.com/time/world/article/0,8599,1882711,00. html [accessed 11 April 2011].

McGregor, Richard (2010), *The Party: The Secret World of China's Communist Rulers*, London: Allen Lane.

Roth, Aleda V., Andy A. Tsay, Madeleine E. Pullman and John V. Gray (2008), 'Unraveling the Food Supply Chain: Strategic Insights From China and the 2007 Recalls', *Journal of Supply Chain Management*, 44(1), 22–39.

Shue, Vivienne, 'Legitimacy Crisis in China', in Peter Hays Gries and Stanley Rosen (2010), *State and Society in 21st Century China: Crisis, Contention, and Legitimation*, Abingdon: Routledge.

Skallerud, Kåre and Kjell Grønhaug (2010), 'Chinese Food Retailers' Positioning Strategies and the Influence on their Buying Behaviour', *Asia Pacific Journal of Marketing and Logistics*, 22(2), 196–209.

Song, Haiying and Kevin Chen (2010), 'Trade Effects and Compliance Costs of Food Safety Regulations: The Case of China', *Agriculture and Agricultural Science Procedia*, 1, 429–438.

Veeck, Ann, Hongyan Yu and Alvin C. Burns (2010), 'Consumer Risks and New Food Systems in Urban China', *Journal of Macromarketing*, 30(3), 222–237.

Wang, Zhigang, Yanna Mao and Fred Gale (2008), 'Chinese Consumer Demand for Food Safety Attributes in Milk Products', *Food Policy*, 33(1), 27–36.

Wishnick, Elizabeth (2009), 'Of Milk and Spacemen: The Paradox of Chinese Power in an Era of Risk', *Brown Journal of World Affairs*, Spring, 211–224.

Xie, Xianghua and Tong La Ga Zhang (2009), 'An Analysis of The Talents Training and Corporate Culture Construction of Mengniu Group', *Journal of Inner Mongolia Finance and Economics*, Vol. 5, at http://en.cnki.com.cn/Article_en/CJFDTOTAL-NMCJ200905034.htm [accessed 3 June 2011].

Yang, Dali L. (2007), 'China's Long March to Freedom', *Journal of Democracy*, 18(3), 58–64.

Zhang, Xiaoyong, Hans Dagevos, Yuna He, Ivo Van der Lans and Fengying Zhai (2008), 'Consumption and Corpulence in China: A consumer segmentation study based on the food perspective', *Food Policy*, 33(1), 37–47.

Zhou, Zhang-yue (2010), 'The Global Financial Crisis – The Asian agrifood market and future trade', *Deakin Business Review*, 3(1), 53–72.

6. The political economy of Chinese food safety regulation: Distributing adulterated milk powder in mainland China and Taiwan[1]

John P. Burns, Jing Li and Xiaoqi Wang

6.1 INTRODUCTION

This chapter focuses on the implementation of food safety regimes, arguably at least as important as the formal rules and regulations that most countries now have in place. We ask why political leaders sometimes fail to enforce food safety regulations and which political and economic incentives have sometimes encouraged them to turn a blind eye to food safety problems. We focus on a single episode (the adulteration and distribution of milk powder tainted with melamine on mainland China and in Taiwan in 2008) and argue that the distribution of the tainted product had similar political consequences in both places (leaders resigned or were fired), but that the participants and process of coming to this outcome differed markedly, reflecting the importance of regime type. In authoritarian mainland China the food safety regime has been set on top of an incentive system for the promotion of local leaders that rewards economic growth and virtually ignores many other issues of importance to citizens, including food safety. These consequences were devastating. In democratic Taiwan competitive party politics and a robust and influential civil society turned what leaders perceived to be a technical issue into a political one. In both systems politicians had established highly fragmented food safety institutional arrangements that gave local officials considerable discretion. The arrangements have imposed costs on politicians, which sometimes have been severe but, especially on the mainland, apparently not severe enough for central authorities to reform the incentive system governing the behaviour of local leaders.

We use agency theory to examine the incentives for information sharing and holding political executives to account for food safety scandals.

Accordingly the relationship of principals and agents is one of conflicts of interest and information asymmetry (Downs 1966; Moe 1984; Horn 1995). Pursuing their own interests, agents seek to hide information and action from principals, which results in adverse selection and moral hazard. We understand that supervisors have influence over promotions, which may help to align incentives between principals and agents (Downs 1966). The chapter is based on archival research and interviews carried out in Beijing and Taipei with food safety officials, commercial operators, market managers, wholesalers, retailers, and NGOs from 2007 to 2009.

6.2   THE FOOD SAFETY REGULATORY SYSTEMS

Across regime types, including the two regimes in our case study, the food safety policy domain shares certain characteristics that include an important role played by experts (e.g., medical doctors, food inspectors, and veterinarians), unsure science (e.g., the relatively unknown health risks of genetically modified food), separate roles for producers and consumers, risks of regulatory capture, globalised food production and processing chains, and periodic food crises that can have global significance (Ansell and Vogel 2006; Toke 2004; Nestle 2003). In both mainland China and Taiwan politicians have put public health authorities in charge of managing food safety policy in regulatory systems that have been highly fragmented in large part because of the need to consider the interests of agricultural producers. We argue that a kind of regulatory capture has been a severe problem in mainland China where local authorities, pursuing rapid economic growth that they themselves are heavily invested in, appear to have undermined the enforcement of food safety regulation. Regulatory capture was less evident in our case in Taiwan.

By the mid-1990s politicians on both the mainland and in Taiwan had established highly fragmented, uncoordinated institutional arrangements for regulating food safety. By 2000, on the mainland at the central level, food safety regulatory responsibilities were shared by many different agencies, including the Ministry of Health, the Ministry of Agriculture, the General Administration of Quality Supervision, Inspection and Quarantine (AQSIQ), the State Administration for Industry and Commerce, and the Ministry of Commerce (Lam 1998). The Food Hygiene Law of 1995 charged the Bureau of Health Supervision of the Ministry of Health (MoH) with 'nationwide food control, formulation of food regulations and registration of new source food and health food' (Tam and Yang 2005). The Bureau was supported by the MoH's National Institute of Food Safety Control and Inspection. The system was characterised by strong vertical communications, overlapping responsibilities, and significant regulatory gaps. Each regulatory agency issued its own rules and standards on food safety within its own jurisdiction, resulting in regulatory confusion. The cross-cutting nature of food safety (crossing the health, rural [agriculture], and commerce policy systems, each with a senior official in charge) militated against strategic coordination. Powerful bureaucracies able to resist change operated in each of these areas. Moreover, China's important 'organizational responsibility system', which laid out performance criteria for the promotion of local government officials, failed to make food safety a high priority (Burns and Zhou 2010).

Enforcement of food safety regulations was the duty of local governments such as Shijiazhuang City, the epicentre of our mainland case study. Each of the agencies mentioned above had a provincial, prefectural/district and county office, which was responsible for implementing their own food safety-related laws and regulations (e.g., the Food Hygiene Law, the Product Quality Law, the Agricultural Law, and the Standardisation Law). We understand that these local agencies were often ill-equipped to carry out their supervisory functions.[2] Although these local government offices took professional guidance from higher level offices (that is the county industry and commerce bureau took professional guidance from the prefectural and provincial industry and commerce bureau (ICB), which in turn took professional guidance from the ICB at the centre), personnel arrangements including promotions were handled by local party committees. We argue that local governments used their power over promotions of local officials to influence (in our case, undermine) local food safety regulatory bodies in the performance of their duties.

In 2003, after years of food safety scandals, central authorities established the State Food and Drug Administration (SFDA), reportedly inspired by the US Food and Drug Administration (SFDA 2009; Tam and Yang 2005). Although the SFDA had wide responsibilities in the area of food safety, it had neither the bureaucratic status nor the political clout to carry them out. Interviewees within the SFDA reported that of the seven major areas that it was charged with coordinating policy and policy implementation, in reality it could only operate in two of them (Jiang 2005, 67). Officially the SFDA was described as the body charged with the 'real implementation' of the policy and comprehensive supervision and coordination. In practice it served as a clearing house for information the other agencies chose to share. Eventually authorities set up SFDAs in each province, and in prefectural-level cities such as Shijiazhuang (figure 6.1). When the head of the SFDA was executed for massive drugs-approvals related corruption in 2007, the continuing weaknesses of the SFDA became

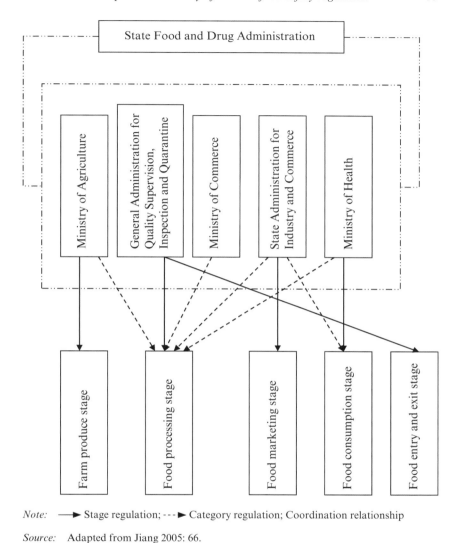

Note: ——▶ Stage regulation; ---▶ Category regulation; Coordination relationship

Source: Adapted from Jiang 2005: 66.

Figure 6.1 Mainland China food safety regulatory system in 2004

public knowledge (*CD*, 10 July 2007). A year later, just before the public became aware of the Sanlu tainted milk powder scandal, discussed below, politicians transferred food safety policy coordination authority back to the MoH (*CD* 26 August 2008). However, they left in place the highly fragmented food safety system that authorities on the mainland have been unwilling to change, principally we argue because they perceived that more effective enforcement would slow economic growth. Further institutional reform such as passing a new Food Safety Law (2009) and establishing a National Food Safety Commission (2010) have failed to address the incentive system discussed in this chapter (see Collins and Gottwald in this volume).

In Taiwan, in spite of the island's unitary political system (Peng 2003; Tan et al. 1996) politicians also established a highly fragmented food safety regulatory regime, again to accommodate food producers and processers. The institutional arrangements and coordination mechanisms for food safety control at the central level in Taiwan in 2008 are illustrated in figure 6.2 (Ye 2010). At the central level, three main agencies of the Executive Yuan had food safety responsibilities: the Department of Health, the Council of Agriculture, and the Environmental Protection Administration. The Department of Health's Food Hygiene Division was responsible for the safety of food in markets and in restaurants, while the Council of Agriculture was responsible for the safety of the farm products. The EPA focused on the environmental impacts of food production, processing, and marketing. Another three ministries also had responsibilities related to food safety control. The Bureau of Standards, Metrology and Inspection under the Ministry of Economic Affairs was in charge of the inspection of imported food. The Ministry of Education was responsible for food safety education. The Mainland Affairs Council was involved when food was imported from mainland China. At the local level, the Food Hygiene Division of the Ministry of Health provided professional guidance to the Public Health Bureaus of Taipei, Kaohsiung and other counties (Ye 2010). Critics observe that the Food Hygiene Division at the central level and its local counterparts were understaffed and underfunded (Ye 2010, 7).

With so many government agencies involved their responsibilities frequently overlapped or conflicted with each other, and no single bureau coordinated regulation enforcement. For example, the Bureau of Standards, Metrology and Inspection under the Ministry of Economic Affairs was in charge of inspecting imported food. When the Bureau failed to screen out tainted products and let them enter the market, public health authorities were supposed to recall, test and remove tainted products from the shops. Public health bureaus would be blamed for implementation failures of the standards and inspection bureau (Ye 2010).

While the regulatory regimes in the two places resemble each other to some extent, they were embedded in very different political arrangements. On the mainland, local government officials were evaluated and promoted based on a centralized performance management system that stressed

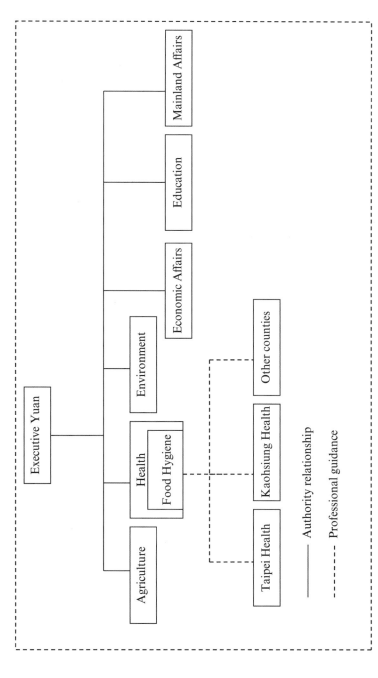

Source: Ye 2010.

Figure 6.2 Taiwan food safety regulatory system in 2008

economic growth and largely ignored food safety (Burns and Zhou, 2010) and civil society played little part in food safety regulation. In Taiwan, competitive elections and party politics determined the fate of local government officials and civil society played an important role in determining who should take responsibility for food safety blunders.

6.3   THE SANLU TAINTED MILK POWDER CASE

In 2008 authorities on both the mainland and in Taiwan discovered that food regulators in both places had allowed tons of contaminated milk powder to be sold in local markets, which caused kidney stones in infants and deaths on the mainland. The milk powder was produced on the mainland under a perverse incentive system that rewarded cost cutting and that paid little regard for building long-term reputation.

6.3.1   China's Dairy Industry

China has a long history of milk consumption but the consumption level has been very low, only about 5.6 kilograms per capita in 2003 (Fuller and Beghin 2004, 10–12). The government, however, made a strong push for people to drink milk (Wang Zhihua 2008). At the same time, to boost rural incomes authorities encouraged individual farmers to raise small numbers of dairy cows, which led to a remarkable expansion of both dairy production and consumption. The contemporary Chinese dairy industry began with cooperatives that owned their own dairy cattle. To cut costs in 1987, the Sanlu Group, a large, well-known brand, majority owned by the Shijiazhuang City government, initiated a reform that gave dairy cattle to farmers and let the Group focus on production and marketing, a move that split farming and processing into two separate operations. Middlemen then stepped in, setting up milk stations run for profit to buy the milk from farmers and sell it on to Sanlu (Schiere et al. 2007). The quality of the milk collected by milk stations varied.

In addition to individual farmers and small farms not having sufficient equipment and professional knowledge to care for the cows, milk collection stations could adulterate the milk.[3] According to a World Health Organization (WHO) investigation:

> In China, where adulteration has occurred, water has been added to raw milk to increase its volume. As a result of this dilution the milk has a lower protein concentration. Companies using the milk for further production (e.g. powdered infant formula) normally check the protein level through a test measuring

nitrogen content. The addition of melamine increases the nitrogen content of the milk and therefore its apparent protein content (WHO 2008).

Chinese industry insiders also confirmed this. Milk collection stations added water and alkali to raw milk, and later animal and plant protein powders that contained melamine (Gong 2008). The adulteration took advantage of a loophole in the regulations, which allowed the volume of nitrogen to represent protein. Such adulteration was common for many years and seems to have been an open secret in the dairy industry. Still, before 2007, dairy enterprises could control the quality of raw milk and refused to buy substandard raw milk because it was a buyer's market.

In China's dairy industry, domestic raw milk competes with imported reconstituted milk. The latter used to be much cheaper than the former. Dairy enterprises used imported reconstituted milk as the raw material for yoghurt and fresh milk production because the quality of reconstituted milk was much higher than raw milk collected domestically. Some dairy products, such as fresh milk and yoghurt, need high quality raw milk, which only a small part of domestic raw milk producers could meet. Moreover, the cost of reconstituted milk was much cheaper than domestic raw milk. In addition, another loophole in China's food safety policy did not require the labelling of reconstituted milk until the end of 2005 and dairy enterprises took their time to comply. Domestic raw milk then had no comparative advantage. Besides, farm feed prices had increased squeezing farmers' profits. Accordingly, by 2006 about 40 per cent of dairy farmers lost money, 30 per cent broke even, and only 30 per cent survived with a slim profit (Gong 2008). As a consequence, many dairy cattle were killed in 2006. By 2007, a world shortage of milk powder saw import prices increase dramatically (BZZERI 2007) and Chinese dairy enterprises began looking for raw milk from domestic sources. But domestic supply was inadequate and a buyers' market suddenly became a sellers' market: dairy enterprises competed to collect domestically produced raw milk. In 2008 to combat inflation, the Chinese government imposed price controls on dairy products, which put dairy enterprises in an even worse position. They had to deal with rising costs and a shortage of supply but could not get a payoff due to price controls. A possible way out was to loosen quality control to reduce costs. With milk collection entering a sellers' market, in which dairy enterprises chose to exercise less quality control over raw milk, milk stations had more bargaining power (Gong 2008).

Dairy enterprises clearly knew about the various quality levels of raw milk during collection and where to sell different grades of product. They paid more money for higher quality raw milk and less for lower quality. (That is, they no longer refused low quality raw milk.) They then used different qualities of milk to produce various kinds of dairy products (figure 6.3). The best raw milk was used to make yoghurt and fresh milk, the suboptimal raw milk to make breakfast or peanut milk, and the worst quality to make low quality infant milk powder for sale in rural areas where government regulation was much weaker. They chose adults as their major consumption target because, dairy enterprises reasoned, adults were better able to tolerate milk containing melamine. At the same time, dairy enterprises knew they should use the best quality milk (melamine-free) for important state events such as the Beijing Olympic Games which were scheduled for August 2008, and thus although melamine was found in most milk products in China in September, no dairy products used in the Olympic Village were found to contain melamine.

Among the largest producers of milk powder, the Sanlu Group was a foreign-invested state-owned enterprise. In 2008 the government-owned Shijiazhuang Dairy Company held 56.4 per cent of shares in the Sanlu Group, while the New Zealand Fonterra Group owned 43 per cent of Sanlu, an investment Fonterra made in 2005 (Fonterra Co-operative Group, Ltd. 2005). In addition another three Chinese companies – Shijiazhuang Hongqi Dairy Company, Chengde Huaning Dairy Company and Tangshan Kangning Dairy Company – each held 0.2 per cent shares of Sanlu. Sanlu Group's assets included a liquid milk plant, a plant in Jinan and three wholly-owned subsidiaries, as well as nineteen joint ventures (*Caijing* 2009). Before the incident, although it had been blacklisted in April 2004 for producing sub-standard milk powder along with forty five other companies caught up in the Fuyang case (*Ming bao* 14 September 2008), its milk powder had a good reputation and it was granted a 'Renowned Chinese Brand Products' certificate. In January 2008 its infant formula received the National Science and Technology Progress Award, the first time a dairy product had won the award in the award's twenty year history (*SCMP* 14 September 2008). As a result of such official recognition, Sanlu's products had also been exempted from government inspections for years because AQSIQ deemed it to have superior quality controls. Even the official China Central Television (CCTV) made a documentary to introduce Sanlu's '1100 quality testing procedures'. In China, with large numbers of counterfeit products available in the market, and where consumers make purchases based on brand names, Sanlu was at the top of its game.

In December 2007 customers began to complain to the Sanlu Group about the quality of Sanlu's baby formula (Wang et al. 2009). Sanlu strongly rebuffed further customer complaints in February and March 2008 (*SCMP* 13 and 14 September 2008; *Ming bao* 14 September 2008). However, in May the Group discovered that the content of non-protein

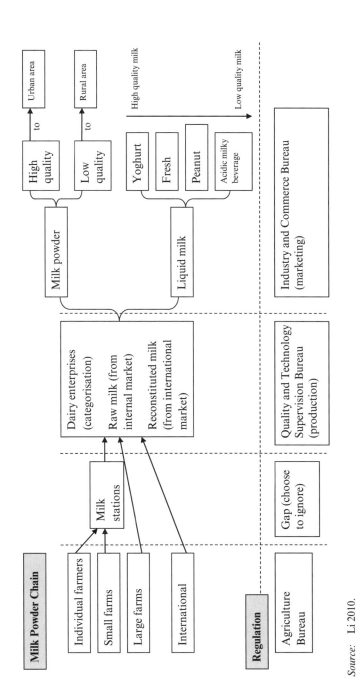

Source: Li 2010.

Figure 6.3 Mainland China dairy industry in 2008

nitrogen in its product was high but, according to reports, doubted that the cause might be melamine. By June 2008, health authorities in Jiangsu province had recorded fifteen cases of kidney stones in infants who had used Sanlu milk powder (*Caijing* 15 September 2008). On 30 June 2008 a member of the public made an inquiry about Sanlu milk powder on the central-level AQSIQ's website. AQSIQ replied that it needed more information and dropped the matter (*SCMP* 13 September 2008). In July 2008, in Changsha, Hunan Province health authorities recorded cases of kidney stones in infants and Hunan Cable TV explicitly linked renal failure in infants to possible contaminated Sanlu milk powder (*SCMP* 13 September 2008). In the same month a hospital in Gansu Province also reported to its Provincial Health Bureau (PHB) that sixteen infants under one year of age were in hospital with kidney problems. A month later the Gansu PHB told the hospital that it was 'still investigating' the case, but publicly the PHB said that it 'could not establish a link' between the kidney failure and Sanlu's product. At the time Gansu PHB's own hospital had admitted more than ten cases of renal failure among infants, an abnormally high number (*Caijing* 15 September 2008; Chen 2008).[4] In July, Sanlu sent a sample of its milk powder to a test centre of the Hebei Entry-Exit Inspection and Quarantine Bureau which on 1 August confirmed that the product did contain melamine. Still in August, in the run up to and during the Beijing Olympics, CCTV continued to identify Sanlu as a 'high quality domestic brand' (*SCMP* 13 September 2008).

The narrative reveals that complaints and doubts about Sanlu's powdered milk had been around for a long time. Local health authorities outside Hebei province did not share their findings or suspicions about the link between Sanlu's milk powder and kidney stones in infants with other regulators. Throughout this time no complaints were released to the public by hospitals or health bureaus in Hebei province. The central-level AQSIQ, apparently satisfied with its own finding that the Sanlu brand was of such high quality that it was exempt from testing, failed to investigate complaints from the public about the product or to bring the issue up with other regulators. While the local media outside Hebei raised concerns, the centre's propaganda machine drowned out any doubters. The period of the Olympics, especially August 2008, was a sensitive time and it is likely that the CCP Propaganda Department in Beijing had banned stories about food safety problems during August.

From 1 August the Sanlu Group, the Shijiazhuang City Government, and the AQSIQ in Beijing covered up the issue. On 1 August Sanlu held a board meeting (undoubtedly attended by representatives of the Shijiazhuang government, the majority shareholder and Fonterra, the largest minority shareholder), from which the Shijiazhuang government learned of the toxic milk situation. In response, on 2 August Deputy Mayor Zhao Xinchao, whose portfolio included public health, led a team of Shijiazhuang government officials to visit the Sanlu Group headquarters for a meeting with Sanlu executives. The team included the City Secretary General and officials from the Supervision and Technology Bureau (local AQSIQ), the Food and Drug Inspection Bureau (local SFDA body), the local Industrial Development Bureau, the Agriculture Bureau, and the City CCP Propaganda Department News Section (Wang et al. 2009). That confirms that, from 2 August, the local AQSIQ and SFDA had the information about the situation in Sanlu. The city officials refused Sanlu's suggestion to recall the milk powder privately. Rather they required Sanlu to exchange the contaminated product for a new product and compensate consumers to keep them quiet. Apparently they intended to keep the issue secret until the end of the Olympic Games (Wang et al. 2009). Accordingly, Sanlu issued no public recall for the product. It is likely that the Shijiazhuang food safety authorities reported this matter to the central-level AQSIQ in Beijing immediately. A food poisoning scare at the Olympic Village would have been a public relations disaster. After the scandal was exposed in September, the head of the central-level AQSIQ, Li Changjiang, stated in a press conference that, 'After the baby formula was found to be tainted by melamine, we conducted immediate tests of the dairy supply for the Olympics and no melamine was found.'[5] No melamine was found because Sanlu knew about the contamination, and supplied only high quality milk for the Olympics. We speculate that the central-level AQSIQ did not share the information about Sanlu (or other dairy enterprises) with the rest of the Central Government. We also speculate that based on its investigations in Gansu Province, some officials of the Ministry of Health may also have had information about the case in August. Still, throughout August and into September Sanlu continued to use contaminated raw milk to produce liquid milk for sale in some markets (Wang et al. 2009).

On 8 September the New Zealand government, having learned of the contaminated milk powder from Fonterra (which had the information from the board meeting on 1 August), reported to the central-level AQSIQ that potentially deadly milk powder was continuing to be sold by Sanlu (Ministry of Foreign Affairs 2008).[6] (We infer from Li Chunjiang's press conference that AQSIQ had known about this case since early August.) The Ministry of Health claims that it only became aware of the problem on 8 September. And on that day the Shijiazhuang government claims that it reported the matter to the Hebei Provincial government (*SCMP* 14 September 2008; *Ming bao* 14 September 2008). On 9 and 10 September, Sanlu continued to maintain publicly that the product was not to blame.

Finally on 11 September, the Gansu PHB held a press conference, naming Sanlu as the producer of milk powder contaminated with melamine (*Mingbao* 13 September 2008). Only then did Sanlu admit that its product had been contaminated. That is, during the thirty eight days from 2 August to 9 September neither the AQSIQ nor other food safety authorities nor Sanlu had taken any effective measures to address the problem (China Food Science Net 2008).

6.3.2   The Milk Scandal reaches Taiwan

In September 2008 authorities in Taiwan discovered that a subsidiary of New Zealand's Fonterra Group, the foreign investor in the Sanlu Group, had imported twenty five tons of the milk powder manufactured by Sanlu into Taiwan (China Milk Scandal 2008) and that mainland sourced tainted milk powder was widespread in many products in Taiwan. The government then banned the import of the tainted milk powder from the mainland and ordered stores to remove the products containing the milk powder from store shelves. At the same time various local health bureaus started to test milk products in the market. Given that melamine was not a compulsory test item before September 2008, various health bureaus adopted their own standards to define toxic products.

6.3.3   The Aftermath

By mid-September Sanlu halted all production as did industry giants Mengniu and Yili when melamine was found in their products, too. In the end, Sanlu was fined, went bankrupt and its assets were sold. The Chairman of Sanlu was fined and sentenced to life in prison for 'producing and selling fake or substandard products' (a violation of Article 140 of China's criminal law). Three other executives were convicted of the same charge and sentenced to five, eight, and fifteen years in prison respectively (*Caijing* 22 January 2009). Numerous Shijiazhuang officials, including the Mayor, Vice Mayor in charge of health, the Vice Mayor in charge of state assets supervision and food safety, the head of the Agriculture Bureau, the head of the Animal Husbandry Bureau, the Director of the local FDA, and the head of the local AQSIQ were also fired. The head of the central government's AQSIQ, Li Changjiang, resigned to take responsibility for covering up this incident (*CD* 18 September 2008). Curiously Li and many other officials have since been reappointed to other senior positions.

In Taiwan, the tainted milk powder import case also had political consequences. Having banned melamine in food products, on 23 September

2008, the Department of Health reversed itself and announced that it would from then on accept 2.5 ppm as the national (Taiwan-wide) uniform standard for melamine in products. The WHO subsequently also adopted this standard (Lui 2008). The change of policy prompted a furious reaction from the trade, the media, consumer groups and legislators of both parties that ultimately forced the Minister of Health, Lin Fang-yue, to resign (*Taipei Times*, 26 September 2008). Industry groups demanded that the government compensate importers and retailers for their losses (Ye 2010, 5). The media played a major role in pressing the government to take responsibility for the policy reversal. The issue became so salient because it highlighted the difference between the two major political parties on relations with the mainland (Ye 2010, 54). Since it lost the presidency in May 2008 to the Guomintang (Nationalist Party or KMT), the Democratic Progressive Party (DPP) in opposition had spared no effort to criticise the KMT's governance and its pro-mainland China stance. The fact that the melamine-tainted milk products were imported from mainland China gave the DPP another chance to criticise the KMT (Ye 2010, 55). According to the DPP, importing tainted food from the mainland demonstrated the danger of the KMT's pro-mainland policies to Taiwan. The DPP saw the policy reversal as more evidence of the KMT government's willingness to sacrifice food safety standards to improve relations with the mainland.

6.4 DISCUSSION

On both the mainland and in Taiwan, the distribution of tainted milk powder had severe consequences for some political executives. Politicians were dismissed on the mainland for covering up the scandal and for failing to take immediate action when they knew the extent of the problem. We speculate that because the local government in mainland China controlled the promotion of officials in local quality control offices, even though they were nominally part of a nation-wide (semi-vertical) quality control system, the local principal's concern for high economic growth (to ensure the principal's own promotion) overrode the formal task of ensuring that quality standards were maintained. Moreover, the local principals' concern for their own promotion which was linked to an overarching performance criteria (high growth and high tax remittances), meant that it was not in the principals' interest to invest in strong quality control capacity, which was perceived to undermine (at least in the short term) achieving the economic goals. Given that many local principals on the mainland expect to stay in a particular office for no more than from five to eight years, their time horizon was mainly short term. Promotion within local government was very competitive and they gambled that no quality problems of serious concern to central-level principals would emerge during their relatively brief watch. Given the nature of the political system which gives taxpayers and consumers relatively little voice,[7] this was a reasonable expectation. If serious problems emerged in the longer term, they would have moved on to a higher post.

Central principals tolerated this behaviour because local principals (their agents) were able to deliver the goods. Accordingly, it was not (at least in the short term) in the interest of central principals to develop strong quality control capacity, especially for the domestic market. The political system gives taxpayers and consumers relatively little voice, and their complaints could mostly be ignored or 'managed' (for example, through the politically dominated courts, side payments or extra-legal means).[8] By this logic the goals of regulatory institutions such as those put in place for food safety were displaced to support the developmental project that highly valued high growth and full employment.

In Taiwan, where principals are elected in competitive elections, the new KMT government mishandled what it perceived to be a technical issue (how much melamine in food was acceptable?). That the food was imported from the mainland made the issue even more sensitive. Consumers (a multiple principals-problem) voiced strong criticism of the reversal of policy on melamine in foodstuffs, and the government accepted the blame. In Taiwan, of course, local officials also look up to their bureaucratic principals but Taiwan's environment of competitive elections and media freedom give voters considerable clout.

The case reveals the impact of regime differences on the institutional arrangements for food safety regulation. The role of the public and pressure from civil society, including interest groups and NGOs, is magnified in competitive systems such as Taiwan's. Principals and agents both must take public pressure into account as part of their calculus.

In spite of the political fallout and further reform in both places the incentives for private operators and government officials to enforce regulations need to be further addressed (see Collins and Gottwald in this volume). On the mainland, local authorities have continued to discover milk powder producers selling products adulterated with melamine and food safety scandals have continued unabated (*Wall Street Journal* 25 April 2011). In Taiwan authorities discovered in May 2011 that local food and drink makers had been adding cancer-causing industrial plasticisers to their products, a practice that had apparently gone on unnoticed since the 1980s (*SCMP* 11 June 2011). Both places continued to have severe food safety problems, illustrating the need to address underlying incentive structures for enforcement of food safety regulations.

NOTES

1. The authors gratefully acknowledge the support of the Hong Kong Research Grants Council in the preparation of this chapter.
2. Interview with a director of Huaxia Dairy, Sanhe County, Hebei, 8 November 2008.
3. Interview with a director, Huaxia Dairy, 8 November 2008.
4. In an interview with Ministry of Health officials we were told that the Ministry sent a task force to investigate the Gansu kidney stone problems, but that they did not link them to Sanlu infant milk powder. Interview 16 December 2008.
5. 'Dairy Supply for Olympics Safe due to "Special Management"', Online. Available at http://news.xinhuanet.com/english/2008-09/17/content_10052104.htm (accessed 27 June 2009).
6. Interview with an official from Ministry of Health on 16 December 2008.
7. In 2011 civil society appeared to be playing more of a role in food safety policy implementation. See http://zccw.info (accessed 22 June 2011).
8. In contrast to the domestic scene, central and local principals had an interest in developing the export quality control system to which foreign trade was tied, reputation was important, and customers (through their overseas governments) had more of a voice.

REFERENCES

Ansell, C. and Vogel, D. (2006), *What's the Beef? The Contested Governance of European Food Safety*, Cambridge, MA: MIT Press.

Baiman, S. (1982) 'Agency Research in Managerial Accounting: A Survey', *Journal of Accounting Literature*, 1, 154–213.

Beijing Zhongjing Zongheng Economic Research Institution (BZSZERE) (2007), *China Milk Powder Market Supply, Demand & Competition Situations Research Report*, Beijing: Beijing Zhongjing Zongheng Economic Research Institution.

Burns, J.P. and Z.R. Zhou (2010), 'Performance management in the People's Republic of China', *OECD Journal of Budgeting*, 2, 1–28.

Caijng (2009), 'Who Owns Sanlu Group?', online. Available at http://english. caijng.com.cn/2009-01-06/110045400.html (accessed 21 January 2009).

Chen, Q. (2008), 'Gansu Shangbao Ying'er Shenjieshi Bingli 59 Li' (Gansu Province Reports 59 Cases of Baby Kidney Stones), online. Available at http://www.caijng.com.cn/2008-09-11/110011817.html (accessed 12 September 2009).

China Daily (*CD*), various issues, available at chinadaily.com.cn.

China Food Science Net (2008), 'Sanlu Manbao 8 Ge Yue, Shijiazhuang Shi Zhengfu Wanbao 38 Tian' (Sanlu Group Hid the Emergency for 8 Months, Shijiazhuang City Government Reported 38 days Late), online. Available at http://www.tech-food.com/news/2008-9-23/n0204406.htm (accessed 18 July 2011).

'China Milk Scandal: Asia, Europe Tighten Controls' (25 September 2008). Online. Available at http://www.monstersandcrits.com/news/asiapacific/news/

article_1433115.php/China_milk_scandal_Asia_Europe_tighten_controls_ Correction, (accessed 26 April 2010).

Downs, A. (1966), *Inside Bureaucracy*, Boston: Little Brown.

Fonterra Cooperative Group Ltd (2005), 'Press Release: Fonterra and San Lu Reach Joint Venture Agreement', online. Available at http://www/scoop.co.nz/ stories/BU0512/S00032.htm (accessed 21 January 2009).

Fuller, F. and J.C. Beghin (2004), 'China's growing market for dairy products', *Iowa Agricultural Review*, 10(3), 10–12.

Gong, J. (2008), 'Hebei Dairy's Messy Supply Chain', *Caijing*, online. Available at http://english.caijing.com.cn/2008-09-22/110014641.html (accessed 22 January 2009).

Horn, M.J. (1995), *The Political Economy of Public Administration: Institutional Choice in the Public Sector*, Cambridge: Cambridge University Press.

Jiang, J.J. (2005), *Rebuilding of China's Food Safety Regulation System*, unpublished PhD thesis, Beijing: Renmin University of China.

Lam, C.C.A (1998), *Consultant's Report on Food Safety and Environmental Hygiene Services in Hong Kong*, Hong Kong: photocopy, paragraphs 3.01–3.06 and Appendix 3(a).

Li, J. (2010), *Policy Coordination in China: The Cases of Infectious Disease and Food Safety*, unpublished PhD thesis, Hong Kong: University of Hong Kong.

Moe, T. (1984) 'The new economics of organization', *American Journal of Political Science*, 28, 739–777.

Ministry of Foreign Affairs (2008), 'Waijiaobu Fayanren Jiu Sanlu Naifen Youguan Wenti Da Jizhe Wen' (13 September) (Ministry of Foreign Affairs' Press Conference on Sanlu Milk Powder), online. Available at http://msn.china. ynet.com/view.jsp?oid+43246454 (accessed 1 January 2009).

Ministry of Interior (2010), 'Taiwan FDA Officially Becomes Operational', online. Available at http://www.moi.gov.tw/english/print.aspx?panel=news&type=tai wan&sn=3718 (accessed 27 April 2010).

Nestle, M. (2003), *Safe Food: Bacteria, Biotechnology and Bioterrorism*, Berkeley: University of California Press.

Peng, H.E. (2003), *Zhonghua minguo zhengzhi tixi* (Taiwan's Political System), Taipei: Fengyun luntan chubanshe.

Qi, L.M. (2007), 'Nainiu Weishenme Neng Channai' (Why Cows could Produce Milk), online. Available at http://blog.cctv.com/html/29/712229-16622.html (accessed 1 March 2009).

Schiere, H., X.Y. Zhang, K. De Koning and H. Hengsdijk (2007), *China Dairy Chains – Towards Qualities for Future*, China/The Netherlands: Wageningen UR.

State Council (2008), 'Guoyuyuan Youguan Bumen Fuze Ren Jiu Sanlu Pai Yingyou'er Naifen Zhongda Anquan Shigu De Youguan Qingkuang Da Jizhe Wen' (State Council Press Conference on Food Safety Incident of Sanlu Baby Formula), online. Available at http://news.xinhuanet.com/newscenter/2008-09/17/content_10047267.htm. (accessed 19 September 2008).

State Food and Drug Administration (SFDA) (2009), 'Main Responsibilities of SFDA on Food Safety' (English translation) from official SFDA website, online. Available at http://former.sfda.gov.cn/cmsweb/webportal/W45255826/ index.html (accessed 27 March 2009).

Tam, W.K. and D.L. Yang (2005), 'Food safety and the development of regulatory institutions in China', *Asian Perspective*, 29(4), 5–36.

Tan, Q.S., P.K.H. Yu and W.C. Chen (1996), 'Local politics in Taiwan: Democratic consolidation', *Asian Survey*, 36(5), 483–494.

Tirole, J. (1986), 'Hierarchies and bureaucracies: On the role of collusion in organization', *Journal of Law, Economics and Organization*, 2, 181–200.

Toke, D. (2004), *The Politics of GM Food: A Comparative Study of the UK, USA, and EU*, London: Routledge.

Wang, H.Y., Z. Tao and D.D. Ye (2009), 'Caijing Zazhi Tebie Baodao: Sanlu Du Naifen Shenpan' (Caijing Magazine Special Report: Sanlu Poisonous Milk Powder Sentences), online. Available at http://www.sachina.edu.cn/Htmldata/news/2009/01/4773.html. (accessed 20 January 2009).

Wang, Z.H. (2008), 'Meitian Yijin Nai Qiangzhuang Zhongguoren, Zhongguo Aixin Xingdong Jianjie' (1/2 Kg Milk Per Day Make Strong Bones, Love in Action), online. Available at http://www.niangzao.net/News/569/56938.html (accessed 11 February 2009).

World Health Organization (WHO) (2008), 'Questions and Answers on Melamine,' online. Available at http://www.who.int/scr/media/faqQAmelamine/en/index.html (accessed 1 January 2009).

Ye, F.G. (2010), *Gonggong zhengce zhiding guochengde junheng yu duanxu – yi dunaifen shijian quli moshi weili* (The Balance and Discontinuity of the Public Policy Making Process: Case of the Handling of the Melamine Contaminated Milk Powder), unpublished Masters' thesis, Taipei: National Cheng Chi University.

PART III

New forms of private food governance

7. Authority and legitimacy in governing global food chains

Peter Oosterveer

7.1 INTRODUCTION

As more food is traded across borders, food regulation is profoundly transforming as well. Conventionally this regulation was based on sovereign nation-states deciding how to secure their economy and feed their population. But nowadays, national authorities can no longer assume effective control over food because the volumes traded have increased dramatically while the structures of production and consumption constitute swiftly changing transnational networks. The emergence of unfamiliar hazards, such as BSE and Avian Influenza H5N1, leading to growing food safety worries among consumers, however, create an intense pressure to control food under the conditions of globalization. It is unlikely that existing multilateral structures, such as the WTO and the Codex Alimentarius, can adequately address present-day food concerns because they necessarily build on existing state structures and capacities. It is therefore not surprising that innovative governance arrangements multiply, notably via private standards and labelling initiatives. However, the involvement of private actors in food governance generates a debate about their authority and legitimacy.

This chapter discusses two conceptual frameworks developed to analyse governance arrangements emerging in the context of globalization. Although these theories by Sassen and Rosenau were not specifically developed for studying the governance of food, they may nevertheless serve as a useful conceptual base for analysing changes in this domain. In the first section, their views are introduced and their potential for analyzing present-day global food governance assessed. In order to illustrate this further, I relate these analytical frameworks to two private food governance arrangements, GlobalG.A.P. and MSC. The principal question to answer is how the challenge to secure authority and legitimacy is dealt with in private global food governance arrangements. In the final section, the answers to this question are elaborated and some emerging issues identified.

7.2 BACKGROUND

For over a century, conventional food politics was the responsibility of national governments. Governments were expected to set standards for food quality and safety on the basis of scientific information and to enforce adherence to these standards through specialized agencies for food safety monitoring and control.

In recent decades, this approach encountered several problems. The emergence of unfamiliar food safety risks such as BSE and GM-food challenged the reliability of science as the primary source for food safety politics. Moreover, many analysts of political thinking (Braithwaite 2008; Arts et al. 2006; Lang et al. 2009) agree that the nation-state is no longer the sole centre of command and control, but has to accommodate other actors and become involved in more collaborative forms of governing. In the present era of globalization, food politics also has to consider market-induced norms, cost-effectiveness, level playing fields for both domestic and foreign companies, as well as equity, justice and fairness from a global perspective and can therefore no longer apply only a national point of view (Oosterveer 2012). New concepts emerge to describe these changing ways of policy-making. Prominent among these concepts is *governance* (Van Kersbergen and Van Waarden 2004), which can be defined as 'the structures and processes that enable governmental and non-governmental actors to coordinate their interdependent needs and interests through the making and implementation of policies in the absence of a unifying political authority' (Krahmann 2003, 331).

In the context of global food governance, national governments increasingly have to share responsibilities with supply chain actors (Marsden et al. 2010). Particularly private companies and civil society organizations become involved in addressing sustainability and food safety in global food supply chains (Boström and Klintman 2008; Hatanaka et al. 2005). Fulponi (2006) observes three trends in present-day food policy:

1. a move towards private, voluntary quality and safety systems which include process as well as product characteristics;
2. emergence of global coalitions for setting standards; and
3. increased use of global business-to-business standards.

Despite the growth in privately-initiated forms of governance, nation-states still play key roles as decision-makers at national and multilateral level and as brokers between competing interests in global food provision. Hence, contemporary food governance in Western countries is an 'interactive process of state and public laws and policy with private interests and actors' (Lang et al. 2009, 81). This process deserves further exploration. For this aim, I introduce two conceptual frameworks that may support a better understanding of food politics in the context of globalization. First, Sassen's 'TAR' which emerged from a broad social science tradition and then, Rosenau's concept 'bifurcation' from a political science background.

7.3   NOVEL ASSEMBLAGES OF AUTHORITY UNDER GLOBALIZATION

According to Sassen (2006, 2008), the conventional regulatory system, based on *harmonized* local, national and supranational arrangements dominated by nation-states, is giving way to different *assemblages* of territory, authority and rights (TAR). This is an epochal transformation because it 'engages the most complex institutional architecture we have ever produced: the nation state' (Sassen 2006, 1). Sassen argues that the process of globalization is not integrated (or co-ordinated) but consists of a number of different processes evolving in a parallel manner enabling the emergence of a global dynamic and destabilizing existing governance practices. Sassen introduces the elements of territory, authority and rights as building blocks that will be connected in novel combinations (assemblages). Globalization can be seen as the re-assemblage of these three elements in global configurations. This new organising logic may be already dominant, while many characteristics from the previous organising logic, the nation-state, remain visible. The nation-state is still important because it is highly formalized and institutionalized but it also enables the emergence of a global scale of governance. At present, the emerging global assemblages (TAR) are highly specialized and partial, compared with previous arrangements. Globalization has not (yet) evolved in a fully developed TAR that completely replaces the nation-state. At the moment we are therefore going through a period of transition and, according to Sassen, we can determine the principal organising logic in the present context only by empirical research and compare the findings with assemblages from previous times.

To study these transformations in regulatory arrangements, Sassen suggests some additional concepts. *Capabilities* refer to 'collective productions whose development entails time, making, competition and conflicts, and whose utilities are, in principle, multivalent' (Sassen 2006: 7/8). Here, she refers to social processes that although emerging under an existing assemblage of TAR may contribute at the same time to the emergence of a novel assemblage. For instance, the rule of law was critical for the development of the nation-state and the interstate system but is at the moment also enabling the formation of a global system of human rights. Different capabilities together form an *'organising logic'* which can jump tracks to form new organising logics. The new organising logic does not invent itself nor is it generated from external pressure only, but a function of capabilities shaped and developed in the preceding period.

In the organizing logic of the global arrangement, Sassen claims that the diverse emergent assemblages of territory, authority and rights have one feature in common, which is that they are denationalized, whether their origins lie in specifically designed *global systems* or in the nation-state. Hence, the state has not become irrelevant as it is also through the state and its institutions that globalization materializes (Spaargaren and Mol 2008). It is therefore important not to oppose the global with the local because the global can be observed in the organising logic of the local.

A typical contemporary structuration of TAR, external to the nation-state, entails the private institutional order linked to the global economy, such as international NGO or private business networks. Even though such structures may partly remain national, they constitute a distinct *geography of power* and alter 'the historically produced distinction between the private and public domains' (Sassen 2006, 411). In this new (private) international order we see an emergent normativity that is not embedded in the state but partly installs itself in the public realm where it reappears as public policy, reorienting state agendas towards the requirements of the global economy (Sassen 2006, 412).[1] There is a proliferation of *subassemblages* bringing together elements that used to be part of different institutional domains within the nation-state or the supranational institutions. Novel types of *bordering capabilities* play a critical role in the formation of these particularized assemblages because under the conditions of globalization, borders are not necessarily only of a geographical character. Today borders can also be of non-geographic origin and for instance be embedded in the product, the individual or the regulatory instrument. Examples are internal transactions within worldwide operating private companies or the production of biofuels in developing countries according to the sustainability requirements defined by the European Union.

Sassen argues for a revision of the traditional notion of authority as based on the formal legal position of the state and suggests to replace it by a more social definition. In the global era, the legitimacy of authority is rather based on acceptance by those addressed than on a formal definition and can therefore be challenged in multiple ways by different social actors.

Sassen explicitly *decentres* the nation-state as the dominant organising logic and replaces it by an expanding number of more specialized global (sub-) assemblages. So, also in the area of food regulations, the coherent national arrangements of the past increasingly have to accommodate multiple private arrangements such as 'organic', 'fair-trade', 'climate neutral', and 'HACCP-safe', initiated by non-state actors. Questions then concern the basis of their authority and legitimacy and the capabilities that enable these arrangements to emerge and function.

7.4 GLOBALIZATION AND GOVERNANCE: 'BIFURCATION' ACCORDING TO ROSENAU

Rosenau (1992) developed an alternative conceptual framework and observes a shift in the location of authority in the process of globalization. He claims that five simultaneous changes have been driving this transition since the 1980s:

1. the shift from an industrial to a post-industrial order focussed on technological change;
2. the emergence of transnational political problems;
3. the reducing intervention capacity of the state;
4. the process of decentralization; and
5. the improved analytical skills and increased self-consciousness ordinary citizens possess when approaching authorities (the 'skills revolution').[2]

Under these conditions a process of *bifurcation* occurs where authority moves away from the nation-state, '"upward" towards transnational organizations and "downward" towards subnational groups' (Rosenau 1992, 256). Van Kersbergen and Van Waarden (2004) add horizontal shifts to these vertical ones, and point at transfers within the public sector towards the judiciary and from public to semi-public organizations. In the same vein they also observe mixed, vertical-horizontal, shifts such as from national public to international private standards. These new levels and arenas of governance lead to different understandings and institutionalizations of governability, accountability and legitimacy.[3]

States are not oblivious to these changes, although it is not their sovereignty or jurisdiction that becomes problematic, but rather the exclusivity and the scope of their competence as multi-centric systems of governance develop. According to Rosenau, nation-states are becoming one level and one actor amidst a plurality of arrangements with multiple levels and multiple actors. This is referred to as *multi-level multi-actor governance* (Arts et al. 2006). Rosenau argues that in the context of globalization authority is de-territorialized and located in multiple *'spheres of authority'*, which may undergo even further disaggregation (Rosenau 2007). Spheres of authority are determined by the issuance of directives from its leadership and the compliance by its adherents. Compliance is the key to determine a sphere and compliance can be either intentional or unintentional, and the result of a host of interactive and reinforcing dynamics but not automatic. The propagation of spheres of authority by private companies and civil society organizations is a consequence of globalization, because this process weakens the state and private initiatives try to fill the emerging void. Such new spheres of authority derive their legitimacy from the voluntary and conditional participation of individuals who can revoke their consent at any time, contrary to the nation-state where citizens are legally bound to honour decisions by governmental authorities. Politics in these new sites of power is more chaotic and informal because there are no political and legal authorities and formally defined governance levels (such as in the nation-state), but mainly unconventional ones where each actor has to redefine and construct his/her own role. Moreover, these actors have to construct their roles while engaging in actual politics at the same time (Van Leeuwen 2010).

Today, governance may materialize in different 'modes', which may be positioned on a continuum between public authority and societal self-regulation involving particular policy instruments, actor constellations and institutional settings (Treib et al. 2007). Opportunities are created for hybrid forms of governance: co-management (between civil society and state), public-private partnerships (between state and market), and private-social partnerships (between civil society and the market). Mechanisms of environmental governance based on the market and economic incentives, i.e. eco-taxes, voluntary agreements, certification, and informational systems are examples of public-private and private-private cooperation that increasingly drive global governance (Stripple 2006). Multilevel, non-hierarchical, information-rich, loose networks of institutions and actors repeatedly prove more effective than state-centric international regimes (Lemos and Agrawal 2006). The current multiplication of different spheres of authority however inhibits the perspectives for a single global governance structure, and leaves only the possibility of multiple overlapping and transnational ones. Rosenau (2007) suggests that despite their number and variety, these spheres of authority co-evolve and thereby become increasingly adaptive to each other so, over time, they may achieve a certain level of (global) harmonization.

Although conventional political theory is less useful under the conditions of hybridity and ambiguity typical for the era of globalization, the classical challenges of legitimacy and authority remain. Rosenau argues that, with the presence of multiple spheres of authority, legitimacy and authority have to be addressed in a novel manner by combining normative with more pragmatic, procedural elements. Rosenau argues for inclusive participation of all relevant stakeholders profiting from the increased awareness and knowledge among citizens (the skills revolution).

When applying Rosenau's views on global food governance one may observe the emergence of a new separate sphere of authority where hybrid modes of governance are developed dominated by private actors and to a lesser extent by national authorities. For instance, a certification scheme for sustainably managed fisheries such as the Marine Stewardship Council (MSC) was initiated by a private company (Unilever) and an international NGO (WWF) and today MSC is globally recognized as a guarantee for sustainable fish (Oosterveer, 2012). Such a sphere of authority is forced to find its place in the midst of already existing global food governance arrangements, dominated by national governments and the WTO. It is therefore an empirical question to determine to what extent global food governance will develop further into a separate sphere of authority with a particular mode of governance or whether these initiatives will become integrated in already existing global food governance arrangements.

The views from Sassen and Rosenau presented here do not diametrically oppose each other as they both notice, together with many other authors, the changing role of the nation-state but not its disappearance, the emergence of hybrid governance arrangements that involve public and private actors, and the presence of multiple spheres of authority (Rosenau) or assemblages (Sassen) without one dominant global governance system. They differ however in their analysis of the process of change: Sassen pays much more attention to socio-historical dynamics, while Rosenau concentrates on the conditions for developing successful modes of governance in the context of the multiple emerging spheres of authority. The most relevant difference concerns their view on how to protect public interest under the conditions of globalization. Rosenau is rather optimistic about the possibilities of skilled citizens influencing the emerging modes of global governance. As authority is less based on formal power and more on voluntary acceptance by the people concerned, authority is immediately undermined when people revoke their consent. Sassen is much less optimistic as she argues that specialized global governance assemblages may emerge from capabilities present among key actors, such as private companies, who have no need for including all stakeholders. Curtailing the power of such assemblages requires the development of alternatives opposing global assemblages.

These perspectives provide a promising framework for analysing the ways in which public interests are incorporated in two different global food governance arrangements that were recently introduced: GlobalG.A.P. and MSC. My focus is hereby on two specific public interests, namely the safety of food and the environmental impact of food provision.

7.5   GLOBALG.A.P.

GlobalG.A.P. (Global Partnership for Good Agricultural Practices; initially introduced as EurepGAP)[4] was established in 1997 by the Euro-Retailer Produce Working Group (EUREP) and combines auditing food safety standards and specific protocols for sustainable food production (Campbell 2005; Van der Grijp and Hond 1999). Before 1997, European retailing firms responded individually to food crises creating confusion about food safety and potentially turning this into a matter of competition. Many firms considered this unhelpful because it would rather confuse consumers and not contribute to trust in food in general. Another consideration for introducing GlobalG.A.P. was that 'organic agriculture' was, at that time, recognized as the only sustainable alternative to conventional food production, while retailers considered 'integrated farming' as another attractive option, which they therefore wanted to promote as well (Campbell 2005).[5] At the same time, the EU developed uniform standards for the maximum residue levels of pesticides in fresh produce (Henson et al. 2009). So, as there was a need for harmonization, the larger European retailers began to discuss 'integrated crop management'. Their objective was to develop common, verifiable environmental and food safety standards that were accessible for groups of mainstream farmers, i.e. requiring their compliance with minimum norms without complicated changes in their businesses (Gawron and Theuvsen 2009). For this purpose, they developed 'good agricultural practices' on the basis of the already existing HACCP-protocol to assure the safety of food in combination with on-farm integrated systems to guarantee environmental sustainability. At first they focussed on fresh fruits and vegetables but later the initiative expanded to other agricultural products as well (Humphrey 2008).[6] As a private, voluntary process standard, GlobalG.A.P. is based on third-party certification and as a business-to-business standard, it has no label to inform consumers nor is it used in advertising.

Concrete protocols were developed between 1997 and 1999 through negotiations within its Technical Standards Committees that included a range of stakeholders[7] and made decisions on the basis of unanimity. This way, private actors created a separate sphere of authority, as it was not the profit-seeking strategy of an individual company nor the general interest defended by a public institution that determined farmer practices. The retailers and food processors participating in the process created a particular sub-assemblage and nominated themselves as authority entitled to make decisions on food production practices all over the world. They introduced a particular mode of governance because formally no farmer was obliged to follow their guidelines, but in practice they had no other option if they wanted to sell their produce to large European supermarkets. This private initiative therefore determined the definitions of food safety and sustainability and how they should be secured, without involving farmers. And although, the GlobalG.A.P. standards are justified as primarily being designed 'to reassure consumers about how food is produced on the farm by minimizing detrimental environmental impacts of farming operations, reducing the use of chemical inputs and ensuring a responsible approach to worker health and safety as well as animal welfare',[8] consumers have not been engaged. The basis of their authority and legitimacy is therefore unclear.

Within only a few years after their introduction, the GlobalG.A.P. protocols were applied by nearly all leading European retailers, followed by many farmers, auditing and agro-input firms, and NGOs. The protocols were initially built on farming practices familiar to the EU's Common Agricultural Policy and hence most easily applicable on European-like models of farming. However, not all food originates from within the EU, so the initiative needed to transform into a worldwide standard for food production within international supply chains. As smallholder participation from developing countries was seriously hampered by the GlobalG.A.P. requirements (Narrod et al. 2008) the organization responded by developing specific instruments to facilitate their access: group certification, a smallholder manual, and feedback opportunities. This process has been successful as the organization has issued over 93 000 certificates to producers in more than 100 countries.[9] The initiative expanded further by including additional members and food products and by benchmarking its standards against international food safety standards, as established in the Codex Alimentarius. Moreover, GlobalG.A.P. actively promotes benchmarked national standards that are regarded as equivalent. This makes it possible to adapt GlobalG.A.P.'s own protocols to national circumstances while maintaining recognition of the international standard's value (Humphrey 2008). Several national working groups are actively pursuing this goal.

Although not legally binding, as a private initiative GlobalG.A.P. has become de facto mandatory for food producers operating on the European market and increasingly beyond it as well. This way a level playing field is being created on food safety and sustainability for all major European (and global) retailers. The standards inserted in GlobalG.A.P. are partly to fulfil official EU-requirements but also involves wider retailer concerns. This initiative has not rendered state systems of governance obsolete, because compliance with state regulations in both the country of origin and the country of destination remains necessary for GlobalG.A.P. certification (Casey 2008). Nevertheless, this collaborative relationship between different private actors shows the emergence of a specific sub-assemblage, outside the conventional food policy arrangement, that gets increasingly institutionalized. The legitimacy of GlobalG.A.P. flows from a combination of the connection with governmental regulations, standards that were based on consumer concerns, and the use of science and scientific experts. On these grounds GlobalG.A.P.'s justification as defending public interests remains largely undisputed and only its procedures are contested because they complicate access for smallholder farmers, especially from developing countries (Humphrey 2008). Public pressure on GlobalG.A.P. has not been widespread, but where exerted this focussed on adapting procedures in order to no longer exclude smallholders.

The GlobalG.A.P. initiative makes clear that a separate governance arena emerges where private actors carve out a particular domain in global food supply where they autonomously position their authority. For instance, only food supplied to consumers in large European and US supermarkets falls under this regime (c.f. Sassen's notion of novel borders in the global era), but in the process the initiative creates global standards and contributes to further emergence of global assemblages. The mode of governance is innovative through the use of voluntary standards and certification, justified by scientific arguments and being based on consumer interests. However, Rosenau's suggestion that this innovative mode of governance could contribute to integrated stakeholder participation is not effectuated as consumers and farmers are not actively involved in GlobalG.A.P. where private company interests seem to dominate.

7.6   MARINE STEWARDSHIP COUNCIL (MSC)

Fish has become an important globally traded food product as annually over 40 per cent (representing a value of US$86 billion) of the world's fish production enters international commerce. The high demand for fish has resulted in widespread over-fishing, and currently 70 per cent of the world's commercial fisheries are considered overexploited (FAO 2009). Therefore, many consider improving fisheries' management to recover endangered fish stocks and conserve the remaining marine biodiversity urgent.

Managing fisheries, especially in marine areas, is complicated, as fish stocks and fishing fleets move easily across national borders and over the high seas. Governments tried to respond to this by creating international commissions under the auspices of the FAO, charged with managing particular species or specific fishing areas (Peterson 1993). However, the impact of these commissions remained modest because governments showed little commitment or lack of capacity to effectively implement their recommendations. Hence, fish have become a globally traded food product without an adequate, well-functioning global governance arrangement (Bush and Oosterveer 2007; Oosterveer 2008).

In 1997, the multinational food processing company Unilever and the environmental NGO WWF founded the Marine Stewardship Council (MSC) to respond more effectively to this challenge. WWF considered the use of a specific label for sustainably captured fish a promising strategy to promote sustainable fisheries. Unilever realized that the future of its commercial fish-related activities would be jeopardized if over-fishing would not end. After being established by these private actors, the MSC rapidly (by 1999) became an independent organization intending to promote sustainable fisheries by harnessing 'consumer purchasing power to generate change and promote environmentally responsible stewardship of the world's most important renewable food source'[10] (MSC 2007).

For this aim MSC introduced its own (MSC) label, which is exclusively environment-oriented whereby its Principles and Criteria for Sustainable Fishing are developed into a standard for voluntary, third-party certification. In the certification process the general principles are translated into a detailed management plan for a specific fishery to assure its responsible and sustainable use.

All relevant stakeholders are invited to participate in the certification process. Governments are invited to engage at the same level as all other stakeholders, but support from environmental NGOs is considered vital to secure public trust (MSC 2002). According to the instructions for the certification process, certifying bodies should therefore actively contact these NGOs and request their participation in the process.

As of June 2014, 237 fisheries had received the MSC-label, most of which are in OECD countries except for some certified fisheries in South Africa, Vietnam and Mexico, while 98 other fisheries were undergoing assessment.[11] When the produce from a certified fishery is sold via an MSC-certified chain of custody, consumers can buy fish with an MSC-label which guarantees its origin from a certified sustainable fishery. In supermarkets and specialized fish retail stores in industrialized countries, currently more than 22000 different MSC-labelled items from certified fisheries are available. The organization claims that in 2014 approximately 10 per cent of the world's total edible wild capture fisheries, representing over 10 million tons of seafood, were part of the MSC-programme.[12] With the MSC-label, a new, 'green' product identity is created in the otherwise anonymous global fish market.

MSC represents an innovative global food governance arrangement that, contrary to GlobalG.A.P., includes producers and engages consumers by inviting them to buy the certified sustainable products. In this respect, MSC fits more in Rosenau's perspective than in Sassen's because it tries to establish a more inclusive sub-sphere of authority and not an exclusionary one dominated by private interests. The social actors involved in MSC are operating at different geographical levels but their common interests converge on creating sustainable fisheries. MSC's private character as a global food governance arrangement intended to protect the environment is underlined by the absence of any formal role for state authorities (Deere 1999). The authority of MSC seems to derive mainly from being a professional, expert-based organization aiming at a publicly recognized goal. Its legitimacy derives from its use of transparent and inclusive (participatory) methods applying a combination of procedural and scientific arguments. All fisheries are entitled to request certification on a voluntary basis and when they engage in the process, all stakeholders participate in a process wherein natural science-based information is applied and improved management guidelines are agreed upon. MSC explicitly claims to apply up-to-date ecological science methods to assess the sustainability of a fishery. MSC is creating an innovative governance arrangement outside formal governmental actions, although building on existing governmental arrangements as legal procedures and fisheries policies. It is a specialized sub-assemblage of territory, authority and rights and there are few indications that it will become part of a larger multi-level multi-actor sphere of authority. In this respect MSC responds more to Sassen's suggestion that multiple sub-assemblages may emerge next to each other in the context of globalization than Rosenau's expectation that a harmonized sphere of authority will emerge.

MSC forms a hybrid global food governance arrangement by combining business and civil society interests and trying to fill the void between national fisheries policies and the global fish trade.

7.7   CONCLUSION

Both GlobalG.A.P. and MSC are private food governance arrangements introduced by private companies and non-governmental organizations in the context of globalization. They are exemplary for a much broader range of initiatives introduced to respond to environmental, social or economic problems that seem insufficiently addressed by conventional state-based arrangements. However, there is no global public authority that can secure democratic decision-making and balance of power in such arrangements, so the basis for authority and legitimacy in these arrangements is not evident.

These private governance arrangements create separate spheres of authority but rather than being the starting point of a process towards integration at trans-national level, as suggested by Rosenau, these multiple spheres of authority seem rather the end-result. Each private governance initiative seems oriented towards constructing its own individual arrangement, justified by its specific goals rather than towards successful integration at higher scales. MSC and GlobalG.A.P. derive their legitimacy from claiming to secure the sustainability and safety of food production and processing for the interest of different supply chain actors and in the case of MSC for consumers as well. The guarantee offered is not limited to the characteristics of the final product, but addresses a wider range of concerns and the argument is based on objective, scientific standards to acquire public trust. To a lesser extent authority and legitimacy also relies on public participation and transparency in the procedures developed and applied by these initiatives. MSC is most explicit on the involvement of all direct stakeholders in the certification process, but also GlobalG.A.P. increasingly pays attention to engaging multiple stakeholders when developing standards and benchmarks.

The cases presented here show that authority and legitimacy of such private governance arrangements are not so much derived from formal procedures, like democracy in the nation-state (input legitimacy), but from their (intended) output (output legitimacy). Both initiatives claim that they respond to widely acknowledged public concerns to which national governments had no answer. GlobalG.A.P. justified itself as an effective way to secure the safety of food and reduce the environmental impact from food production, while the MSC claims that it will assure the longer term sustainability of fish provision. By creating separate spheres of authority (Rosenau) or a specific sub-assemblage of TAR (Sassen), these initiatives position themselves as a more adequate response to the challenges of sustainable development than formal government arrangements. Their voluntary and science-based procedures preclude the imposition of their measures without consultation and voluntary consent from the producers involved.

Countervailing power to private interests in these governance arrangements can be found partly within the arrangements themselves, as stakeholders are involved and can express their concerns through the official procedures. So, more than Sassen suggests, such global governance arrangements include different actors and interests and are not only based on singular private company interests. Hence, countervailing power does not necessarily have to be generated external to such global assemblages. For instance, MSC makes all reports publicly available and encourages comments from all relevant stakeholders to strengthen its attractiveness for fisheries. In the case of GlobalG.A.P., on the other hand, the countervailing power is located outside the arrangement because its activities are hidden from the general public and only visible within the companies involved. In this respect, GlobalG.A.P. fits Sassen's concept much more than MSC. Nevertheless, both initiatives have been subject to external criticism for excluding producers in developing countries and for protecting private company interests (c.f. Campbell 2005; Casey 2008; Constance and Bonanno 1999/2000). Both initiatives responded by pointing at their procedures and scientific basis but they nevertheless revized their procedures to facilitate the inclusion of small-holders.

This chapter presented the emergence of unfamiliar food governance arrangements in the context of globalization and discussed their authority and legitimacy, and whether they allow for countervailing power. It became clear that such initiatives are not uniform but they seek to justify their authority on the basis of their procedures and the use of scientific instruments. Both Sassen and Rosenau offer useful conceptual framings on this process whereby Sassen is more helpful in positioning these arrangements in a wider perspective and Rosenau when analysing their internal dynamics. Surprisingly, both frameworks did not incorporate the crucial role science plays in such arrangements as the main source of legitimacy although this may be specific for the case of food.

NOTES

1. 'Since 1980, states have become more occupied with the regulation part of governance and less with providing (of services such as education and social security). Yet non-state regulation has grown even more rapidly' (Braithwaite 2008, 1). Braithwaite claims it is best to conceive our era as one of *regulatory capitalism*.
2. The 'skills revolution' refers to the increasing ability of people to know their own values and perceive where they are *best* articulated in the *global arena* as a consequence of improved education and progress in ICT. This has generated possibilities for more horizontal forms of networking, a diminution of hierarchy and disaggregation of authority.
3. In response, alternative governance mechanisms are suggested, such as 'deliberative democracy' (Hirst 1994; Miller 1992), intended to re-establish authority by involving all those governed in the relevant policy decision-making processes.
4. The renaming occurred in 2007 to underline the global aspirations of the initiators (Henson et al. 2009).
5. Integrated farming aims to produce agricultural products that do not contain pesticide residues, and are operated under strict protocols within audit systems (Campbell 2005).
6. Today, GlobalG.A.P. encompasses five key themes: food safety, environmental protection, occupational health, safety and welfare, and animal welfare.
7. 'Retailer and producer/supplier members are represented equally on the organisation's sector committees and the board also has equality of representation from the two groups' (Humphrey 2008, 32). Consumers and primary producers (farmers) are not represented.
8. See: www.globalgap.org (accessed 4 January 2012).

9. See note 8.
10. This 'consumer power' is often translated into using retail power to force fisheries to become more sustainable. For instance, the complete Dutch retail sector declared in 2007 that by 2012 they would only sell sustainable fish, such as certified by MSC. See: http://www.cbl.nl/activiteiten/duurzaamheid-en-gezondheid/cbl-duurzaamheidsagenda/duurzame-vis/, accessed 4 January 2012.
11. See: www.msc.org, accessed 11 June 2014.
12. See note 11.

REFERENCES

Arts, B., P. Leroy and J. Van Tatenhove (2006), 'Political Modernisation and Policy Arrangements: A Framework for Understanding Environmental Policy Change', *Public Organization Review; A Global Journal*, 6(2), 93–106.

Boström, M. and M. Klintman (2008), *Eco-Standards, Product Labelling and Green Consumerism*, Houndmills: Palgrave MacMillan.

Braithwaite, J. (2008), *Regulatory Capitalism; How it Works, Ideas for Making it Work Better*, Cheltenham, UK and Northampton, MA: Edward Elgar Publishing.

Bush, S.R. and P. Oosterveer (2007), 'The Missing Link: Intersecting Governance and Trade in the Space of Place and the Space of Flows', *Sociologia Ruralis*, 47(4), 384–99.

Campbell, H. (2005), 'The Rise and Rise of EurepGAP: European (Re)Invention of Colonial Food Relations?', *International Journal of Food and Agriculture*, 13(2), 1–19.

Casey, D. (2008), 'Three Puzzles of Private Governance: Global GAP and the Regulation of Food Safety and Quality', paper presented at the Conference '(Re)Regulation in the Wake of Neoliberalism. Consequences of Three Decades of Privatization and Market Liberalization', Utrecht, ECPR Standing Group Regulatory Governance.

Constance, D.H. and A. Bonanno (1999), 'Contested Terrain of the Global Fisheries: "Dolphin-Safe" Tuna, The Panama Declaration, and the Marine Stewardship Council', *Rural Sociology*, 64(4), 597–623.

Constance, D.H. and A. Bonanno (2000), 'Regulating the Global Fisheries: The World Wildlife Fund, Unilever and the Marine Stewardship Council', *Agriculture and Human Values*, 17, 171–87.

Deere, C. (1999), *Eco-Labelling and Sustainable Fisheries*, Cambridge and Rome: IUCN and FAO.

FAO (2009), *The State of World Fisheries and Aquaculture 2008*, Rome: FAO.

Fulponi, L. (2006), 'Private Voluntary Standards in the Food System: The Perspective of Major Food Retailers in OECD Countries', *Food Policy*, 31, 1–13.

Gawron, J.-C. and L. Theuvsen (2009), 'Certification Schemes in the European Agri-Food Sector: Overview and Opportunities for Central and Eastern Europe', *Outlook on Agriculture*, 38(1), 9–14.

Hatanaka, M., C. Bain and L. Busch (2005), 'Third-Party Certification in the Global Agrifood System', *Food Policy*, 30, 354–69.

Henson, S., O. Masakure and J. Cranfeld (2009), *Do Fresh Produce Exporters in Sub-Saharan Africa Benefit from GlobalGAP Certification?*, Guelph (Canada):

Department of Food, Agricultural and Resource Economics, University of Guelph.

Hirst, P. (1994), *Associative Democracy: New Forms of Economic and Social Governance*, Cambridge: Polity Press.

Humphrey, J. (2008), *Private Standards, Small Farmers and Donor Policy: EUREPGAP in Kenya*, Brighton: IDS (Institute of Development Studies).

Krahmann, E. (2003), 'National, Regional, and Global Governance: One Phenomenon or Many?', *Global Governance*, 9, 323–46.

Lang, T., D. Barling and M. Caraher (2009), *Food Policy: Integrating Health, Environment and Society*, Oxford: Oxford University Press.

Lemos, M.C. and A. Agrawal (2006), 'Environmental Governance', *Annual Review of Environment and Resources*, 31, 297–325.

Marsden, T., R. Lee, A. Flynn and S. Thankappan (2010), *The New Regulation and Governance of Food: Beyond the Food Crisis?*, New York and London: Routledge.

Miller, D. (1992), 'Deliberative Democracy and Social Choice', *Political Studies*, 40(s1), 54–67.

MSC (2002), *Fish 4 Thought; The MSC Quarterly Newsletter* 2.

MSC (2007), MSC website: www.msc.org, accessed 8 January 2007.

MSC (2009), *Marine Stewardship Council 'Risk-Based Framework and Guidance to Certification Bodies'; Version 1*, London: MSC.

MSC (2010), *Annual Report 2009/10*, London: MSC.

Narrod, C., D. Roy, B. Avendano and J. Okello (2008), 'Impact of International Food Safety Standards on Smallholders: Evidence from Three Cases', in E.B. McCullough, P.L. Pingali and K.G. Stamoulis (eds), *The Transformation of Agri-Food Systems; Globalization, Supply Chains and Smallholder Farmers*, London: Earthscan, pp. 355–72.

Oosterveer, P. (2002), 'Reinventing Risk Politics: Reflexive Modernity and the European BSE Crisis', *Journal of Environmental Policy & Planning*, 4, 215–229.

Oosterveer, P. (2008), 'Governing Global Fish Provisioning: Ownership and Management of Marine Resources', *Ocean & Coastal Management*, 51, 797–805.

Oosterveer, P. and Sonnenfeld, D. A. (2012), *Food, Globalization and Sustainability*, Londen and New York: Earthscan.

Peterson, M.J. (1993), 'International Fisheries Management', in P.M. Haas, Robert O. Keohane and Marc A. Levy (eds), *Institutions for the Earth. Sources of Effective International Environmental Protection*, Cambridge, MA: MIT Press, pp. 249–305.

Rosenau, J.N. (1992), 'The Relocation of Authority in a Shrinking World', *Comparative Politics*, 24(3), 253–272.

Rosenau, J.N. (2007), 'Governing the Ungovernable: The Challenge of a Global Disaggregation of Authority', *Regulation & Governance*, 1, 88–97.

Sassen, S. (2006), *Territory, Authority, Rights: From Medieval to Global Assemblages*, Princeton and Oxford: Princeton University Press.

Sassen, S. (2008), 'Neither Global nor National: Novel Assemblages of Territory, Authority and Rights', *Ethics & Global Politics*, 1, 1–2.

Spaargaren, G. and A.P.J. Mol (2008), 'Greening Global Consumption: Redefining Politics and Authority', *Global Environmental Change*, 18(3), 350–359.

Stripple, J. (2006), 'Editorial. Rules for the Environment: Reconsidering Authority in Global Environmental Governance', *European Environment*, 16, 259–264.

Treib, O., H. Bähr and G. Falkner (2007), 'Modes of Governance: Towards a Conceptual Clarification', *Journal of European Public Policy*, 14(1), 1–20.

Van der Grijp, N.M. and F. De Hond (1999), *Green Supply Chain Initiatives in the European Food and Retailing Sector*, Amsterdam: IVM (Institute for Environmental Studies).

Van Kersbergen, K. and F. Van Waarden (2004), '"Governance" as a Bridge between Disciplines: Cross-Disciplinary Inspiration Regarding Shifts in Governance and Problems of Governability, Accountability and Legitimacy', *European Journal of Political Research*, 43, 142–171.

Van Leeuwen, J. (2010), *Who Greens the Waves? Changing Authority in the Environmental Governance of Shipping and Offshore Oil and Gas Production*, Wageningen: Wageningen Academic Publishers.

8. The effectiveness of private food governance in fostering sustainable development

Agni Kalfagianni and Doris Fuchs

8.1 INTRODUCTION

Today's global agrifood system is highly unsustainable. Problems exist with respect to carbon emissions, effluents, pesticide use, soil erosion and acidification, animal welfare, farm worker standards and farmer incomes, to name just a few. These problems have yet to be politically addressed with any degree of effectiveness.

At the same time, private actors, especially transnational food corporations, have become key players in global agrifood governance (Clapp and Fuchs 2009). Today private food governance is a reality which exerts powerful influences on the sustainability of the global agrifood system. In consequence, science and politics urgently need to gain a better understanding of the relationship between agrifood sustainability and private food governance.

Advocates of private governance often argue that it can effectively and efficiently contribute to the provision of public goods in areas where governments are unwilling and unable to do so. Critical views, however, have pointed out that the impact of private food governance on sustainable development is highly ambivalent (Clapp 1998; King and Lennox 2000). This also applies to private food governance, where previous studies have shown that private standards may be able to improve food safety in some aspects and address selected environmental problems, while more fundamental environmental aspects as well as the issues of social equity and sustainable incomes tend to be ignored and often worsen (Fuchs, Kalfagianni and Arentsen 2009).

Against this background, we clearly need to identify the determinants of an effective contribution of private food governance to agrifood sustainability. Under which conditions can this contribution occur? An answer to this question will allow us to better decide how likely a positive contribution of private agrifood governance to agrifood sustainability is in specific contexts as well as in general. Moreover, such an answer would provide us with better insights into how a sustainable agrifood system can be further fostered.

In this chapter, we therefore set out to identify the determinants of the effectiveness of private food governance in fostering the sustainability of the global agrifood system. To this end, we define effectiveness in terms of the stringency of private food standards. We argue that this effectiveness will be a function of external pressure, internal collaborative structures, the characteristics of available solutions as well as the size and heterogeneity of the group of actors designing and implementing the given private governance institution.

The chapter proceeds as follows. The next section provides a brief background on private food governance as such. Section three then presents our core argument and identifies and operationalizes the independent and dependent variables. In section four, we attempt a first empirical illustration of the argument using the GlobalG.A.P. as an example. Section five discusses our findings and concludes the chapter with a brief outlook on research needs and political necessities.

8.2 BACKGROUND: PRIVATE FOOD GOVERNANCE

Private governance – the rules and institutions developed by private actors to structure and direct behaviour in a particular issue-area – has proliferated in recent years. Quality assurance schemes, certification and labelling programmes, private standards and codes of conduct at the national and, increasingly, transnational levels have spread to different domains, including politically sensitive ones (Lock 2001). These novel activities by private actors signify their new political role as rule-setters in global governance that goes beyond well-established activities such as lobbying and awareness raising. This phenomenon reflects a general trend in governance as political capacity and functions have shifted from state to non-state actors in the context of globalization and the popularity of neoliberal norms (Graz and Nölke 2007).

One policy domain where private governance rapidly replaces traditional forms of steering is agrifood (Fuchs, Kalfagianni and Havinga 2011). Traditionally the domain of governmental and intergovernmental actors, the governance of food and agriculture is increasingly being not just influenced, but also 'created' by private actors. Two sets of actors are of interest in this respect: business actors and civil society organizations. Business actors, in particular food retailers, are emerging as key players shaping the agrifood sector on the basis of private standards and the creation of own brand products (Lawrence and Burch 2007). Accordingly, retailers have been described as the 'new food and lifestyle authorities' next to the traditional authorities of government, church and professional bodies (Dixon 2007, 30). Likewise, producers and their associations are also engaged in governance activities in the agrifood sector, albeit to a smaller extent. Examples of producer-led governance efforts include, for instance, the creation of alternative food initiatives and organizations dedicated to the promotion of organic agriculture (Morgan et al. 2006). Further, many of the private governance initiatives developed by retailers, producers or cooperative arrangements between the two also include the participation of civil society organizations. Examples of civil society organizations participating in the governance of agrifood include Oxfam, with a special focus on development issues and the World Wild Fund for Nature (WWF), a leading environmental conservation organization.

Private governance initiatives may use different mechanisms to achieve their goals. We can currently identify three distinct types of private governance mechanisms in the agrifood sector: corporate social responsibility reporting (CSR), codes of conduct (CoC), and private standards (see also Fuchs, Kalfagianni, Clapp and Busch 2011). Corporate social responsibility efforts include measures to raise corporate awareness as well as reporting business activities which touch on social and human rights, as well as environmental themes. The idea is that such reporting will foster transparency, and ultimately improve firms' performance on these fronts (Gupta 2010). Codes of conduct can be understood as written guidelines on the basis of which companies deal with their workforce, suppliers, state authorities and external stakeholders in their host country (Greven 2004, 142). Standards are agreed criteria by which a product or a service's performance, its technical and physical characteristics, and/or the process, and conditions under which it has been produced or delivered, can be assessed (Nadvi and Wältring 2002). Standards usually represent the strictest form of private governance as they typically require regular internal and external auditing processes and include disciplinary penalties and/or rewards. However, some codes of conduct are also certifiable. In sum, with these private governance mechanisms, private actors are increasingly involved in the design, implementation and enforcement of rules and principles governing the global food system at various points in the sector from inputs to production to sale.

8.3 CONDITIONS FOR AN EFFECTIVE CONTRIBUTION OF PRIVATE FOOD GOVERNANCE TO AGRIFOOD SUSTAINABILITY

In exploring determinants of effectiveness we adopt a rational institutionalist perspective (Hurd 1999; Jönsson and Tallberg 1998; Scharpf 1997). This perspective allows us to treat private actors as central nodes in our analysis in contrast to, for instance, structuralist perspectives, which emphasize the role of the broader political and economic context in shaping policy outputs. Specifically, we assume that the fundamental units of analysis are utility-maximizing private actors who endorse private governance institutions on the basis of self-interest calculations (see also Abott and Snidal 1998). We argue that the patterns of adoption and support of private rules as well as the stringency and strictness of such rules are determined largely by the preferences and capacities of private actors. In other words, private actors create and endorse private governance institutions in so far as the latter enable them to pursue their own (common) goals.

Two functions performed by private governance institutions gain the support of private actors according to the rationalist perspective: (i) the reduction of transaction and other types of costs; and (ii) the provision of reputation and financial benefits. In terms of costs, more specifically, private governance institutions are considered pivotal in reducing information asymmetries and uncertainty, costs associated with negotiation (i.e. with whom and what to discuss, when and on what terms) and costs of enforcement (i.e. establishing the conditions and instruments for punishment when a contracted transaction is not completed) (see Cutler, Haufler and Ronit 1999). In terms of benefits, rational institutionalist approaches emphasize reputation and financial gains as pivotal incentives in endorsing private governance. Examples include the payment of less expensive premiums and increased access to capital from lending institutions to firms adopting ISO 14000 due to the enhancement of the firms' environmental image to consumers, other firms and investors (Clapp 1998). On a similar note, Hedberg and Von Malmborg (2003) underline the improved access to banks' and insurance companies' funds by companies listed under the Dow Jones Sustainability Group Index.[1]

Cost and benefit calculations might differ for different actors. Characteristics such as position in the market, vulnerability to NGO campaigns, sector characteristics, cultural origin, proximity to consumers but also a genuine concern for social and environmental improvement within senior management are factors which affect firms' decisions to adopt voluntary regulation (Courville 2003; Fuchs 2006). In the forestry certification, for instance, actors with high commercial and/or reputational benefits, such as niche and higher-end producers, appear more likely to adopt private voluntary programmes in relation to low cost operators (Auld et al. 2008; Marx and Cuypers 2010). Similar observations are made for the certification of coffee and fisheries where 'good quality' producers and suppliers usually situated in countries with well regulated and controlled environments appear to have higher incentives to adopt voluntary programmes (Gulbrandsen 2010; Muradian and Pelupessy 2005).

In sum, the rationalist perspective emphasizes the self-interest of private actors as the foundation of private governance. This chapter draws on this theoretical context in exploring the conditions for effective contribution of private food governance to agrifood sustainability. Moreover, the chapter complements the rationalist perspective by underlying the significance of learning and education processes for the fostering of effective private governance.

8.3.1   Defining and Explaining Effectiveness

We define effectiveness in terms of the ability of a private food governance institution to improve the sustainability of the agrifood system. We further argue that this ability is reflected in the stringency of private food standards, in other words the extent to which the standards entail strict prescriptions for environmental and social conduct. Without strict prescriptions we expect that behavioural changes by the targeted actors tend to be weak (on average) and, accordingly, the overall impact of the private governance institution lower than desired. Such prescriptions can be reflected in clear and verifiable/measurable targets, ambitious targets, monitoring and sanctioning mechanisms (including the aspects of third party auditing and the public accessibility of reports) and the comprehensiveness of the sustainability dimensions addressed by the standards. Sustainability dimensions include different types of environmental (input, output, and preservation), social (farmer incomes, labour standards, gender issues), and animal welfare aspects.

We argue that the effectiveness of private food governance is likely to be a function of external pressure, internal collaboration and the characteristics of the available solutions, as well as the heterogeneity of the target group. External pressure may arise due to the visibility of the initiative, the visibility of actors in the initiative or the visibility of a problem. We operationalize the visibility of the initiative or actors in it via their size (for the initiative: membership and market coverage; for the actors: workforce and turnover), the existence of previous scandals or NGO campaigns targeting the standard as such or relevant actors in it, and the proximity to consumers, i.e. the retail end of products' cycles. Moreover, we consider the home of actors in the initiative, as Northern/Western consumers have a larger track record of boycotts and political consumerism. We operationalize the visibility of the problem via its media uptake and/or its presence on the political agenda of governmental or intergovernmental actors as well as large NGOs.

Next to external pressure, we argue that internal collaborative aspects are likely to influence the stringency and uptake of an initiative. Internal collaboration refers especially to the type of involvement of civil society actors in the private governance institution. Here we ask, who gave the initial impulse for its creation, whether civil society actors participate in the governing boards of the institutions and in what function (observer status, decision making power) and with what degree of potential influence (minor, equal, major share of votes).[2] Moreover, we explore the existence of processes fostering learning and best practice transfer.

We further argue that the availability of solutions to a given problem will affect the stringency of a private governance institution. After all, it is much easier for actors to agree on a stringent standard, when cheap solutions, either technological or organizational, are available. If instead systemic changes would be needed to solve a problem, a level of stringency fostering such changes is much less likely. Finally, the stringency of a standard is likely to be a function of the size and heterogeneity of the group designing and adopting the standard.

In sum, we argue that the following relationships exist (see table 8.1 for a summary of the operationalization of the different variables):

Stringency = External pressure + internal collaboration + availability of solutions + size and heterogeneity of membership

In the next section, we illustrate these 'hypotheses' using the GlobalG.A.P. as an example. We will focus on our core variables of interest: external pressure and internal collaboration, in particular, and neglect the other ('control') variables at this point (table 8.1). While discussing the case of the GlobalG.A.P., we will also identify the variables more easily assessed and those which would require more in-depth research in the form of a larger research project.

8.4 EMPIRICAL ILLUSTRATION: THE GLOBALG.A.P.

The GlobalG.A.P. is a private sector body that sets voluntary standards for the certification of agricultural products around the globe. The

Table 8.1   Variables and their operationalization

Variable	First level of operationalization	Second level of operationalization	Third level of operationalization
Stringency	Targets	Clear and verifiable/ measurable Ambitiousness	
	Comprehensiveness	Environmental	Input Output Conservation
		Social	Farmer incomes Labour standards Gender issues
		Animal welfare	
	Compliance	Monitoring mechanisms Sanctioning mechanisms Third-party auditing Public accessibility of reports Learning mechanisms	
External Pressure	Visibility of initiative	Size Scandal/NGO campaign Consumer segment	
	Visibility of participating actors (esp. TNCs)	Size Scandals/NGO campaigns Consumer segment Northern home base	Turnover Workforce
	Visibility of problem	Media uptake On political agenda(s)	
Internal Collaboration	Initiative taken by		
	Participation of civil society	Status	Not given/observer Status/voting power
		Degree of voting power	None/minor/equal/ dominant
Characteristics of available solutions	Availability of solutions	Technological solutions available Need for systemic change	Costs of technological solutions
Membership in Initiative	Size Heterogeneity		

standard (first known as EurepGAP) was initiated in 1997 by retailers belonging to the Euro-Retailer Produce Working Group (EUREP). It aims to establish one standard for Good Agricultural Practice (GAP) with different product applications capable of fitting to the whole range of global conventional agricultural products. GlobalG.A.P. is a pre-farm-gate standard, which means that the certificate covers the processing of the certified product from farm inputs like feed or seedlings and all the farming activities until the product leaves the farm. Moreover, it is a business-to-business label not directly visible to consumers.

To apply the standard for one product, a series of documents is needed. These include the General Regulations, the Control Points and Compliance Criteria (CPCC) Protocol and the Checklist. The general regulations set out the rules by which the standard is administered. The CPCC Protocol is the standard with which farmers must comply and against which they are audited to verify compliance. Checklists replicate the control points and are used by farmers to fulfil the annual internal audit requirement and also form the basis of the farmers' external audit. The most important checklist is the one used for inspecting producers, which contains all the Control Points. It *must* be used during inspections by the Certification Board and *can* also be used by the producer/group when performing self-assessments. This checklist is divided into 41 'major musts', 122 'minor musts' as well as 91 recommendations ('shoulds'). For major musts 100 per cent compliance is compulsory, whereas for minor musts 95 per cent. Shoulds have the status of recommendations that must be inspected by certification bodies, but are not a prerequisite for the granting of a GlobalG.A.P. certificate. The status of standards is relevant in relation to the sanctions that are available in case of non-compliance (Van der Grijp 2010).[3]

GlobalG.A.P. membership consists of three groups: retailers and food service members, suppliers and associate members (table 8.2). Membership has varied during the years, with new members joining in and some dropping out (see also Van der Grijp 2010). At the moment, the geographic coverage of the standard is universal. Europe, however, clearly dominates in all three categories. Especially in the retail sector it represents almost 85 per cent of the members. In the other two categories, the percentage of European presence is slightly lower, with 67 per cent of the supplier members and 57 per cent of the associate members. In total, Europe represents 66 per cent of total GlobalG.A.P. membership.[4]

8.4.1 Assessing and Explaining Stringency

The GlobalG.A.P.'s stringency changed over time with a trend towards the softening of the standard (Van der Grijp 2010). Today, the standard

Table 8.2   Membership of GlobalG.A.P. in 2010

Continent	Retailer and Food Service member	Supplier* member	Associate member	Total
Africa	1	12	10	23
Asia	1	10	14	25
Australia and New Zealand	0	3	3	6
Europe	39	112	66	217
Middle East	0	3	2	5
North America	5	10	10	25
Latin America	0	16	11	27
Total	46	166	116	328

Note: * Suppliers can apply both as individuals and as groups.

Source: www2.gobalgap.org/members (16.12.10).

sets very detailed qualitative targets and has institutionalized compliance and sanctioning mechanisms. Moreover, the standard seems to be quite comprehensive, at first glance. A closer look, however, reveals a different picture. So let us discuss the state of affairs in some detail.

If we assess stringency in terms of targets, we find that the GlobalG.A.P. standard prescribes a long list of rather detailed qualitative targets. These appear mostly clear as well and, thus, relatively easy to verify in the auditing process. When it comes to the ambitiousness of the targets, however, the standard's stringency becomes questionable. The qualitative targets introduced by GlobalG.A.P. focus predominantly on communication and recording. Quantitative targets, however, would allow for a measurement of performance beyond such requirements, i.e. not just demand the documentation of pesticide use but also set limits to it. In that sense, quantitative targets can demonstrate more clearly departure from past performance and achievement of demanding goals. Clearly, quantitative targets are not always appropriate and therefore not always preferable to qualitative ones. In contexts allowing for quantitative targets, however, we would argue that a provision of such targets tends to demonstrate a higher degree of ambitiousness of the standard. With respect to GlobalG.A.P., the predominately qualitative nature of its targets, even in easily quantifiable aspects such as pesticide use and emissions reduction, illustrates a lack of ambition, in our view.

A recently introduced module (since 2009) in GlobalG.A.P. certification showing relatively more ambitious targets is aquaculture. In this module, environmental goals include biodiversity impact assessment, preservation of high conservation value areas, water usage, water, escapees, predator control, biosecurity and to prohibit the use of GMOs. Social issues include occupational health and safety and animal welfare concerns, as well as GRASP, an optional protocol covering a broad range of social concerns. However, again, the standard does not include quantifiable targets. Aspects that can be quantified such as the Maximum Residue Limits are determined according to the market(s) where the farmed product is traded (domestic or international). Similarly, the standard does not specify effluent limits and water quality indicators but allows them to vary according to local (often weak) legislation.

At the same time, a number of challenges for the assessment of the ambitiousness of targets become clear, however. First, it becomes obvious that a thorough assessment of ambitiousness would require a broad range of expert interviews for better evaluation and thus would require a larger research project. Expert views, for instance, would be needed on the question of what is necessary, feasible and under which conditions to assess ambitiousness of standard prescriptions. Secondly, the case of GlobalG.A.P. reveals the difficulty of assessing ambitiousness in a global context. Some of the standard's elements seem easy to achieve for Northern industrialized farmers, while they may appear highly ambitious for small farmers in the South.

Evaluating stringency in terms of the comprehensiveness of the standard, i.e. its attention to different dimensions of sustainability, we find that the GlobalG.A.P. appears comprehensive at first sight, addressing food safety/animal health, environmental and social aspects. However, the relevance of the different dimensions differs. While hygiene as well as animal related aspects such as stocking density are 'major musts', most environmental and social issues are relegated to the status of 'minor musts' if not 'shoulds'.[5] Moreover, fundamental social sustainability challenges such as farmer incomes and gender issues are excluded.[6]

Importantly, previous research tracing developments in the standard underlines a shift in the weights among the different criteria represented in GlobalG.A.P. towards less stringent sustainability targets (Kalfagianni and Fuchs 2011). Specifically, while issues related to record keeping, internal self-inspection and hygiene have been strengthened in the new versions of the standard, others, such as recycling and re-use, impact of farming on the environment and wildlife and conservation policies, have been reduced to 'recommendations'.[7]

When turning to stringency with regards to compliance and sanctioning mechanisms, finally, we find that the GlobalG.A.P. overall appears to have rather strict compliance methods consisting of monitoring and sanctioning mechanisms as well as third-party auditing. Specifically, the scheme is controlled annually by 130 GlobalG.A.P. approved Certification Bodies (CBs) supervised by an independent surveillance body, the Integrity Surveillance Committee. Internal self-assessment is also possible and must be carried out at least once a year under the responsibility of the producer. 'Unscheduled' Surveillance Inspections of a minimum of 10 per cent of all certified producers per annum are carried out (see also below).

There are two types of GlobalG.A.P. violation of rules: non-compliance and non-conformance. Non-compliance occurs when a control point in the checklist is not fulfilled according to the compliance criteria. Non-conformance occurs when a rule that is necessary for obtaining the certificate is infringed. For all types of non-conformance a warning is issued first, which allows for correction in a time period negotiated between the producer and the CB (maximum 28 days). If the cause of sanction is not resolved within the set time period, a suspension is imposed. During the period of suspension, the producer is prevented from using the GlobalG.A.P. logo. The suspension can be lifted when there is sufficient evidence of corrective action. Finally, a cancellation of the contract is issued when the CB finds evidence of fraud and/or lack of trust to comply with GlobalG.A.P. requirements. A cancellation results in the total prohibition of the use of logo or any device related to GlobalG.A.P. A producer that has received a cancellation cannot be accepted back to GlobalG.A.P. within 12 months.

The role of the compliance and sanctioning mechanisms is limited by three constraints, however. First, the categories of 'minor must' and mostly 'shoulds' already allow a considerable degree of non-compliance. Secondly, information on certification assessments, audit reports, and especially the specific instances of non-compliance is not publicly accessible. Thirdly, 'unscheduled' visits are still announced 48 hours in advance and there is only a 10 per cent chance of receiving such a visit.[8]

To sum up, GlobalG.A.P. is a relatively comprehensive standard with diverse levels of stringency. The implementation requirements differ for different issues, with animal welfare being the strictest and environmental conservation the weakest categories. What explains these observations?

Looking at external pressure, two factors appear to have played an important role. First, GlobalG.A.P. emerged in the mid-1990s in a period where food safety concerns were mounting as a result of the BSE crisis, while environmental and social issues were also starting to capture the attention of an increasingly aware consumer segment. In comparison, however, food safety and the realization that one can actually die from the consumption of contaminated products has attracted more attention by the media, politicians and the general public and continues to dominate public discourse today.[9] Moreover, health epidemics have proven to be much more costly for businesses in relation to environmental degradation, for instance. In terms of our argument, then, we would expect the higher stringency of GlobalG.A.P. elements related to food safety and public health concerns, which we found above.[10]

Second, while GlobalG.A.P. is not visible to consumers it is visible among the food chain actors, civil society, governments and experts. This is enhanced by the fact that important market actors have endorsed the initiative from its inception until today. While it is difficult to provide an evaluation of collective market share of GlobalG.A.P. members, indicatively, we can say that from the producer side, some of the biggest agricultural companies, e.g. Del Monte, Cargill and Frosta, participate in the initiative. Likewise, the leading global retailers and food outlets with large turnovers, store numbers and workforces are also represented. These include:

1. Walmart with USD$405 billion net sales in 2009, 8400 stores in 15 countries around the world, and a workforce of 2 million people;[11]
2. Ahold with total sales of €28 billion in 2009, 2909 stores, 206000 employees;[12]
3. Carrefour group with net sales €86 billion in 2009, 15661 stores and the seventh employer worldwide in the private sector in 2009;[13] and
4. Tesco with £59 billion in 2009, the third largest supermarket in the world, with 4331 stores and employing 470000 people.[14]

Moreover, Marks and Spencer and the MacDonald's corporation are members of the GlobalG.A.P.

Such visibility has attracted scrutiny of the standard and at times created pressure for higher stringency. The following example illustrates this point. In 2006, Greenpeace issued a report revealing illegal pesticides and minimal risk levels for hazardous substances exceedance on fruits and vegetables in German supermarkets that were members of GlobalG.A.P., e.g. REWE, Edeka, Kaisers.[15] In response to these revelations, GlobalG.A.P. upgraded three CPCC requirements from 'minor' to 'major musts' and introduced an Integrated Pest Management Toolbox (a checklist and a document that give guidance to producers, advisors, certifiers).[16] Observers warn, however, that in cases where stringency requires technical changes that prove costly for the farmers (e.g. use of low chemical but more expensive pesticides) and in the absence of premium payments for the implementation of such rules, violations cannot be ruled out.[17]

With respect to the role of internal collaboration in influencing the stringency of the standard, we can note the following. As mentioned above, the GlobalG.A.P. was created by European retailers and is highly business dominated. Specifically, the GlobalG.A.P. is a business standard shared equally by suppliers and retailers. Decisions are taken by the Board with elected representatives from both groups while civil society organizations are excluded from decision-making. The latter can participate in consultative roles in the annual meetings, however. In addition, GlobalG.A.P. provides the opportunity to interested parties to participate in public consultations regarding revisions of the standard on the web. In the case of aquaculture, moreover, GlobalG.A.P. participates in the WWF Aquaculture Dialogue standards, a series of dialogues aiming to create standards that will minimize key negative environmental and social impacts for a number of fish species. Such interactions, then, are important in that they provide opportunities for mutual learning and knowledge transfer between the parties. The relatively more ambitious targets of the GlobalG.A.P. aquaculture standard is an indication that the GlobalG.A.P. board makes use of the views exchanged in such forums, to some extent.

Given these collaborative characteristics, our argument would lead us to expect that the GlobalG.A.P. is not very stringent. In consequence, the absence of clear and measurable targets, and the relegation of most environmental and social issues to 'minor musts' and 'should,' again, should not come as a surprise. A larger degree of decision-making power of environmental and social NGOs in the GlobalG.A.P. governance mechanisms would likely have led to a different outcome.

8.5 CONCLUSION

In this chapter, we identified likely determinants of the effectiveness of private food governance for agrifood sustainability and illustrated the application of our argument using the GlobalG.A.P. as an example. We argued that the effectiveness of private food governance is reflected in the stringency of the respective standards. Moreover, we postulated that stringency is a function of external pressure and internal collaborative structures (as well as the characteristics of available solutions and the size and heterogeneity of the group designing and adopting the standard). In our empirical illustration, we found that the expected relations between dependent and independent variables were largely supported. External pressure, particularly stemming from the visibility of the members participating in the initiatives, promises to be influential in rethinking targets and enforcing sanctions to a certain extent. Likewise, our inquiry suggests that internal collaboration has been influential and reflects the interests of respective actors in the targets set.

There are some limits to our analysis that need to be acknowledged and which constitute areas where further research is required in the future. First, we need to establish clearer correlations between the dependent and independent variables of our framework. While the GlobalG.A.P. case served to test the plausibility of our hypotheses, bigger and more detailed studies are required to provide a more thorough and systematic understanding of the conditions for effective TNC governance for the sustainability of the global agrifood system.

Second, one may argue that our definition of effectiveness via stringency captures only part of the picture. In our approach to effectiveness, we assume that a standard's impact on agrifood sustainability is correlated with the actual prescriptions for conduct made by the standard as well as their enforcement. Critics may claim that this is not necessarily the case. Thus, actors may adopt weak standards, but be pushed to make major changes in behaviour via learning processes, i.e. on a voluntary rather than mandatory basis. We do address the presence of mechanisms fostering learning among the independent variables in our argument, of course. Nevertheless, one could argue that, irrespective of the presence of institutionalized mechanisms, learning may occur and that we do not consider it sufficiently among our measures of effectiveness, i.e. the dependent variables. Two potential arguments exist against the claim that we underestimate the existence of learning as a measure of effectiveness. First, if such learning processes did indeed occur among a large share of standard takers, it is highly likely that the standard's target would be improved in turn. After all, the supporters and adopters of private governance institutions tend to use them as an instrument for communicating their achievements and a more stringent standard would allow for better image shaping. In this case, the effectiveness of the standard, even if initially achieved via learning processes, should still be reflected in its stringency. We do not capture the outperformance of the standard by individual companies via stringency, of course, but would argue that those individual companies cannot reflect the standard's impact on agrifood sustainability as such. Secondly, numerous standards with varying degrees of stringency exist by now in many areas of the agrifood system. If a company did indeed greatly outperform a given standard due to learning processes after a while, it is similarly likely that this company would adopt an additional, more stringent standard. Again, this would allow a better communication of achievements and thus reaping of benefits of the standard in terms of self-advertisement. In this case, the effectiveness of the standard would show in the following uptake of more stringent standards by the relevant actors. This potential process was not part of our analysis and therefore would require further investigation for us to be able to reject this potential effectiveness of the given standard via learning processes with confidence.

Third, further research will have to address standard uptake as an additional element influencing the overall effectiveness of a private governance institution. After all, the most stringent standard will have little effect on the pursuit of sustainable development if it is only adopted by a tiny share of the relevant market. Moreover, stringency and uptake are likely to interact. Standard uptake is likely to be a function of its stringency, as actors can more easily achieve compliance with weaker standards than with stringent ones.[18] As we suggested above, stringency, in turn, is likely to be a function of the size and heterogeneity of the group designing and adopting the standard. In the case of the GlobalG.A.P., we also find indicators of such an interaction between stringency and uptake. A large and heterogeneous membership appears to come at a cost. The stringency of the standard dropped as participation broadened, especially to actors beyond the Northern sphere. The causal nature of the relationship requires more detailed inquiry. At first sight, it appears that the standard was intentionally softened to allow for broader membership. However, new members may also have demanded the softening after joining the standard. Moreover, certain types of actors may have been pushing for a softening of the standard. The participation of big market players with large supply needs can create pressure for relaxing the stringency of standards due to production constraints. This has occurred in other private initiatives, such as the Forest Stewardship Council (FSC), where the participation of big retailers led to the introduction of varying levels of stringency in the FSC due to the inability to meet the market demand of their supply chains (Van Waarden 2010).

In terms of political needs, the analysis has shown that private governance may entail desirable contributions to sustainability governance only under certain conditions and can therefore not be a panacea for sustainability. In consequence, there is a need for greater involvement by public actors. At the very least, public actors such as states and intergovernmental organizations can try to foster some of the conditions for effective private governance. Examples include the creation of external pressure by bringing private initiatives under scrutiny and fostering greater awareness in society. Public actors can also facilitate the uptake of stringent standards by introducing appropriate financial incentives, such as state contributions to the costs of implementation, particularly for the financially weak. We acknowledge, however, that in the current circumstances such a scenario is very unlikely. Simultaneously, public actors can try to create a 'race to the top' by setting minimum environmental and social standards for global food supply chains. Again, we are not very optimistic that this might happen any time soon. In any case, our analysis indicates that market based instruments will almost always face tradeoffs between broader uptake/larger market share vs. higher stringency. As such, it is unrealistic to rely on them as the core strategy in the pursuit of the transformations required for an environmentally and socially sustainable food system.

NOTES

1. Of course, business actors are not the only ones engaged in private governance. Civil society organizations as well as public actors are often part of these arrangements. Regarding civil society (and/or public) actors participating in private governance arrangements, rational institutionalist approaches point out that positive perceptions about goal attainment, e.g. sustainability, constitute incentives for the mobilisation of support even if such goals are narrowly defined and might not address fundamental critiques or concerns (see also Cashore 2002). Our focus in this chapter, however, lies specifically with business actors.
2. Public actors may also be involved in public-private governance institutions, but their impact on the stringency and uptake of the standard cannot be predicted as easily, due to the potential for rent-seeking and capture of public interests by private ones. Moreover, in the cases studied in this chapter, public actors were not present.
3. Other checklists include the Quality Management Systems Checklist used for auditing producer group Quality Management Systems (QMS) and the Benchmarking Cross-Reference Checklist (BMCL) or the Approved Modified Checklist (AMC) used by applicant scheme owners applying for benchmarking against GlobalG.A.P. to show equivalence.
4. These percentages are lower than they were in 2009, however. See Kalfagianni and Fuchs 2011.
5. Environmental inputs, such as use of fertilizer and irrigation, are targeted by the standard but are considered 'minor musts'. Outputs include one 'major must', related to the clearance of farm and premises of litter and waste to avoid establishing a breeding ground for pests and diseases which could result in a food safety risk. In the conservation category, a number of requirements exist but these are almost all 'recommendations', except for one 'minor must' regarding the establishment of a management of wildlife and conservation plan for the enterprise that acknowledges the impact of farming activities on the environment.
6. GRASP (GlobalG.A.P. Risk Assessment on Social Practices), a recently introduced module which covers a broader range of social issues, including children rights, legal status of employees, working hours etc. is completely voluntary and, therefore, not required for GlobalG.A.P. certification.
7. GlobalG.A.P. publishes a new version of the standard every three years to account for technological and market developments.
8. Compared to a 20 per cent chance in the case of the Ethical Trading Initiative (ETI), for instance.
9. The most recently reported food safety incident is the dioxin animal feed scare in January 2011 which shut down more than 4700 German farms. See http://www.bbc.co.uk/news/world-europe-12133361, accessed 7 January 2011. A larger research project could support such arguments with a systematic discourse analysis.

10. However, this discussion also reveals a challenge with respect to the overall research design. Here, we identify (the visibility of) the problem post-hoc and, in consequence, focus only on those problems that have received at least some visibility. In principle, we would need to identify the range of relevant problems first, via literature searches and expert interviews, in order to then identify their visibility and try to link that to the stringency of corresponding elements of the GlobalG.A.P. standard. The same challenge applies to the control variable of availability of solutions, as well as to the identification of the presence of (clear and measurable as well as ambitious) targets of the standard.
11. http://walmartstores.com/sites/annualreport/2010/financial_highlights.aspx, accessed 15 January 2011.
12. http://www.annualreport2009.ahold.com/documents/reports/Ahold_AR_2009.pdf, accessed 16 December 2010.
13. http://www.carrefour.com/docroot/groupe/C4com/Pieces_jointes/Assemblee_generale/RFI_VGB_BAT_def_ve.pdf, accessed 16 December 2010.
14. http://www.tescoplc.com/annualreport09/abouttesco/financial_highlights, accessed 15 December 2010.
15. http://www.greenpeace.de/themen/chemie/pestizide_lebensmittel/detail/artikel/essen_ohne_pestizide-1/, accessed 18 December 2010.
16. www.globalgap.org/. . ./101007_Bolckmans_GLOBALGAP_Summit_London.pdf, accessed 18 December 2010.
17. http://www.biocontrol.ca/pdf/Bio13EN-FinalRev.pdf, accessed 20 December 2010.
18. Of course, a standard may also be so weak that actors would not even want to adopt it. Thus, there may be a somewhat ambivalent relationship between stringency and uptake here.

REFERENCES

Abott, K.W. and D. Snidal (1998), 'Why States Act through Formal International Organizations', *The Journal of Conflict Resolution* 42(1), 3–32.

Auld, G., L.H. Gulbrandsen and C.L. McDermott (2008), 'Certification Schemes and the Impacts on Forests and Forestry', *Annual Review of Environment and Resources* 33, 187–211.

Cashore, B. (2002), 'Legitimacy and the Privatisation of Environmental Governance: How Non-State Market-Driven (NSMD) Governance Systems Gain Rule-Making Authority', *Governance* 15(4), 503–529.

Chasek, P., D.L. Downie and J.W. Brown (2006), 'Effective Environmental Regimes, Obstacles and Opportunities', in P. Chasek, D.L. Downie and J.W. Brown (eds), *Global Environmental Politics*, 4th edition, Boulder: Westview Press, pp. 197–232.

Clapp, J. (1998), 'The Privatization of Global Environmental Governance: ISO 14000 and the Developing World', *Global Governance* 4, 295–316.

Courville, S. (2003), 'Social Accountability Audits: Challenging or Defending Democratic Governance?', *Law and Policy* 25(3), 269–297.

Cutler, A.C., V. Haufler and T. Porter (1999), *Private Authority and International Affairs*, New York: SUNY Press.

Dixon, J. (2007), 'Supermarkets as New Food Authorities', in D. Burch and G. Lawrence (eds), *Supermarkets and Agrifood Supply Chains*, Cheltenham: Edward Elgar Publishing, pp. 29–50.

Fuchs, D. (2006), 'Transnational Corporations and Global Governance: The

Effectiveness of Private Governance', in: S. Schirm (ed.), *Globalization. State of the Art of Research and Perspectives*, London: Routledge.

Fuchs, D., A. Kalfagianni, J. Clapp and L. Busch (2011), 'Introduction to Symposium on Private Agrifood Governance: Values, Shortcomings and Alternatives', *Agriculture and Human Values* 28(3), 335–344.

Fuchs, D., A. Kalfagianni and T. Havinga (2011), 'Actors in Private Food Governance: The Legitimacy of Retail Standards and Multi-Stakeholder Initiatives with Civil Society Participation', *Agriculture and Human Values* 28(3), 353–367.

Graz, J.C. and A. Nölke (2008), *Transnational Private Governance and its Limits*, London: Routledge.

Greven, T. (2004), 'Private, Staatliche und Überstaatliche Interventionen zur Verankerung von Arbeitnehmerrechten', in: H. Bass and S. Melchers (eds), *Neue Instrumente zur Sozialen und Ökologischen Gestaltung der Globalisierung: Codes of Conduct, Sozialklauseln, nachhaltige Investmentfonds*, Münster/Hamburg/Berlin, pp. 139–371.

Gupta, A. (2010), 'Transparency in Global Environmental Governance: A Coming of Age?', *Global Environmental Politics* 10(3), 1–9.

Gulbrandsen, L. (2010), *Transnational Environmental Governance: The Emergence and Effects of the Certification of Forests and Fisheries*, Cheltenham: Edward Elgar Publishing.

Hale, A. (2000), 'What Hope for "Ethical" Trade in the Globalised Garment Industry?', *Antipode* 32(4), 349–356.

Hale, A. and L.M. Shaw (2001), 'Women Workers and the Promise of Ethical Trade in the Globalised Garment Industry: A Serious Beginning?', *Antipode* 33(3), 510–30.

Hedberg, C.J. and F. Von Malmborg (2003), 'The Global Reporting Initiative and Corporate Sustainability Reporting in Swedish Companies', *Corporate Social Responsibility and Environmental Management* 10, 153–164.

Hughes, Alex (2001), 'Multi-Stakeholder Approaches to Ethical Trade: Towards a Reorganisation of UK Retailers' Global Supply Chains?', *Journal of Economic Geography* 1, 421–437.

Hurd, I. (1999), 'Legitimacy and Authority in International Politics', *International Organisation* 53(2), 379–408.

Jönsson, C. and J. Tallberg (1998), 'Compliance and Post-Agreement Bargaining', *European Journal of International Relations* 4(4), 371–408.

Lawrence, G. and D. Burch (eds) (2007), *Supermarkets and Agrifood Supply Chains*, Cheltenham: Edward Elgar Publishing.

Lock, P. (2001), 'Sicherheit à la carte? Entstaatlichung, Gewaltmärkte und die Privatisierung des Staatlichen Gewaltmonopols', in: T. Brühl, T. Debiel, B. Hamm, H. Hummel and J. Martens (eds), *Die Privatisierung der Weltpolitik*, Bonn: Verlag J.H.W. Dietz Nachfolger, pp. 200–231.

Kalfagianni, Agni and Doris Fuchs (2011), 'The GlobalG.A.P.', in A. Reed, D. Reed and P. Utting (eds), *Business, Non-State Regulation and Development*, London: Routledge.

Marx, A. and D. Cuypers (2010), 'Forest Certification as a Global Environmental Governance Tool: What is the Macro-Effectiveness of the Forest Stewardship Council?', *Regulation and Governance* 4, 408–434.

Mitchell, R.B. (2002), 'A Quantitative Approach to Evaluating International Environmental Regimes', *Global Environmental Politics*, 2(4), 58–83.

Morgan, K., T. Marsden and J. Murdoch (2006), *Worlds of Food*, Oxford: Oxford University Press.

Muradian, R. and W. Pelupessy (2005), 'Governing the Coffee Chain: The Role of Voluntary Regulatory Systems', *World Development* 33(12), 2029–2044.

Nadvi, K. and F. Wältring (2002), *Making Sense of Global Standards*, INEF Report 58/2002, Duisburg: University of Duisburg-Essen.

Schaller, S. (2007), *The Democratic Legitimacy of Private Governance: An Analysis of the Ethical Trading Initiative*, INEF Report 91/2007, Institute for Development and Peace, Duisburg: University of Duisburg-Essen.

Scharpf, W.F. (1997), *Games Real Actors Play*, Colorado: Westview Press.

Van der Grijp, N. (2010), *Regulating Pesticide Risk Reduction: The Practice and Dynamics of Legal Pluralism*, Amsterdam: Free University Press.

Van Waarden, F. (2010), 'Governing Global Commons: Public-Private Protection of Fish and Forests', *Jerusalem Papers in Regulation & Governance*, Working Paper No 17. June 2010, http://regulation.huji.ac.il/papers/jp17.pdf, accessed 6 January 2011.

9. Food quality through networks in the European wine industry[1]

Federica Casarosa and Marco Gobbato

9.1 INTRODUCTION

In recent times, state regulation concerning food safety and quality has been progressively replaced by self- or co-regulatory arrangements requiring that companies, within the whole food chain or in a given phase, implement their own food safety and quality systems. This shift, encouraged by States that rely on higher compliance with private regulation, has triggered the adoption of private standards drafted by private firms within the food chain. These standards mainly relate to food safety, but they can also focus on food quality standards, which move from the default level defined by 'safe' products towards a higher one, where the decision concerning the type of products and the methods of processing can also become an added value embedded in the final product. In this latter case, the standards usually go beyond the requirements established by public standards as, for instance, requirements for more stringent or more extensive rules concerning the selection of raw materials are defined. Additionally, quality standards may extend vertically, controlling either upper or lower layers in the value chain.

The purpose of this chapter is to analyse a sector where quality standards have a fundamental role to play, namely the wine sector, in order to show the regulatory strategies that firms adopt defining and implementing quality standards. The chapter will describe the findings of a research project concerning inter-firm networks in the wine supply chain, focusing on transnational networks that are quality driven. The cases available will show how the balance between cooperation and competition has been struck through organisational and contractual network models, in order to achieve higher levels of compliance with the quality standard.

9.2 THE ROLE OF INTER-FIRM NETWORKS IN IMPROVING QUALITY STANDARDS

Since the 1990s, the food sector has become the preferred area in which private sector initiatives have proliferated, in particular in the form of standards and certification programmes defining methods of production and processing to be used by suppliers of agricultural products. The increased interest and activity by enterprises were, on the one hand, a reaction to a more informed and demanding consumer (Feenstra 1998) and, on the other, a response to a less interventionist state approach (Gereffi, Humphrey and Sturgeon 2005, 79). This evolution should be viewed within its historical context, where the concentration of food production and trade in large companies was faced with the globalisation of food supply and the differentiation of agricultural practices in the production chains. In order to govern such differences and to overcome the potential harm in cases of limited control over the production process, agri-food enterprises have developed single-industry standards or common rules to define good practices that can be monitored and controlled directly or by third party certifiers (Casey 2009). Thus, food safety and quality have become criteria that cannot be understated, neither in the process of production, nor in distribution.

Given the exponential increase in the number of schemes and programmes focused on food safety, the current academic debate focuses on the problems of overlapping amongst them, and in particular on the burden that such standards place on suppliers, especially in developing countries (Henson and Humphrey 2009; Meidinger 2009; Beauvais 2010). Less attention has been paid so far to the different objectives and characteristics of food quality standards in comparison to safety ones.

Food safety standards usually focus on control and compliance in respect of production, transport and processing standards. They are based on a shared definition of 'safe' product that is qualified at its minimum level by national regulations[2] (Hodges 2005; Schepel 2005; Cafaggi 2009), while private standards can increase such levels by providing for additional or stricter criteria (Henson and Humphrey 2009).

Food quality standards, though implying a default level of safety, address a different concern, namely the achievement of an added value to the final product, including criteria on the type of the raw products and the methods of processing. For instance, food quality standards can focus on more extensive, and usually stricter, rules concerning the selection of raw materials, or they can require the adoption of technically advanced processing machines.[3] The overlapping between the two types of standards is illustrated by table 9.1: the dichotomy flowing from the food safety

Table 9.1   Overlap between quality and safety standards

	High quality	Medium quality	Low quality
Safe	Marketable	Marketable	Marketable/*unmarketable*
Unsafe	*Unmarketable*	*Unmarketable*	*Unmarketable*

standards, i.e. safe versus unsafe, can be easily applied to any product notwithstanding its categorisation within either the higher or lower quality level category. For instance, the methanol crisis in the late eighties showed that (presumed) high quality wines with this component could also be unsafe and have negative effects on consumers' health, requiring their immediate withdrawal from the market.

The difference between the two types of standards, then, is related to the fact that where, in the case of safety, national regulation provides for a minimum level that is to be applied as a limit for the commercialisation of food products. In the case of quality, it depends on the type of product, whether national or international regulation defines the boundary between high, medium and low quality level, and eventually the minimum level for their commercialisation.

Given this framework, this chapter focuses on the wine sector, where quality standards have a fundamental role to play. In general, wine quality has always been the element upon which producers rely in order to gain reputation and consequently the favour of consumers.

From the legal point of view, a level playing field has also been defined by national and European regulators, through the appellation system which distinguishes between 'quality wines produced in a specified region' (QWpsr) and table wines (TW), following the traditional French approach (O'Connor 2004, 27). The distinction therefore provides both the criteria upon which quality can be evaluated, acknowledging high and low quality types of production, and also the minimum level of quality that can allow marketability of the final product (table 9.2, with adapted matrix for the wine sector).

Wine producers in most of the cases rely on the legal distinction, eventually including internal subcategories, which can provide further

Table 9.2   Matrix of quality and safety standards in the wine sector

	Quality wines	Table wines	Other wines
Safe	Marketable	Marketable	*Unmarketable*
Unsafe	*Unmarketable*	*Unmarketable*	*Unmarketable*

intermediary levels through national regulation.[4] However, wine producers have recently started to prefer not to base their production and market strategies on such a quality scale, instead building their reputation on their brand names and consequently on internally drafted quality standards (Federvini 2007).

These standards can be drafted differently in terms of their legal form, for instance through the inclusion of specific clauses in the purchase contract, or through the application of a specific standard along the supply chain, etc. Moreover, standards can involve different types of actors from grape-growers to final producer, including wine-makers and bottlers, with different roles, as standard setters or regulatees, and can be driven by simple or multiple purposes (e.g. in respect of access to new market sectors or to foreign markets, or in respect of the distinction of production for different distribution channels, etc.).

The objective of this chapter will be to present the way in which enterprises encompass such quality standards and requirements within their production and distribution agreements, taking into account the aforementioned elements of differentiation. In particular, the chapter will use the concept of inter-firm networks in order to describe the cases in which the relationships among the enterprises can overcome the mere market exchange, and rely on interdependent relationships that also include quality requirements.

Moreover, as will be briefly described, the choice of the types of networks is not neutral, given that it would affect both the regulatory output and the costs to comply with the quality standards. The chapter will verify which type of network could increase the flow of information along the chain and which type of network could enhance compliance. Previous research provides evidence that a balance between competition and cooperation is not easily struck, and can be affected by the structure of the network, namely whether it is hierarchical or horizontal, and on the degree of integration among the firms along the supply chain (Cafaggi 2008; Cafaggi and Iamiceli 2012).

The hypothesis is the following: the organisational network model (e.g. a cooperative) is selected where the competition level is low and the quality standard is defined by the network members (or by a third party), whereas the contractual network model (e.g. linked bilateral contracts) is selected where the competition level is high and there is a lead actor that controls the whole supply chain.

The hypothesis will be tested on the cases found in European research on the wine supply chain, taking as point of reference the quality-driven transnational networks.

9.3   INTER-FIRM NETWORKS

In our view, inter-firm networks are collaborative settings created by firms for the purposes of pursuing one or many common projects and for managing interdependencies emerging from their resources, intangible assets, strategies, etc. (Cafaggi 2008; Cafaggi 2011a). The interdependencies induce mutual learning, collective practices and peer monitoring but call for coordination.

Within networks, resources and/or products of one firm are specific to the resources or products of other firms. Thus, each firm may exit the network only at a positive cost – for instance, the cost of adapting the assets produced for the network to alternative uses. At the same time, as the withdrawal of a firm occurs, the other partners may face high costs of replacement. These reasons drive parties to set up legal devices for improving collaboration and ensuring both the stability and flexibility of the network (Cafaggi 2008, 539). They usually include alternative risk allocation schemes in order to reduce the consequences of possible unforeseen events – as a fall in demand of products produced by the networks – or of the possible impossibility of performing by one or more parties.

Inter-firm networks may be very attractive, even in the presence of positive governance costs. By avoiding vertical integration among the firms, they preserve the autonomy and legal independence of partners. To such an extent, they may be considered as hybrid forms located between markets and hierarchies (Powell 1990). They also promote flexibility: thus, by using networks, parties may collaborate in some projects or in some markets while competing in others. Thus, firms may select the appropriate degree of involvement.

The array of network models may vary significantly (Menard 2004; Williamson 1996). Basically, a network may be governed by one or many contracts (contractual networks), by an organisation (organisational networks) or, finally, by a combination of the aforementioned legal devices (mixed networks). Contractual networks may be formed by a unique, multilateral contract entered into by several firms or may be the result of a combination of many bilaterally linked contracts (Cafaggi 2008). Organisational networks, instead, take the form of new legal entities (corporation, association, foundation, etc.) in which several firms participate. In this case, hierarchical control by one single firm can be imposed, but there can also be cases in which none of the firms participating in the network are entitled to control the overall organisation, as the power is shared among the all the participants.

The research on the wine sector shows that contractual networks formed by a set of bilateral contracts are widespread among firms operating at different levels of the supply chain. Multilateral contracts are very few and regulate networks formed by competing firms usually operating at the final stages of the supply chain. The majority of networks detected are organisational: mutual organisations prevail (in the form of cooperatives), while for-profit and non-profit networks are less diffused.

9.4   EVIDENCE FROM THE RESEARCH PROJECT ON WINE

The cases that will be discussed in this chapter are based on a European research project focused on inter-firm networks in the wine sector (Cafaggi and Iamiceli 2010). The project provided information from seven geographical areas in five European countries: Loire (France), Hungary, Trentino, Verona and East Sicily (Italy), Douro (Portugal), and Valencia (Spain). Almost two hundred firms were interviewed (precisely 193) among which the following can be counted: 19 grape-growers, 149 final producers and 25 distributors.[5] The majority of firms are micro- and small-sized (126), while fewer are medium (36) and big (26) firms.[6] The information was collected through interviews and questionnaires, which allowed for the gathering of qualitative information on several organisational aspects of inter-firm collaboration and its governance.

The data collected showed the existence of many cases of inter-firm networks within the wine sector,[7] but not all of them were focused entirely on the control over quality of the production. As a matter of fact, in many cases quality control is also coupled with other rationales, namely fragmentation of land, access to specific products, access to new markets or different segments of the market, reduction of costs, innovation, increase of bargaining power and so on. The analysis of all these cases of inter-firm networks is beyond the scope of this chapter, yet the study will focus on inter-firm networks that are mainly triggered by quality and, among them, those that show a transnational dimension. Among the whole body of interviews, the ones that are relevant here are limited to thirteen final producers and one distributor. The class of transnational inter-firm networks includes networks that list, as among their members, enterprises from different countries, or that predominantly provide their services in a foreign country, e.g. the distribution of the wines of the participants abroad. Although this would seem to be a very wide definition, it still embeds both the formal and substantial facets of the network that will also be used as criteria to differentiate the different hypothesis.

9.4.1   Taxonomy of Cases

As previously mentioned, the cases that are included in this chapter focus on quality networks. The criteria used to distinguish between them are the following:

1. legal form, which includes contractual, organisational and mixed forms of networks; and
2. type of participants, which distinguishes among distributors, final producers (such as private firms and cooperatives), and nationality of the partners and of the network.

From table 9.3, it is clear that the type of participant is predominantly final producers, with a limited intervention of distributors; this is due to the fact that quality requirements are mainly developed and applied in the production phase, from grape-growing to bottling, thus predominantly involving those actors engaged in such activities. Moreover, the transnational dimension of the networks requires an enterprise dimension that cannot be too small, rather it should be sufficiently large to allow for the investment of part of its revenues in respect of facilitating access to foreign markets. Thus, grape-growers are not present among these networks, as the average dimension of grape-growers' enterprises is very small in the countries analysed (Eurostat 2007).

9.5   CONTRACTUAL NETWORKS

The simplest model of contractual networks is based on linked bilateral contracts for the sale of grapes or bulk wine (see cases 01 and 02 in table 9.3). Although the supply of grapes is very common within each country (Cafaggi and Iamiceli 2010), this is not the case in the transnational networks. Rather, here, contracts generally have as their object the supply of bulk wine (figure 9.1). Different models may be acknowledged according to the final aims undertaken and the compliance devices adopted.

In the case of grape supply networks, the final producer develops stable relationships with his suppliers, usually used for producing high quality wine (figure 9.1). In fact, the final producer buys grapes to complement its own production and will require a high level quality from the grape-growers. Due to fragmentation of land, each supplier does not provide for a large quantity of grapes. The relationship is usually defined through a written contract where basic quality requirements are set,[8] which provides

Table 9.3   Food quality networks in European wine sector

Name	Nationality of network	Type of members	Legal form	Objectives
Case 01	FR	Final Producer (FR) Final Producers (EU)	Linked bilateral contracts	– Supply of grapes – Stable and guaranteed quality
Case 02	PT	Final Producer (PT) Final Producer (ES) Final Producer (FR)	Linked bilateral contracts	– Supply of high quantity of bulk wine – Stable and guaranteed quality
Case 03	IT	Intermediary (IT) Final Producers (IT) Distributor (UK)	Linked bilateral contracts	– Supply of high quantity of bottled wine – Stable and guaranteed quality
Case 04	A	Final producer (A) Final producers (HUN)	Linked bilateral contracts	– Supply of high quantity of grapes – Stable and certified DO quality
Case 05	G	5 Final Producers (IT)	For-profit company	– Access to foreign market – Present high quality wines
Case 06	INT	11 Final producers (EU)	Association	– Increase reputation – Present high quality wines
Case 07	IT	Final producer (IT) Grape growers (IT) Final producers (EU)	Linked bilateral contracts and for-profit company	– Supply of high quantity of grapes and bulk wines – Stable and guaranteed quality
Case 08	PT	5 Final producers (PT)	Informal group	– Access to foreign market – Present high quality wine from specific DO region

Glossary: A – Austria; ES – Spain; EU – Europe; FR – France; HUN – Hungary;
IT – Italy; PT – Portugal; UK – United Kingdom.

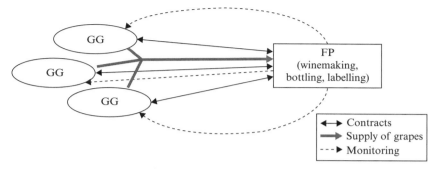

Figure 9.1   Contractual network for the supply of grapes or bulk wine

for penalties in the event of non-compliance.[9] Further, exclusive dealing arrangements that are binding for the suppliers may also be included in the contract.

Compliance in respect of quality standards is ensured by a combination of formal and informal devices. The grape-growers are required to be subject to controls provided by local institutions (e.g. in Italy by the local Chamber of Commerce) concerning public standards (i.e. certification of the denomination of origin of the grapes supplied). In order to improve the quality and ensure that it satisfies the final producer's requirements, incentives are also included – such as remuneration related to the sugar content of the grapes supplied. The monitoring of the grape-growers also plays a remarkable role in compliance. Because of the notion of spatial proximity, agronomists and oenologists of the final producer may monitor and advise the grape-growers on the most important phases of production (e.g. the decision to thin out the grapes, the time to harvest, etc.). These functions – including the service supply – allow the final producer to coordinate the network, ensuring the uniformity of the grapes produced, and also the further improvement in respect of the requirement of compliance with the relevant quality standards.

The same level of formalisation is achieved in respect of bulk wine supply; in this case, however, the quantity of product supplied by a single producer is higher. The final product may be of a different quality, according to the needs of the final producer, usually also reflecting the commercialisation strategies. In such a case, the final producer is more interested in securing a stable quantity of wine, characterised by a uniform quality. The hierarchical element of the relationship is also significant, as the buyer defines precisely the type of wine to be provided. Since monitoring can be costly – the farm of the supplier may not be close to the final producer company – and the suppliers usually have the know-how for producing the wine – they may be well-known final producers and also cooperatives – the compliance is based more on the fulfilment of requirements included in the contract clauses. The quality is defined in detail by the purchaser, usually providing the supplier with some technical requirements that should identify the elements for the production of the final product. The contract negotiation is very detailed and the compliance with the standard required may call for specific investments in the relationship undertaken by the supplier. Sometimes the supply is based on samples submitted by the supplier and tested and accepted by the final producer.

To a lesser extent, direct monitoring is provided by repeated visits to the farm of the supplier both in respect of the grape-growing and the wine-making process, and in terms of coordination between the agronomy and oenology experts of the seller and purchaser, etc.

A noteworthy case is represented by transnational networks for the supply of bulk wine (see case 03). The network is governed by a set of coordinated bilateral contracts. A large-scale distributor enters into a contract with an intermediary enterprise for the supply of a high quantity of wine. The intermediary selects final producers and organises the production of the wine, identifying, if required, the bottlers that are also in charge of labelling. The wine is produced under the label of the distributor, which may also be the label's owner or the licensee of a label created by the intermediary enterprise. The network is run by the distributor, who decides exactly what kind of wine will be provided. The intermediary enterprise is in charge of monitoring during the production process and of ensuring full consistency with the distribution contract.

The compliance with quality standards is achieved by setting up contractual obligations. During the negotiation with the distributor, the combination of quality and price is established and the contract is concluded. Then, the intermediary has to organise the production process accordingly. He is further required to periodically submit samples to independent laboratories in order to achieve the eligibility for the commercialisation. The non-fulfilment of the obligations concerning certification leads to the application of penalty clauses, which, in this case, have also been applied. The quality of the wine supplied may also be detected by the tasting of some samples provided by the intermediary. At the time of the harvest, the intermediary, together with the distributor, supervises the quality of the product, eventually providing instructions for the wine-making process.

Consider that, even if contracts are annually renewed, the relationship with the distributor may exist over many years. Usually, even before the contract has been concluded, the intermediary enterprise monitors the Italian market, providing the distributor with the relevant information

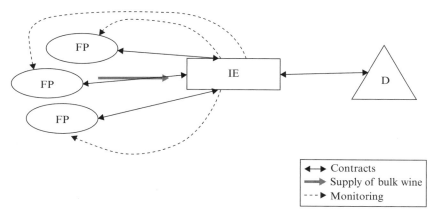

Figure 9.2   Contractual network for the supply of bulk wine through an intermediary

in advance as to which wine can potentially be supplied and the expected quality of the year. Long-term relationships with distributors facilitate the accumulation of such knowledge, which cannot be completely formalised through the definition of standards.

An exceptional and interesting case is a Hungarian one (see case 04 in figure 9.2), which involves a Hungarian final producer and an Austrian cooperative. Divergent from the previous cases, in this case quality standards rely fully on the 'denomination of origin' (DO) as defined within the Hungarian region. The cooperative negotiates specific linked bilateral

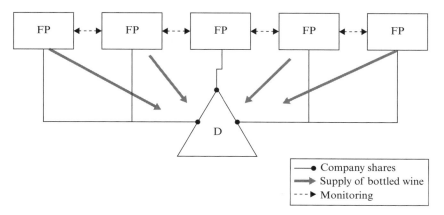

Figure 9.3   Organisational network for distribution abroad of bottled wine

contracts with foreign grape suppliers concerning Hungarian DO grapes, which are then collected and processed by the Austrian cooperative so as to produce Hungarian DO wine. In this case, the private initiative could not have been achieved without the intervention of the two national governments and of the two producers' associations. The preliminary agreements provide a special exception for production carried out abroad, due to the proximity of wine production regions. Quality standard is embedded in the linked bilateral contracts but it is mainly defined upon the existing national regulation concerning DO wine.

9.6   ORGANISATIONAL NETWORKS

9.6.1   For-Profit Networks

For-profit networks are created when many firms create a new company in order to carry out a specific activity and when no firm is entitled to control over the company (i.e. the decision power is shared among the participants). The research detected for-profit networks performing both the production and the distribution of wine (Cafaggi and Iamiceli 2010).

In one case, a for-profit company in which five Italian high quality wine producers from different regions of Italy participate, is formed for the purpose of exporting their wine to Germany, specifically through the 'hotel, restaurants and catering' (Ho.re.ca.) channel (figure 9.3).[10] In order to foster cooperative behaviour and restrain internal competition among similar products from different producers, the network has a very narrow focus: that is, it aims at distributing a limited selection of wines for each member of the network, under the assumption that those selected are complementary and not alternative to those produced by any other partner. Some exclusivity clauses are also included in order to enhance the collaboration. According to participants, shareholders may not export the same wine to Germany through other imports as distributed by the company.

The quality of the wine is basically ensured by each producer. However, internal competition is also the driver for the monitoring of compliance in respect of quality standards. On the one hand, internal competition pushes for the implementation of high quality requirements, not defined in the statute, but rather negotiated internally each time. On the other hand, it triggers peer monitoring among the members of the network concerning the quality of the bottled wine to be distributed abroad. Again, monitoring is not formalised through any legal tool, rather it is informally exercised by members, given that a lower quality of wine produced by one of the members could affect the whole network to the extent that not only could the collective offer of members' wines be refused by retailers,[11] but also the reputation of the other products could be downgraded as a result.

This balance at the governance level was then challenged by the proposal for the distribution of additional high quality wines. Initially the choice was clear: the network company could not distribute the wine of producers competing with the five shareholders. However, subsequently the shareholders debated the option, given that one of the members is also the distributor (in the Italian market) of French champagne, and suggested distributing such a product in Germany through the network. However, the similarities with the sparkling wine produced by one of the other members provoked an internal debate on the opportunity to distribute members' competing products through the network. Finally, a positive solution was adopted allowing for the distribution of non-members' wines, requiring those wines to be sufficiently differentiated from those of the members and in terms of compliance with the same quality requirements as demanded of members' wines.

In this case, it is clear that the achievement of strategies grounded on quality may contribute to the enhancement of collaboration, although specific governance devices are needed for containing competition among partners.

9.6.2 Non-Profit Networks

Within the category of transnational organisational networks we should also include the case of a not-for-profit network that exists in an association form (see case 06). The primary objective of this transnational network is the supply of promotional services, which is seen as constituting the basis for access to new markets. The association, founded in the early nineties, relies on twelve European producers with complementary brand portfolios, to leverage the international promotion of their wine and spirits.[12] The selection of participants is based on the type of enterprise, which should be family-owned, and the quality of products, which should fall within the super-premium category. It should be underlined that, while specific criteria are defined in the chapters of the association, in this case the reputational factors are mostly important in respect of access to the association, given that membership is by invitation only and that all decisions should be approved unanimously.

The association itself has a promotional objective, which is carried out through the collective presentation of the highest quality wines in limited edition cases. Nonetheless, such organisation provides a forum which not only provides the sharing of experience among members concerning the issues related to the transmission of the family business, it also enhances the creation of collaborative ties between producers.[13]

A feature of this association is the low level of competition among the members due to the different types of wines supplied by each producer, with each representing DO regions, even though they are all operating in the same segment of the market.

9.7   MIXED NETWORKS

Mixed networks are governed by a combination of contractual and organisational devices (figure 9.4). The research found few examples of such devices in Italy. They are established in order to produce high quality wines while increasing the 'wine portfolio' of the final producer in charge of the coordination of the network (Cafaggi et al. 2010).

In one case, a final producer of one region of Italy enters into several bilateral contracts with suppliers who are in charge of providing grapes and bulk wine. Some suppliers are located in the same region of the final producer, thus integrating its production with wine of the same DO.

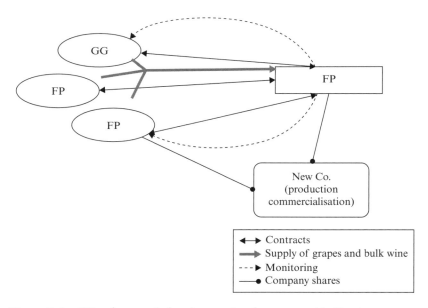

Figure 9.4   Mixed network for the supply of grapes and bulk wine

However, in order to enlarge its wine portfolio, the final producer may also enter into several contracts with suppliers operating in other regions.

The need to increase interdependence with high quality producers, eventually increasing monitoring and decision power of strategic choices, is the trigger for more complex legal structures where contractual and organisational devices are used. When the supply of bulk wine becomes pivotal for commercial reasons, mainly in respect of the relationship with distributors and the need to integrate a certain wine portfolio, then the interdependence is governed through a combination of contractual, property and corporate devices. Beside the contractual relationship regulating the supply of wine, the final producer and the supplier – who in turn may also be a final producer – also create a new company in charge of producing and distributing the wine produced under a co-owned common trademark.

In another case, the creation of the network is even more clearly grounded on a strategy for improving quality. The final producer coordinates the network for pursuing the project focusing on 'noble' wines. Again the interdependences between the final producer and the various suppliers are governed through different legal devices.

The final producer entered into long-term contracts with a few selected and well-known final producers providing substantial control over the activity of each party. The final producer may rely on the famous trademarks of the partners and is in charge of the distribution of its own wine as well as of the wine produced by them. In turn, partners take advantage of oenological services supplied by the final producer and also of its commercial expertise. With one of the suppliers, the final producer created a new company that, in this case, only owns the land. Subsequently, a bilateral contract is entered into for the supply of bottled wine, produced with oenological consultation of the network coordinator, which ensures compliance with quality standards. Each party holds the ownership of its trademark as the exploitation of product complementarities is realised at the commercial level through joint marketing strategies.

9.8 INFORMAL NETWORKS

Within the cases of transnational networks focused on quality, the case of a promotional network not based on a specific legal form should also be briefly discussed. In respect of the situation identified in the Portuguese case study (see case 08), members of the network are producers of DO wines that cooperate in order to increase the reputation of Portuguese wines, apart from Port wine. In particular, the network is used as a forum for the sharing of knowledge, technology and experience among members, which is perceived as pivotal in the promotion of the production of quality wines.

Although the network works on the basis of common interests, the individuality of members is very strong and raises the level of competition among the participants, resulting in a lack of coordinated strategy for the distribution of wine, not only nationally but also abroad.

9.9   CONCLUSION

The cases presented above show the significant role that networks play in the definition and implementation of quality standards.

Within networks, parties may use a variety of legal tools to define and introduce food quality standards and requirements within their production and distribution relationships.

In some cases, these requirements are detailed and strictly monitored during the overall production process, while, in others, food quality is used as a criterion in the selection of the partners to the network. This differentiation is also due to the concurrent rationales that drive the network, which is never focused exclusively on quality matters.

The choice concerning the type of network model used to govern enterprises' relationships can also affect the implementation of food quality standards, either providing comprehensive monitoring functions or stronger enforcement mechanisms within the supply chain.

Table 9.4 summarizes the research findings. While due to the limited number of cases available, the findings cannot allow for generalisation of the results, but they can be used to test the initial hypothesis. It is clear that the choice between contractual and organisational networks provide different legal tools to achieve the highest level of compliance. In the case of contractual networks, the hierarchical structure is preferred as the suppliers are usually located in different countries and the link between all of them is the purchaser, eventually substituted by a professional intermediary. The organisational networks are mostly used in horizontal networks, where peer monitoring is used to verify compliance with quality standards by network members, although this activity is not formalised. Mixed networks can be widely different depending on the type of legal tools selected by network members; the cases available are mostly hierarchical where contractual links are supported by organisational tools, which increase suppliers' involvement and improve the level of compliance. Informal networks base their flexibility on exogenous factors in respect of the lack of a formal legal framework, which reduces their capability to react to

Table 9.4 *Summary of research findings*

	Contractual	Organisational		Mixed	Informal
		For-profit	Not-for-profit		
Phase in the supply chain	Mostly production or inter-phase	Distribution	Service supply (promotion)	Production	Service supply (promotion)
Power allocation	Hierarchical (purchaser sets the standard)	Horizontal	Horizontal	Hierarchical	Horizontal
Coordination	– Ex ante instructions by purchaser – Economic incentives – Eventual delegation of coordination to intermediaries	– Exclusivity clauses – Decision by unanimity	– Information sharing – High level of autonomy – Decision by unanimity	– Ex ante instructions by purchaser – Provision of production services – Involvement in suppliers' activity	– Information sharing
Monitoring	– Inspections – Enforcement of contractual remedies (product refusal, contract renovation refusal)	– Peer monitoring	– Peer monitoring	– Inspections – Enforcement of contractual remedies	– Low level of peer monitoring

endogenous problems, including, for example, the decline in the quality level of wines.

Even if further research is needed, the evidence provided suggests that standard setting is less costly in contractual networks than in organisational networks, since in contractual networks such a task is performed by a single firm (usually the final purchaser or the distributor), whereas in organisational networks, the common use of the unanimity rule in decision-making increases the cost of standard setting.

However, implementation may be troublesome in contractual networks where the fragmentation increases (e.g. in transnational networks). Since quality standards are usually hard to codify, their implementation should be based on monitoring rather than on contract clauses, which link the breach of (hard-to-codify) standards to classic remedies.

In these cases, regulation may affect the network shape. For instance, delegation to intermediaries reduces the monitoring costs. Thus instead of directly controlling the first-tier enterprises (i.e. the grape-growers) the purchaser monitors only the intermediary. Alternatively, we also observe that contracts are reinforced with organisational devices that align the parties' behaviour favouring the exchange of knowledge and a deeper implementation of quality standards.

Moreover, the choice of networks affects the regulatory output: contractual networks are based on command-and-control regulation in most cases, while organisational networks are more inclined to responsive regulation. However, this is not a general assumption, as contractual networks can also not be hierarchical, but they have to provide specific incentives to suppliers so as to participate in the improvement of quality levels (FAO 2011, 90; Cafaggi and Iamiceli 2012).

The current analysis is only the first step in wider research concerning food quality standards, but it provides useful insights in respect of the framework hypothesis through which enterprises embed quality requirements in the production chain. However, further research is still required to generalise the above-mentioned results, in particular in respect of providing a better understanding of the relationship between regulation and contract law tools (Cafaggi 2011b). Specifically, further research questions could include which legal forms provide better incentives for enterprises in guaranteeing higher quality standards, which concurring rationales can hinder the quality requirements to be adopted or expressly defined, and whether, in general, the choice over the different legal forms can provide better devices to govern implementation of quality standards.

NOTES

1. This chapter has been drafted within the research project on 'Inter-firm Networks in the European Wine Industry' realized under the Sixth Framework Program – Integrated Project 'Reflexive Governance in the Public Interest' [REFGOV] (2005–2010). Sub-network: Corporate Governance; Sub-section: 'Corporate Governance and inter-firm networks'. We wish to thank all the members of the European research group and, in particular, the coordinator, prof. Fabrizio Cafaggi, and prof. Paola Iamiceli, Matteo De Gasperi, Chiara Ferrari and Massimo Iori and all the researchers in charge of the responsibility of national cases: prof. Sandrine Clavel (Loire), prof. Peter Hardi and prof. Krisztina Büti (Hungary), prof. Ana Lourenco (Portugal), and prof. Juan Ignazio Ruiz (Spain). Though the chapter is the outcome of a common understanding, Federica Casarosa was in charge of drafting paragraphs 9.2, 9.4, 9.6.2 and 9.8 while Marco Gobbato drafted paragraphs 9.3, 9.5, 9.6.1 and 9.7. Conclusions were jointly drafted.
2. See European Directive 95/2001/EC on the general product safety, where the definition of safe product is 'any product which, under normal or reasonably foreseeable conditions of use [. . .] does not present any risk or only the minimum risks compatible with the product's use, considered to be acceptable and consistent with a high level of protection for the safety and health of persons, taking into account the following points in particular:

   1 the characteristics of the product, including its composition, packaging, instructions for assembly and, where applicable, for installation and maintenance;
   2 the effect on other products, where it is reasonably foreseeable that it will be used with other products;
   3 the presentation of the product, the labeling, any warnings and instructions for its use and disposal and any other indication or information regarding the product' (Art. 2 (b)).

3. In this case, the allocation of the cost of investments in innovative techniques could be borne by the standard setter or shifted to the intermediate producer. For instance, in wine making, the cost could be shared by producer members of a cooperative, or could be completely charged to the wine producer where the distributor requires the use of specific innovative techniques without providing them.
4. For example, Italian legislation distinguishes between *Vino da tavola* (table wine) and *Vini a denominazione di orgine controllata e garantita* (DOCG), *Vini a denominazione di origine controllata* (DOC), and *Vini ad indicazione geografica tipica* (IGT), which are all included in the QWprs. See Casarosa and Gobbato 2008.
5. Considering the high number of final producers interviewed, this definition is very wide and includes all the actors involved in the activities that occur between growing the grapes and producing the final product.
6. See Reg. 2003/361/EC; Reg. 363/2004/EC; Reg. 264/2004/EC. For four firms it was not possible to ascertain the size.
7. The output of the research showed a total of 129 inter-firm networks, which can be distinguished as production networks, distribution networks and networks for the supply of services (see Cafaggi and Iamiceli 2010).
8. The contract form may vary remarkably according to the countries. For instance, in the case of Douro (Portugal) and Valencia (Spain) the written form is seldom used. See Cafaggi and Iamiceli 2010.
9. Penalties are usually based on a reduction of the final price of the grapes. They are not only formally defined but also applied in practice, and eventually adapted.
10. See that the two distribution channels are the Ho.re.ca., or traditional channel where hotels, restaurants and cafés are included, and the large distribution chains (LDC) or modern channel that includes convenience stores and supermarkets.

11. A common practice of distributors is to offer a bundle of wines of the same quality, from different regions, to satisfy the consumers' requests as much as possible.
12. The association is by internal rules limited to a maximum of twelve members.
13. In particular, mixed networks arise at the bilateral level: for instance, the participating Portuguese producer has built up a contractual and organisational relationship with the Spanish producer concerning distribution in Spain and in another foreign market (Lourenço and Casarosa 2010). The other types of agreements among the members include joint ventures, distribution agreements, promotion agreements and technical support.

REFERENCES

Beauvais, J. (2010), 'Food Safety Private Regulation and the Role of Developing Economies', Paper Presented at the Conference 'Food Safety and Transnational Private Regulation', Florence, March 2010.

Cafaggi, F. (2008), 'Contractual Networks and the Small Business Act: Towards European Principles?', *European Review of Contract Law*, 4, 943.

Cafaggi, F. (2009), 'Product Safety, Private Standard Setting and Information Networks', in F. Cafaggi and H. Muir Watt (eds), *The Regulatory Function of European Private Law*, Cheltenham: Edward Elgar Publishing, p.207.

Cafaggi, F. (ed.) (2011a), *Contractual Networks, Inter-firm Cooperation and Economic Growth*, Cheltenham: Edward Elgar Publishing.

Cafaggi, F. (2011b), 'Transnational Governance by Contract – Private Regulation and Contractual Networks in Food', available at http://ssrn.com/abstract=1874749.

Cafaggi, F. and P. Iamiceli (2012), 'Private Regulation and Industrial Organisation: the Network Approach', Working Paper – LAW 2012/21, Florence: European University Institute, available at http://ssrn.com/abstract=2136634.

Cafaggi, F. and P. Iamiceli (eds) (2010), 'Inter-Firm Networks in the European Wine Industry', Working Paper, Florence: European University Institute.

Cafaggi, F., P. Iamiceli, F. Casarosa, M. Degasperi, M. Gobbato and C. Ferrari (2010), 'Inter-Firm Networks in the Italian Wine Industry: Three Case Studies in North East and South Italy (Trentino, Verona, Catania and Ragusa)', in F. Cafaggi and P. Iamiceli (eds), *Inter-Firm Networks in the European Wine Industry*, Florence: European University Institute, p.43.

Casey, D. (2009), 'Three Puzzles of Private Governance: GlobalG.A.P. and the Regulation of Food Safety and Quality', UCD Working Papers in Law, Criminology & Socio-Legal Studies, Research Paper No. 22/2009, available at http://ssrn.com/abstract=1515702.

Eurostat (2007), 'Farm Structure Survey', available at http://epp.eurostat.ec.europa.eu/portal/page/portal/farm_structure_survey/data/Database.

FAO (2011), 'Private Standards and Certification in Fisheries and Aquaculture: Current Practice and Emerging Issues', 55 FAO Technical Papers on Fisheries and Aquaculture, available at http://www.fao.org/docrep/013/i1948e/i1948e.pdf.

Feenstra, R.C. (1998), 'Integration of Trade and Disintegration of Production', *Journal of Economic Perspectives*, 12(4), 31.

Gereffi, G., J. Humphrey and T. Sturgeon (2005), 'The Governance of Global Value Chains', *Review of International Political Economy*, 12, 79.

Henson, S. and J. Humphrey (2009), 'The Impacts of Private Food Safety Standards on the Food Chain and on Public Standard-Setting Processes', Paper prepared for FAO/WHO, May 2009, available at ftp://ftp.fao.org/codex/CAC/CAC32/al329Dbe.pdf.

Hodges, C. (2005), *European Regulation of Consumer Product Safety*, Oxford: Oxford University Press.

Lourenço, A. and F. Casarosa (2010), 'Inter-Firm Networks in the Portuguese Wine Industry: The Case of the Douro Region', in F. Cafaggi and P. Iamiceli (eds), *Inter-Firm Networks in the European Wine Industry*, Florence: European University Institute, p.64.

Meidinger, E. (2009), 'Private Import Safety Regulation and Transnational New Governance', in C. Coglianese, A.M. Finkel and D. Zaring, *Import Safety: Regulatory Governance in the Global Economy*, Philadelphia: University of Pennsylvania Press, p.233.

Menard, C. (2004), 'The Economics of Hybrid Organization', *Journal of Institutional and Theoretical Economics*, 160, 345.

O'Connor, B. (2004), *The Law of Geographical Indications*, London: Cameron May.

Powell, W.W. (1990), 'Neither Market nor Hierarchies: Network Forms of Organization', in L.L. Cummings and B. Staw (eds), *Research in Organizational Behaviour*, Greenwich: JAI Press, p.295.

Schepel, H. (2005), *The Constitution of Private Governance: Product Standards in the Regulation of Integrating Markets*, Oxford: Hart Publishing.

Williamson, O. (1996), *The Mechanisms of Governance*, Oxford: Oxford University Press.

10. Markets regulating markets: Competitive private regulation by halal certificates

Frans van Waarden and Robin van Dalen

10.1 INTRODUCTION: THE HALAL MARKET AND THE ABSENCE OF THE STATE

History abounds with market failures: asymmetric information, absence of regulation, and products that are easily tampered with. These all give rise to markets in which goods cannot be easily traded, or they can even lead to a complete absence of trade, as was theorized by Akerlof in his discussion of the 'lemons problem' (Akerlof 1970). The absence of trust in such markets does not only reduce prosperity as economic activity decreases, but has also consequences for society at large. Distrust is sand in the cogs of society, in the economy, politics, and government administration. Many have already pointed out the dangers of a decrease of mutual trust for the social structure in society (Fukuyama 1995; Putnam 1993). Problems of certificate inflation, product laundering, and collective action produce calls for a higher or more respected authority to back the reputation of the certificates or even to take over the responsibility for the certifying itself. Such an authority could in principle be anyone who the customers consider an authority, varying from God and His representatives on earth to expert scientists, and even pop stars, film stars, soccer heroes or other charismatic figures. A critical press broadcast such as the Dutch TV programmes *Zembla* or *Keuringsdienst van Waarde* could also be a contributing factor.

However, in our secular society the state has sooner or later become the authority in last resort or 'the ultimate risk manager' (Moss 2002) with, in principle, the power to enforce its standards. Furthermore, most citizens believe the state to be more neutral and objective than private actors with their particularistic self-interests, because: (i) the state does not need to be directly paid by those seeking to be certified, as it can fund its work out of general tax income; and (ii) the state is accountable to the general public, i.e. to the control institutions typical of a democratic constitutional state. After all, in such a democratic country the state is 'from us all' and therefore expected to represent the 'public interest'. What is more, as long as citizens trust the state to do so, public certification can help potential transaction partners to trust each other and hence also their markets.

Given the public interest in facilitating and encouraging economic transactions, states early on assumed a role in ordering markets. The centuries old process of state formation went hand in hand with an increase in transactions and economic growth, where one facilitated the other and vice versa. The increase in trade and prosperity created surplus, which could be taxed to fund the state and its regulatory and enforcement organisations. Conversely, the market ordering by the state reduced the risk of transactions, thereby facilitating and increasing them.

However, recent developments such as globalisation pose a threat to this classic position of the state. How to regulate flows of products and money that cross several boundaries and even continents? And how to regulate 'public' interests that are only interesting for some groups of the public, and perhaps even work against the interest of others?

In this chapter we try to give an answer to both these questions by focusing on a specific category of products: the emerging market for halal goods, products that are safe for Muslims to consume or use. This market for halal goods is interesting for several reasons. First, the nature of the quality of the goods is such that the market – both in the Netherlands, which we focus on, as well as globally – suffers from serious information problems. Secondly, a frequently used solution, quality regulation by the state, has not been available here. Western non-Muslim states have not considered it their business to regulate and enforce religious product standards. This has largely left the markets to regulate themselves. They have tried to come up with a commercial regulatory solution for this information problem, namely private certification. How successful has this been?

The halal case forms an exception to the historical experience in that where public interest is involved, sooner or later public regulation, in one way or another, has come about. There is a clear public interest involved here (albeit a different one for different 'public groups') but as yet, in Western states there has been no involvement of public authorities or employment of public resources, such as tax revenue, the neutral reputation of the state, or binding regulations backed by criminal or administrative sanctions. The Dutch state has refrained from intervening, at least with economic public law measures. (It does, of course, back private contracts by civil law.) It only feels a responsibility for the physical well-being of its citizens and hence controls whether food – an important halal product – is safe for the body, not whether it is safe for the soul.

Even if the state did get involved, it is questionable whether it could solve the problems that plague the halal market. Ever longer food chains that extend across the globe cannot be controlled by a nation-state, and certainly not for the process standards that define halal products. Moreover, it is questionable whether the specific public (Muslim consumers and traders) would even want secular Dutch state authorities to get involved, whether they would trust them enough, or even see a use for them in the enforcement of their religious standards. These standards are unclear, as they are set and regulated by actors with different perspectives who live and hence consume in different countries.

Whether state intervention would be a solution or not (a question we will address later in this chapter), it has been absent so far. Consequently, a market for private halal certification and product information is evolving, both in Western European countries and globally. This forms an interesting case for studying both the ups and downs, strengths and weaknesses, problems and solutions of a newly emerging market, as well as for studying its capacity as a private regulator for another market, that of the halal products that it certifies.

10.2   PROBLEMS IN THE MARKETS FOR HALAL PRODUCTS

On 21 January 2010, the Dutch TV programme *Keuringsdienst van Waarde* ('Inspection of Value/Commodities') aired a critical documentary on the quality of döner kebabs under the title, 'Investigating the exotic ground-meat stick'.[1] The journalists bought a random sample of ten such Turkish sandwiches, sold as made of '100 per cent lamb', from different snack shops and had them analyzed in a laboratory. Only one of them turned out to be 100 per cent lamb. Of the others, one was 100 per cent mutton, one was 100 per cent beef, one was 100 per cent turkey, one was 100 per cent chicken, five were a mixture of mutton and beef, and, believe it or not, one sandwich, sold as lamb, was made of 100 per cent pork. Now, getting cheated is always upsetting for any consumer. But for a practicing Muslim to buy lamb and get pork is a far more serious affair. Lamb is 'halal' or pure; pork is 'haram', unclean or even sinful. This is almost the worst thing that can happen to a devout Muslim. Even to be around pork products or to eat something that has been transported in the same truck as pork is a threat to their salvation.

The kebab story is only one of many cases of fraud and deception involving the sale of supposedly 'halal' food to Muslims. In November 2009, the Dutch General Inspection Service (*Algemene Inspectiedienst AID*) from the Dutch Ministry of Agriculture raided Fasen Meat Trading, a meat wholesaler from Breda. Using forged documents, the company sold several thousand tons of meat incorrectly identified as halal to Muslims in France.[2] In October 2009, the Belgian halal federation claimed that 60 per cent of all halal products sold in that country were impure.[3] In short, the expanding market of halal products is plagued by fraud and other problems.

There are many reasons for these problems, but we have identified five aspects of the halal market that are particularly problematic for the proper functioning of the market, especially in this combination:

1. religious diversity within Islam;
2. the importance of process standards in addition to product standards;
3. the globalisation of food chains;
4. the increasing importance of composite products; and
5. the presence of Muslim minorities in Western countries.

10.2.1 Confusion about the Precise Religious Food Standards due to Religious Diversity

As mentioned, it is not always clear what is considered halal and what is considered haram, for two reasons: 1. the historical context of the concept of halal; and 2. the diversity among Muslims (Regenstein, Chaudry and Regenstein 2003; Riaz and Chaudry 2004; Rippin 2005).

As regards the historical context, the Koran is holy for Muslims in a manner that goes beyond the holiness of the Bible for Christians. The book, letters, and words themselves are holy and, as such, so are their literal meanings. Deviance from these meanings is, in principle, impossible. But how do we translate rules formulated in the seventh century AD to our rather different modern society? Two concepts are used to this end: *ijmā* (consensus) and *qivyās* (analogy). If the Ummah (the Muslim community) decides that something is haram, then this becomes a new rule: it is *ijmā*. But, given the diversity of that Muslim community, such a consensus is quite rare. Therefore, also *qivyās*, or analogy, is used. Modern drugs like XTC and hashish are considered by many to be haram, because they are said to be comparable to alcohol, which is forbidden in the Koran. These concepts make Islam flexible, but also produce different interpretations of the rules. Moreover, some Muslim scholars, witnessing the diversity, have argued that if there are three different opinions (*fatwas*) of Muslim scholars, a Muslim is allowed to follow the opinion that suits them best. Hence not only orthodox theoretical arguments play a role in the interpretation and application of historical rules, but also some forms of curious pragmatism.

As regards the diversity among Muslims, after Mohammed's death the Ummah lost its central authority and gradually became more decentralised. Furthermore, the enormous geographic expansion of Islam across a variety of cultures added to the heterogeneity of the Muslim community. This decentralisation and heterogeneity have produced different interpretations of the Muslim rules, including food standards. Shiites have different interpretations than Sunnis. And Muslims in Saudi Arabia have norms that differ from those of Indian, Surinamese, Chinese and Malaysian Muslims. Their varying physical living conditions and cultural customs – values, food, local laws, etc. – have, over time, influenced their specific interpretations of the religious and worldly duties of Muslims, including their food laws. And as in other religions, there are also more liberal and more orthodox interpretations of Islamic laws, called Sharia law.

Some of the rules in Sharia law allow for further confusion. It does make a distinction between what is allowed for Muslims – called *halal* – and what is sinful and should be avoided – *haram*. However, in between these clear extremes there is a more or less 'official' grey area, called *makruh*, or objectionable. Many Muslims also have such a grey category for themselves, as in, 'It would be better not to, but I'm not going to make a big deal out of it'. Table 10.1 lists several important halal rules and related uncertainties that provide opportunities for different interpretations.

10.2.2   The Importance of Process Standards

It is especially problematic for Muslims that their dietary laws do not only relate to the composition of their food, but also to the processes according to which it has been cultivated, harvested, slaughtered, processed, preserved, conserved, and transported.

Product norms can be tested on the product itself and at the place of transaction or consumption, although this may require expertise and technological aids. With advanced modern technology, even the slightest traces of pork and other ingredients can be discerned in food.

This is not the case with process standards, such as the living space of the animal, the precise manner in which it has been slaughtered, and how the meat or other products have been stored and transported. These processes are unobservable from the final product which a Muslim consumer considers buying. It is a problem that prospective halal consumers share with those who intend to buy organic or fair trade products. These products have so-called, 'credence quality attributes' (Grunert 2005; Darby and Karni 1973).

Such process norms are particularly important for Muslims. Not only

Table 10.1   Possible uncertainties in the interpretation of halal rules

General halal rules	Grey area (examples)
Only meat from specific animal species; among others no pigs, carnivores, insects, birds or animals with claws	Shellfish? In some areas – Mediterranean –halal, elsewhere haram
No products that may have been in contact with haram animals, like pigs and pork	The same slaughtering machines after thorough cleaning? In the same transport vehicle even if packaged in separate plastic?
No alcohol	Can it be used as a detergent? Is 'alcohol free' beer or champagne halal?
No carrion and hence cadavers. Humans should not be scavengers. Hence the animal must be alive when slaughtered	Is stunning permitted? If yes, which type? Irreversible as with a pin in the brain? Or only reversible such as electric shock?
Food of 'the people of the book' (Jewish and Christians) is allowed	Does this automatically render meat from Dutch slaughterhouses acceptable? What if the butcher may be Muslim, but one who does not follow the rules, e.g. slaughters under the influence of alcohol.
Allah's name must be hailed during slaughtering ('bismillah Allahu akbar')	For every individual animal? What if 100 chickens are simultaneously slaughtered? Can it be played from a cassette? Must a Muslim start the cassette?
Slaughtering should be done with the animal's head facing Mecca	This is often categorised as 'recommended' (*mandub*), thus not haram if not followed, although many disagree

must the animal be slaughtered according to religious norms, its meat or other products may not have come into contact with anything that might be considered haram along the whole chain of production and distribution – from farm to fork, so to speak. Ideally, there should be separate slaughtering lines, machines, knives, trucks, containers, warehouses and distribution centres, preparation kitchens and dining halls for halal and non-halal products and services. Even the personnel handling the halal products should refrain from eating a ham sandwich at lunch.

Having separate systems for the production and distribution of halal and non-halal products can be very costly. It may be only affordable for companies that specialise in halal, or for very large companies that can afford several production and distribution lines. Thus, the scale of the Port of Rotterdam has allowed for the investment of what is essentially a separate harbour with storage and transport facilities used only for halal goods.

This implies that costs can be lower and revenue increased by being less strict with the separation of production and distribution lines, and using a more commercially efficient process, than by mixing cheaper ingredients with the product, as with classical adulteration. But such classical adulteration can usually be detected at the point of final sale, whereas this is not often the case with halal fraud.

These problems are amplified by several other factors and trends that, although they also affect non-Muslim goods, increase the risks and uncertainties for Muslims.

10.2.3   Globalisation of Food Chains

The increasing internationalisation of markets, made possible thanks to new transport, communication, and conservation technologies, has led to ever longer food production and distribution chains. Our food suppliers have become anonymous. Personal contact between cultivators of crops and livestock and the final consumer has become extremely rare. Consequently, it has become practically impossible for the consumer at the end of these long chains to trace where the products that they consume have come from, and if the aforementioned process standards have been meticulously followed at every stage.

The older Muslim generation, who used to buy its meat from the local Muslim butcher, could still ask him and take his word for it. Even more so knowing that, according to Muslim teaching, Allah would punish the butcher if he lied to his clients, rather than the innocent buyer who might unknowingly consume something haram. This religious belief is considered to be a deterrent for pious Muslims and thus forms the basis for mutual trust among Muslims. However, who can be asked and trusted in the large anonymous supermarket or fast food chain restaurant?

10.2.4   The Increasing Importance of Composite Products

Globalization has gone hand in hand with new methods of decomposition and recombination of natural products, resulting in an enormous supply of synthetically composed foodstuffs and ready-made products, made from ingredients that are likely to have originated from a great diversity of biological (plants and animal) and geographical sources. This adds to the information problems of the contemporary Muslim consumer concerned about process standards. Today's huge modern supermarket assortment would have been unimaginable in Mohammed's time.

The consumer cannot possibly be aware of everything that may be in his food. Chewing gum, candy, and chocolate contain gelatin used as a thickener, which could have come from pig bones. By now many Muslims are aware that this may be used as an ingredient in sweets, but it is less well known that it may also be used as an ingredient in chocolate. Sausages, hamburgers, frikadellen, meat products, and the like are in essence combinations of ground meat, offal, herbs, spices, preservatives, pigments, flavours and other additives. These ingredients could all, directly or indirectly, originate from haram sources. Some red pigments, for example, come from scale insects that are haram. Additives, such as the E numbers 472, 441, 485 and 471 are presumably haram. It would require an extremely devout Muslim consumer to check each product against a list of E numbers.

Halal norms also concern non-food products, in particular products that affect the body in different ways to food, such as medicines, cosmetics, shampoos, and even clothing. These are also usually composite products, which may contain traces of haram animals: gelatin in pills, or starch and pigments in clothing.

10.2.5   Muslim Migration to Western Multicultural Societies

Risks and uncertainties also increase for Muslims who migrate and settle in Western countries. In Islamic countries there are usually only halal products on sale. Hence distinguishing halal from haram is less of a problem. However, there it is a problem for the import authorities. Muslim minorities in non-Islamic countries, however, do not have this certainty. They are confronted with an ever increasing choice of consumer products; an abundance that eventually becomes a temptation also for them. By contrast, the amount of halal products available is minimal, made even more so because the local population views halal slaughtering as an animal-unfriendly practice that does not fit in with its value. Muslims in such countries face the far greater challenge of separating the good from the evil, much more so than those in Islamic-ruled countries.

10.2.6   The Consequences: Greater Risks and Uncertainties for Muslims

All these factors have increased the risks and uncertainties in transactions for Muslims. These risks and uncertainties have fueled a demand for information and for some guarantee that what is offered by food suppliers purporting to sell halal food is actually what it claims to be. Essentially, it is a demand for reliable information that guarantees that the product is absolutely halal.

10.3   CERTIFICATION: A POSSIBLE PRIVATE SOLUTION?

As a consequence of the uncertainties involved in buying halal products, the growing demand for halal food has also produced a growing demand for confirmation that the product is what it purports to be. Such confirmation can be summarized in and represented by a certificate or halal hallmark. Hence parallel to the market for halal products, a derived market for halal quality certificates has developed. This has become a market because the demand is being met by more than one supplier. It is a curious market which brings together different worlds, something akin to the uneasy 'combination of fire and water', as several interviewees called it: commerce with religion, and informal trust relations with the formal world of inspections, record keeping, paperwork, and certification.

There are about 30 to 40 halal certifiers in the Netherlands, including self-certifiers and local imams, as estimated by our interviewees and some news media. The chairman of the Turkish Food Auditing and Certification Research Association (GİMDES), Hüseyin Büyüközer, reported in the English language Turkish newspaper *Sunday's Zaman*, that 'his organisation discovered 30 certifiers in the Netherlands and another 13 in Germany, which give away "fake halal certificates"'.[4]

Among these 30 to 40 certifiers are several more official and professional organisations that certify products that are exported by large food producers. These organisations, HVV, HQC, Halal Correct, Halal Audit and HIC, have multinationals such as Unilever and Nestlé as their customers. Together with a few affiliated institutions, the total number of these organisations is seven. The remainder is comprised of small, informal, often sole proprietors, including self-certifiers, imams and do-it-yourself websites. Table 10.2 gives an overview of the different certifiers on the halal market and their features.

Interestingly, the different certifiers seem to target different categories of customers. Thus different certification submarkets have come about, with different features and problems. Some certifiers target mostly small-scale businesses while others focus mainly on the modern, large-scale multinationals and the export market. As such, a distinction can be made between the local 'uncle and aunty' market, the professional domestic market and

Table 10.2   Overview of the important players in the Dutch halal certification market

HVV/HFFIA (Halal Feed and Food Inspection Authority)	Important player One of the oldest, active since the sixties Official certifier since 1994 Founded by first generation immigrants, mainly from Surinam Religious conservative Strict norms and inspection Considered most expensive Reasonably professional However website is unprofessional Employees: 23 Certifies for large MNOs Exports Recognised by the Indonesian MUI and Malaysia JAKIM
HQC/COHS (Halal Quality Control/Control Office of Halal Slaughtering)	Important player Founded in 1983 Run by the Honorary Consul of Syria in the Netherlands Active in international trade, recognised by Muslim countries Reputation based on position in the international diplomatic network Unprofessional website Levels of strictness unknown Regarded as cheaper Employees: 1+ Uses volunteers and external laboratories Exports Recognised by JAKIM and also claims to be recognised by the Indonesian Imam Org. MUI
TQ HCC (Total Quality Halal Correct Certification)	Important player Founded in 2000 by a Tunisian immigrant, active since 1995 Regarded by competitors as the largest commercial company Professional website Very strict Professional in controls, documentation and archiving Expensive Employees: 6 Accredited by Malaysian JAKIM, Indonesian MUI and Islam Univ. Rotterdam

Table 10.2   (continued)

Foundation National Halal Keur	Has a hallmark Inspections are done by HAC
HAC (Halal Audit Company)	Recently founded by Muslim accountancy graduates of polytechnics Among others, origin in Bosnia Audits the Foundation Halal certificates (below) Professional website Controls based on professional auditing Employees: 5 (youth) Also offers training for in-company halal controls
HIC (Halal International Control)	Founder Wahid is from Surinam Founded as self-certifier for Wahid's meat-products business Now officially separated, but still connected to Wahid Certification is an additional function of the meat-products business Therefore less commercial Certifies mainly for the domestic market Less strict; accepts anaesthetisation during slaughter Works with 'volunteers' that already work in slaughterhouse Relatively cheap Certifies for supermarkets (AH, C-1000, Super de Boer, Jumbo) that do not want non-stunned halal slaughtered meat Claims recognition by Cairo's Al Azhar University
Foundation Halal Certificates	Active since the 1970s Own estimation market share 10% Both exports and imports Also provides halal information Least strict: 'Nederlandse slachtwetgeving [Dutch slaughtering legislation] = Islam' Cheaper

the export market. Each of these submarkets includes different consumers, producers and certifiers, and thus exhibits different problems.

10.3.1 The Local 'Uncle and Aunty' Market

The 'uncle and aunty' market is mainly a local phenomenon in which the local butcher sells halal food to a member of the same social or ethnic group on the basis of personal trust. None of the professional certifiers provide professional certificates for this market segment. Certification is mainly done on the basis of informal self-certification (e.g. putting a note on your door stating that your products are '100 per cent halal'), word-of-mouth certification (e.g. aunt Salima to uncle Muhammad: you can really trust butcher X!), or certification by the imam (e.g. the imam telling the community during the Friday afternoon-prayer that butcher X is reliable).

Even though – or probably because of – the local character of this market, its total market share of the halal market seems to be far ahead of the international, organised market. The leading research organisation in the halal market, KasehDia, stated in its report on the European halal market that the total market share of international trade is 'below ten per cent of the potential size' (KasehDia, 2009). This seems to be due to issues of trust that are involved in moving to the professional – and thus anonymous – market, in which supermarkets and wholesalers are the main players, issues that have not yet been solved by the certification market: how can you trust a label, instead of a person?

10.3.2 The Professional Domestic Market

The formal and anonymous domestic market is served by large organizations such as supermarkets and wholesalers. In particular the younger generations born in the Netherlands or other European countries buy here: halal in the supermarket is convenient and fast for the younger generations, but for the older generations who are often more religious and do not trust labels and institutions as easily as their children who have grown up with them, Alberth Heijn halal is still often a no-go. Certification by a local imam is the only thing that can convince them to buy their halal products in an anonymous supermarket, as we have seen in Belgium where Carrefour managed to access this market through such informal certification. The problem with this type of certification is that the imams are usually tied to specific groups of people with a similar, often ethnic, background. Thus, being approved by one imam only gives access to part of the market, and getting access to an imam requires a lot of inside information about the local scene, as well as establishing a trust relationship.

For many Western food organizations this is not an option and therefore they direct themselves to the official, established bodies such as the Dutch HVV and HQC. Unilever, for example, uses HVV as a certifier, while AH, the largest Dutch supermarket chain, gets HIC to certify its meat. The certifiers offer great potential to their customers: their certificates could form the bridge between the large, but still informally regulated 'uncle and aunty' market and the large multinationals and wholesalers that aim to access this large market.

An interesting example of the power of certificates is the case of the large snack food producer, Mekkafoods, which has used professional self-certification (in modern terms called 'branding') to gain access to the traditional Muslim consumer who distrusts large, anonymous multinationals and food chains. Mekkafoods sells halal snacks, such as hamburgers, sausages, croquettes, and pizzas, mostly in small, local supermarkets and tokos, where it has acquired a market share of 60 to 70 per cent of such products. The owner and operator is a Dutchman, Mr René van Appeldoorn, who has built a reputation from scratch through a personal approach towards the Muslim consumer over the years. He has managed to establish Mekkafoods as a reputable brand *without the explicit use of any halal certificate*. The company has informal certificates from, or is supported by, several imams and Islamic agencies, who have visited the factory to check the halal status of the food. Yet Mr Appeldoorn advocates not to 'advertise' this information to the public, unless someone requests it, as such information might alienate other potential customers, like non-Muslims, or Muslims from different backgrounds. Therefore, he prefers to rely on his brand reputation. This case shows the potential of a halal certificate in convincing customers of the halal status of a product, although it might have more to do with the place where the Mekkafoods products are being sold: at the local butcher (the informal halal certificate is automatically transferred to the product) rather than in anonymous Western, supermarkets.

10.3.3   The Export Market

When we move from the professional domestic market to the export market, the degree of impersonality rises as the meat travels thousands of kilometres across many borders, with ever increasing complex food chains and the creation of complicated composite foods with a high level of additives – many of which could be haram. The export market, however, is, far more organised than the domestic market, exactly because of these complex production chains and the crossing of borders. More regulations are necessary and central checkpoints such as national customs prevent an unorganised market from emerging. This market is big and booming, with the most commonly cited estimate showing that it is made up of around 1.69–1.8 billion Muslims, with a total market value of $634.6 billion, which is around 16 per cent of the total global food industry.

However, as discussed before, the international Muslim world is fragmented, dispersed across the globe and lacks central authority. There are many different organisations active in different places, and they differ in belief, opinion, and operation. Organisations are often linked to national governments, who may support or even steer these organisations for both political, religious, commercial and professional reasons, expecting legitimacy from these sources – religious authorities and economic prosperity – in return. Operational authorities such as those of Malaysia and Indonesia compete for market leadership of accreditation agencies with religious authorities that set the norms of halal products, mostly those of Egypt and Saudi Arabia. This leads national accreditors to accept different international accreditors depending on the origin of the (Muslim) consumer they aim to address: different ethnic groups prefer accreditation from the country of origin, and secular meat producers for foreign countries prefer the Westernised accreditation methods of Malaysia.

Marco Tieman, owner and director of LBB Logistics, a subsidiary of MDS Logistics, which is building the global 'Halal SuperHighway' and a huge Global Halal Hub in Malaysia, explains:

> 'Companies that want to participate in this attractive market need halal certification. And that is precisely where the problem lays. Every country has its own interpretation of what halal is, which is why there are different halal hallmarks. The Malaysian halal hallmark, however, has a much broader acceptance in different Muslim countries than other hallmarks. Therefore many large industries that want to increase their market position in the Middle East and Asia choose to do their halal production in Asia' (Westra 2007, 37).

He implies that if the Netherlands or other European countries want to compete in the growing global halal market, they will have to solve the problem of certification confusion.

10.4 MARKET FAILURE IN THE DERIVED CERTIFICATION MARKET?

The price competition, combined with the information asymmetries in the market as to the value of the certificates, and the presence of both malicious dabblers as well as well-meaning, socially concerned Muslims who feel 'that fellow Muslims should not be forced to pay too much for their meat and other products', could produce a 'race to the bottom' as regards the quality and reputation of halal certificates in general. A few bad apples are enough to infest the whole basket.

This has all the elements of a typical collective action problem, familiar from other cases, varying from cartels to strikes. Everyone profits from the good reputation of certification – just like everyone profits from the higher prices produced by the cartel or the higher wages produced by a strike. Yet for the individual, there is a temptation to free ride: offering the goods at a price just below the price agreed in the cartel allows the individual supplier to increase his market share; and by not actively participating in the strike, an individual worker may be able to remain in good standing with his employer, and be rewarded in the future by a promotion or other individual pay raise. Similarly here, the halal certifiers have a collective interest in establishing trust in the market in the value of their certificates; but by lowering their own price a bit, at the cost of less expensive inspections, they may attract more customers for their label and thus increase their market share. The diversity of halal certificate suppliers and the lack of transparency of this market – no one seems to publish publicly available annual reports – allow for that. The overall result is the bad reputation of the certification sector.

The problem is exacerbated by outright illegal copying, where certificates from reliable certifiers are illegally copied, and other fraud. In 2009, the meat wholesaler Fasen Meat Trading in Breda was accused of selling several thousand tons of meat in France that was improperly sold as halal with falsified documents.[5] In the same year, the certifier HQC claimed that Kentucky Fried Chicken misled Muslim customers, by selling as halal, meat products with a document that only proved that a certain slaughterhouse *could* produce halal meat, not that this batch was slaughtered in that manner. Inquiries by the *Volkskrant* proved HQC right. Certificates which are downloadable free from the internet, and which may be used by local butchers, do not help the reputation of halal certificates. The average final consumer has difficulty distinguishing the good from the bad.

Neither is that reputation helped by another form of self-certification, namely the form supplied by HIC for its sister-organisation Wahid Meat. In principle, there may be nothing wrong with it, as long as it is transparent to the customers for whom the certificate is meant. Such a form of self-certification is akin to developing a brand reputation. The Dutch supermarket chain AH does it as well, with its own certificates for 'healthy choice' (*gezonde keuze*) or 'AH pure and honest biological' or 'sustainable fish . . . from a guaranteed quality chain' (*duurzame vis . . . uit een geborgde kwaliteitsketen*). It becomes a problem when the self-certifier either explicitly or implicitly suggests with the hallmark/certificate that this product has been investigated and rated by an independent third party. AH also uses recognised external certificates, such as those of Fair Trade/Max Havelaar, the MSC (for fish, although most of its fish only carries the company hallmark), Nordic Swan and Blue Angel (for ecological food), EKO and Skal (for biological food), and Better Life (for free roaming chickens and eggs).

Distrust has indeed been spreading. Various Dutch TV programmes and newspaper articles already referred to earlier in this chapter have indicated such distrust, and the reasons for it. Hüseyin Büyüközer, chairman of the earlier mentioned GIMDES, said:

> 'From our meetings with consumers in different European countries, we have found that people are complaining about unauthorised certifiers. Some unauthorised certifiers are issuing halal certificates without even seeing the face of the owner of the production facility. This is not how it should be. Having experienced similar misuses in the past, most Muslim consumers do not trust the halal labels on products and expect to see order in the market. This also causes unfair competition and discourages other certifier institutions who exert extra effort to ensure halal standards. The opportunism has reached worrisome levels and should be stopped.'

'Another major problem', he emphasized, 'is that some certifiers sell certificates for excessive prices. There are companies who must procure their halal certificates for 5000 to 10 000 euros. This is high and way above normal costs.'[6]

Participants in the interviews we conducted described the market as being 'anarchy'; 'craziness', and where 'fighting and fierce competition prevail'.

> 'It is a real *who* you know, not *what* you know culture, this world of many little certification businesses. If you are not in one of their acquaintance circles, you'd better not start with it. You can get a certificate without any problems, if it is an acquaintance.'

Many also pointed out what they considered 'objectionable practices', such as 'issuing halal certificates without even checking whether it is actually halal'; nepotism; 'butchers that certify their own meat' (referring to Wahid Meat and HIC); exorbitant prices; and certifiers who are far too lenient or unprofessional. 'The Dutch halal market is chaos' was the headline of an extensive article by a Dutch news magazine.[7]

The confusion over different certificates is not only a problem domestically, but also on the international market. The Netherlands has made a good head start with developing Rotterdam as the 'halal gateway to Europe', however, for the time being the distribution centres are still largely empty, due in part to the lack of trustworthy certification.

The distrust and the confusion surrounding halal certificates indicates that this market is in danger of failing. As distrust spreads and reputations decline, the value of the certificates disappears and so will the willingness of customers to pay a price for such certificates.

10.5   HOW MUCH OF A PUBLIC GOOD AND FOR WHICH PUBLIC?

Certificates are not seen to be 'good enough'. They fail to prove that sufficient inspection has taken place. This is interesting, in a time in which certificates, a form of private market regulation, have greatly increased in popularity and have had to become an alternative for a receding government, inspired by neo-liberalism. The halal case is not alone in this, although the issue becomes here specifically clear because it concerns process norms that are difficult to audit and due to the separation of church and state, which has kept the secular government at a distance. But most markets cannot exist without trust and that is lacking. Just look at the recent problems in the financial markets.

To solve the problem what is really needed is an audit of the auditors, i.e. accreditation. However, even then the homunculus problem remains. Because how can we trust the accreditor? Fundamentally, the chain of accreditors of certifiers of products is endless, if the suspicion in the market is great enough. In reality, this is of course not possible. All these levels of control add to the transaction costs of the original product, and when these become prohibitive, one of two things occurs: either transactions may no longer take place, or the buyer will have to take some risk. In the end, the consumer will have to trust the highest level of certification (Van Waarden 2006a).

The question is on what basis do we do this, can it be achieved by the market and if it can, under what conditions? This halal certification case illustrates that in the case of a completely free market – free entry, price competition, 'race to the bottom' – this is not likely. Inexperienced dabblers try to get a piece of the pie, take fewer pains and undermine the reputation of the product when the customer is not able to distinguish valid certificates from fake ones. The underlying issue of a lack of transparency, along with asymmetric information, can also be a product of the market. Participants of the market often have an interest in making it harder for customers to compare products, because it enables them to obtain a larger profit. The examples are endless: cars that are equipped with all kinds of gadgets in order to distinguish between them, mobile telephones that are offered with a great diversity of subscriptions. It seems an overabundance of choices for the customer. However, because the customer can no longer see the wood for the trees, it is hard to make an optimal choice and the producer or seller can take advantage of this. Certainly, the misrepresentation of the validity of some products is easier to achieve than others. Especially in the case of products that distinguish themselves on the basis of process characteristics (halal slaughtering, biological cultivation, a famous brand), the chance of fraud, and therefore customer distrust, is high.

10.5.1   Asymmetric Public Good

Fundamentally, it is more difficult for a market to produce an independent quality certificate because it has two typical characteristics of a *public good*. The certificates are non-rival: the information they provide is accessible/readable by all. Is it also non-excludable?

In principle information can be excludable. One can charge a price for it, as is the case for a book or a patent. However, in this case it becomes more difficult. The one who benefits the most from reliable information, that is to say the user of the certificate, is the buyer of the product. He or she should therefore be the one to pay for the certificate. However, this raises two issues. He cannot, and is generally unwilling to do so. But the consumer does pay for certification, albeit indirectly, because the price of certification is included in the consumer price.

He cannot because before the transaction, before he has reached the point of becoming a buyer, he is unknown. He is part of the 'shoppers', at least in the case of mass markets such as those for halal products. Because he is unidentifiable before the transaction has occurred, he cannot be charged directly for the costs of the information.

He is unwilling to do so because the information is generally freely available. Although in principle it is excludable, this is not the case in practice. Once the certificate has been attached to the product, it is visible to everyone, provided that it is publicly displayed by the seller, and the seller has an interest to do so. In this sense, such certificates are also a 'public good': they are publicly visible and intended for shoppers.

Theory says that a public good cannot be produced by the market. If no price tag can be attached to it, no one will want to produce it. Nonetheless certificates are made. This is because – although the buyer is the primary consumer – the seller also profits from the certificate, and just because the seller makes it available to potential buyers free of charge. Unlike the buyer, the seller is known before the transaction. After all, he is in possession of the product that is to be traded. Because he is identifiable, he can, in principle, be charged for the costs. He also wants that, because it is an important form of advertising. And for him, unlike for the buyer, the certificate is excludable and rivalrous. He is a rival of competitors who would like to exclude others from using a quality certificate. For him it is a private good, so it is one he is willing to pay for.

That is, however, where the problem lies. The seller has an interest in inducing the buyer to make a purchase, but not necessarily in providing him with the correct information about his product. The buyer is in need of the correct information and knows that he may not be able to trust the seller. For that reason, he wants a certificate from an independent, and therefore also a reliable, institution. The buyer is aware of the usual advertisements and expects them to have a bias. He does not expect this from a quality certificate, which should offer objective information. As long as both the certificate and the services of the certifier are paid for by the seller, a reasonable chance of bias exists. The wisdom of proverbs teaches us this: 'He who pays the piper calls the tune.' Suspicion suffices to undermine the value of the certificate entirely. It is a problem that is also encountered by many other types of certifiers, varying from accountants to institutions of higher education, some of whom have been known to hand out diplomas to students despite the fact that they failed.

10.5.2 Public Financing

In short, objective quality certificates that are traded as private goods and are paid for by those who are being certified are actually an oxymoron. They may be produced, but in the end they do not fulfill their function because they are suspicious by definition. A private sale to those for whom it is a private good, is detrimental in terms of both objectivity and reliability. In this case, something that is considered by consumers to be a public good is still produced by the market, but due to the manner of how it is financed it is simultaneously in danger of losing its worth. Therefore the vital component of these certificates – trust – is not produced within the market.

As such it would be better, if the – from the buyer's point of view seen – public good is not financed by the seller for whom it is a private good. What then is the best way for such a public good to be financed and produced? An obvious solution is to turn to a similar method as is used for other public goods: through a public that is obliged to do so by some or another authority. Such as publicly funded streets, squares and parks – but also certificates such as school diplomas – which are financed through taxation, which the state obliges us to pay.

10.5.3 Public Interest

This is only acceptable if a *public interest* is involved, which seems to be the case. Reliable certificates facilitate transactions. Although at first this may seem a private interest of the parties involved, it also involves a public interest which is the correct functioning of markets. Importantly, there is a public interest for satisfying private interests, namely the interests of the transaction partners to reduce the risks and uncertainty caused by asymmetric information. These individual risks promote individual behaviour – in addition to transactions, commercial, judicial and even violent social conflict – that causes unwanted results at the collective level: distrust, crimes, social unrest, fewer transactions, less employment, and less growth. Think of the export to Muslim countries; fraud is not only unfair and immoral, it is also dysfunctional.

Besides public interests of the general public, there are also public interests of particular publics. These are primarily local halal consumers, for whom halal certification is a public good, followed by the producers for these markets and lastly, the Muslim countries that would like to import from the Netherlands. They all have an interest, either as a consumer or a supplier, to promote trust in the market and its products.

10.5.4 Public Task and Public Authority

In cases where a public interest exists but the market is not really able to deliver it, there could exist a public task for public authorities. The essence of this public task lies in giving a sense of reliability to halal certificates. What exactly this public task should be we leave an open question: either public provision of halal certifications, or the certification of certifications, generally termed accreditation.

Public authorities are all those agents who are regarded by a certain public as having sufficient 'authority', in other words, weight and credibility, partly due to neutrality. For most people, the highest authority is a god. He is, therefore, often called upon for help. His name or symbol is engraved on coins to instil confidence. Muslims may not use an image of Allah or Mohammed, but an illustration of the Koran, a Qur'an stand, or a minaret embellishes many halal certificates. We cannot audit the support of God – He is not accountable – so He can be used for negotiations. Consequently, sooner or later national public authorities have resorted to global authorities.

To facilitate trade public authorities have developed property and contract rights, commercial laws, and also economic criminal law. Selling something as something else is misleading and misuse of information advantages similar to insider trading on the stock market is seen as fraudulent trading and theft. In principle, the legislation concerned with unlawful acts should provide protection, but employing this legislation is laborious and costly, especially if a customer does so on his own initiative. When it concerns relatively cheap products, the costs outweigh the benefits. However, over time civil law has been supplemented with social and economic public law in order to protect the weaker parties within markets and in terms of public health. As a result, many public laws for product norms and controls came into existence, for example for medical products. Will this soon be the case for halal products?

The US has a history of public involvement with religious food standards. Since 1915, 22 US states have enacted Kosher Fraud Statutes under pressure from Jewish lobby groups. These laws were a reaction to problems, similar to those currently being experienced in the halal market. Non-kosher foods were being sold as kosher, and the states felt a responsibility to protect their Jewish citizens from such fraud. It is a form of private-public cooperation. Orthodox Hebrew rabbis define what kosher is, but the enforcement of these standards is a public responsibility (Havinga 2010).

The American Jewish population had faith in the American state. It is questionable whether a Dutch secular state has sufficient weight and trust among those of the specific 'public' who primarily benefit from reliable halal certificates: Muslims living both domestically and internationally. As a non-Muslim state, the Netherlands is neutral. The country has no affiliation with a specific interpretation of Islam. The secular Christian western identity of the state can, through creating a large normative distance, cause the spread of distrust. On the other hand, the Netherlands does have a reputation of doing its job well, in an efficient and effective manner, and its constitutional state is known to provide predictability and reliability. This reliability can be transferred by the state to recognised certificates. It is anything but a *failed state*. This cannot be said of many Muslim countries in the world. Although they embody the correct belief for Muslims in their rules, their effectiveness, efficiency and reliability are less apparent, which is not unimportant in these countries. The threat or even suspicion of corruption can taint the reputation of a quality certificate.

10.5.5   Public Tasks For Which Public?

However, the Dutch people do not make up the only relevant public, and its government is not the only possible authority. Several specific publics were distinguished above, which could take on such a public task. As it is not unusual in the Netherlands either for specific public goods to be produced or financed by a specific public that has an interest therein, this process is simplified by using the means of the state; for example, car owners pay road taxes which are used to finance the building of new roads.

The most typical of these is probably the Dutch statutory trade association (PBO), famous for its marketing boards. These are essentially community groups who derive their identity from a certain product and market, and who, through recognition and support from higher (public) authorities form a small state within the larger state. With this 'mini-state-authority' they are able to regulate their own economic sector, for example the Horticulture Marketing Board. All horticulturalists and flower culti-vators are required to be a member. They choose their board (indirectly) and pay an obligatory fee that is used to finance public goods for the sector. The 50 million Euros that they collected in 2010 is spent on, among other things, collective product promotion (e.g. 'why not buy flowers more often?') (53 per cent), research (24 per cent) and quality management and the environment (13 per cent). The board also decrees binding rules, such as HACCP-based hygiene codes and obligatory controls for insecticide residues at auctions.

There is also a Marketing Board for Cattle and Meat (PVV). It has already faced some halal issues, just like the Netherlands Food and Consumer Product Safety Authority (NVWA) and the Ministry of Agriculture (LNV). These organisations issue export certificates for veteri-nary safety of the export of chickens to Algeria, veal to Egypt and Saudi Arabia, and cow sperm to Morocco. These cases occasionally face 'issues on the level of halal interpretation'. Furthermore, several forms require the 'signature of a halal authority', probably one of the discussed halal cer-tificate providers. This shows that some form of connection already exists.

It is conceivable that, over time, an organisation (or network) like the PBO could be established, where organisations of several specific publics play a role: public Dutch organisations such as the PVV, NVWA and the Dutch Accreditation Council; private Dutch ones, such as several halal hallmarks; and international Muslim authorities.

A start has already been made with the establishment of international connections. The leading Dutch halal certifiers have sought and found support from some of the national halal certification authorities abroad: the MUI in Indonesia and JAKIM in Malaysia. The three leading Dutch halal certifiers are also recognised by the Halal Industry Development Corporation of Malaysia, which has been working hard to make Malaysia the global hub for the trade of halal products. Malaysia combines the advantages of being a Muslim country with being an effective state, and has the ambition to develop the global standard of halal. That could imply that it will soon impose these halal standards as a condition for exporting to this hub. In a way this is a kind of 'California effect', a concept developed by David Vogel (1995): imposing standards via trade relations. But now 'from the East to the West', instead of the other way around, as is the case with Vogel's concept. A 'Malaysia Effect', so to speak, through which Malaysia would become the ultimate authority – and indeed a public one – regulating the Western halal markets.

10.6   CONCLUSION: MARKET REGULATION BY THE MARKET?

Can markets regulate other markets? The case of the market of halal quality certificates trying to do so for the market for halal products is not very promising. Competition in the market for quality certificates has also produced a kind of 'adulteration' of certificates, analogous to the adulteration problems familiar in the primary markets of foodstuffs. Consumers do not know how to value quality certificates, which is similar to their problems with valuing the halal products in the first place.

The only trustworthy actor in the halal market seems to be the Muslim butcher with whom the customer has a personal trust relationship. This is even more the case as Muslim belief allows the buyer to place the burden of the dangers of haram food to the soul on the butcher's shoulders. Both know that a cheating Muslim butcher will be punished by Allah in paradise. All halal transactions that lack this personal trust relationship, as in mass retailing, the wholesale sector, and the long value chains of transactions in global markets (where the bulk of the profits are earned), can never be regarded as entirely trustworthy for Muslims. Thus globalisation of food chains poses a hindrance to the governance of Muslim food quality. The derived market for halal certificates has not been shown to be a reliable source of market governance.

Furthermore, the proliferation of suppliers of quality certificates has not only more or less led to a 'race to the bottom' of lower prices and lower quality of the quality certificates; the abundance has also made the market far less transparent. Thus the 'invisible hand' of the market has not given very clear directions for steering the choices in the market for both halal consumers and halal producers.

Eventually, even in this market a supreme authority seems to be required to bring order, instil trust relations, and facilitate transactions. This authority has however not surfaced domestically. It seems likely that it will come from abroad, from a Muslim country that combines Muslim religious authority with experience in developing and running an efficient and prosperous economy. This country may be Malaysia, which combines both religious and economic legitimacy. But such an interdependence between states may fit the ongoing globalisation of markets.

NOTES

1. 'Keuringsdienst van Waarde onderzoekt de exotische gehaktstaaf', http://sites.rvu.nl/page/7202.
2. *Volkskrant*, 26 November 2009.
3. http://islamineurope.blogspot.com/2009/10/belgium.
4. Hüseyin Büyüközer, 13 January 2010.
5. *Volkskrant*, 26 November 2009.
6. Hava in *Sunday's Zaman*, 13 January 2010.
7. *Vrij Nederland*, 'Herrie om Halal', 1 December 2007, 1.

REFERENCES

Akerlof, G. (1970), 'The Market for "Lemons": Quality Uncertainty and the Market Mechanism', *Quarterly Journal of Economics*, 84(3), 488–500.

Berger, P. and T. Luckmann (1967), *The Social Construction of Reality*, New York: Anchor Books.

Bartley, T. (2007), 'Institutional Emergence in an Era of Globalization: The Rise of Transnational Private Regulation of Labor and Environmental Conditions', *American Journal of Sociology*, 113, 297–351.

Bonne, K. and W. Verbeke (2008), 'Muslim Consumer Trust in Halal Meat Status and Control in Belgium', *Meat Science*, 79, 113–123.

Darby, M. and E. Karni (1973), 'Free Competition and the Optimal Amount of Fraud', *Journal of Law and Economics*, 16, 67–88.

De Koning, M. (2008), *De 'Zuivere' Islam. Geloofsbeleving en Identiteitsvorming van Jonge Marokkaans-Nederlandse Moslims*, Amsterdam: Bert Bakker.

Elias, N. (1977[1939]), *Über den Prozesz der Zivilisation. Soziogenetische und Psychogenetische Untersuchungen*, Baden-Baden: Nomos/Suhrkamp.

Elster, J. (1989), *The Cement of Society: A Study of Social Order*, Cambridge: Cambridge University Press.

Gourevitch, P. (2011), 'The Value of Ethics: Monitoring Normative Compliance in Ethical Consumption Markets', in Jens Beckert and Patrik Aspers (eds), *The Worth of Goods. Valuation and Pricing in the Economy*, Oxford: Oxford University Press, pp. 86–105.

Grunert, K.G. (2005), 'Food Quality and Safety: Consumer Perception and Demand', *European Review of Agricultural Economics*, 32, 369–391.

Hava, E. (2010), 'New Organization to Sort out Rotten Apples in European Halal Food Market', *Sundays Zaman*, 13 January.

Havinga, T. (2010), 'Regulating Halal and Kosher Foods: Different Arrangements between State, Industry and Religious Actors', *Erasmus Law Review*, 3(4), 241–255.

KasehDia, (2009), *World Halal Forum Report*, KasehDia.

Merton, R. (1995), 'The Thomas Theorem and The Matthew Effect', *Social Forces*, 74(2), 379–424.

Regenstein, J.M., M.M. Chaudry and C.E. Regenstein (2003), 'The Kosher and Halal Food Laws', *Comprehensive Reviews in Food Science and Food Safety*, 2, 111–127.

Riaz, M.N. and M.M. Chaudry (eds) (2004), *Halal Food Production*, Boca Raton: CRC Press.

Rippin, A. (2005), *Muslims: Their Religious Beliefs and Practices*, London: Routledge.

Vogel, D. (1995), *Trading Up. Consumer and Environmental Regulation in a Global Economy*, Cambridge, MA: Harvard University Press.

Van Waarden, F. (2006a), 'Taste, Traditions, Transactions, and Trust: The Public and Private Regulation of Food', in C. Ansell and D. Vogel (eds), *What's the Beef? The Contested Governance of European Food Safety*, Cambridge: MIT Press, pp. 35–59.

Van Waarden, F. (2006b), 'Werk in Een Wantrouwende Wereld. Omvang en Oorzaken van Een Uitdijende Controle-Industrie', *Beleid en Maatschappij*, 33(4), 232–251.

Van Waarden, F. (2011), 'Varieties of Private Market Regulation: Problems and Prospects', in D. Levi-Faur (ed.), *Handbook on the Politics of Regulation*, Cheltenham: Edward Elgar Publishing, pp. 469–485.

Van Waarden, F. (2012), 'Governing Global Commons: The Public-Private Protection of Fish and Forests', in J. Swinnen, J. Wouters, M. Maertens and A. Marx (eds), *Private Standards and Global Governance. Legal and Economic Perspectives*, Cheltenham: Edward Elgar Publishing.

Van Waarden, F. and R. Van Dalen (2010), 'Het Homunculusprobleem van Vrije Markten. Over het Halal-Geval van Handel in Vertrouwen', *Beleid en Maatschappij*, 37, 259–278.

Westra, J. (2007), 'Halal is Hot. Nederlanders worden Dijkenbouwers van Halal-Logistiek', *Supply Chain Magazine*, 10, 36–39.

Wirzba, N. (2011), *Food and Faith. A Theology of Eating*, Cambridge: Cambridge University Press.

PART IV

How public and private regulation meet

11. Are we being served? The relationship between public and private food safety regulation

Elena Fagotto[*]

11.1 INTRODUCTION

Foodborne illnesses sicken and kill hundreds of thousands of people every year. As many as 30 per cent of all infections in the last sixty years originated from pathogens transmitted through food (Jones, Patel et al. 2008). The Centers for Disease Control and Prevention estimate that in the United States alone there are approximately 48 million cases of foodborne illnesses every year, 128 000 hospitalisations and 3000 deaths, resulting in significant costs for consumers, healthcare and the private sector.[1] In Europe, 2009 data show about 325 000 cases of reported infections and 5550 foodborne outbreaks, mostly attributable to salmonella (EFSA and ECDC 2011). The true burden of foodborne illnesses is likely to be higher because causality is often difficult to establish, leaving myriads of cases unaccounted for. Ensuring the integrity of foods is a critical priority for governments, consumers and the private sector. This chapter analyses the industry's role, specifically the contribution of private food safety standards (henceforth PFSS) in providing safe foods to consumers, and explores the relationship between public and private safety regulation.

Most of the foods we consume must comply not only with government regulation, but also with strict PFSS that buyers impose on their suppliers. GlobalG.A.P., International Featured Standards-Food (IFS), and the British Retail Consortium Global Standards for Food Safety (BRC) are just some examples of such private initiatives.[2] These standards are *transnational* because they transcend national boundaries to apply to the multiple private actors involved in the food value chain. They are *private* and *voluntary* because they are generally set up by industry associations and enforced through third-party certification mechanisms. Nowadays, standards are so widespread they have become *de facto* mandatory because most buyers are unwilling to accept products unless they are certified. In parallel to public regulation, private standards play a critical role in ensuring the safety of the foods we consume.[3]

Scholars have documented a surge in private regulation in fields ranging from the environment to labour and the professions (Ogus 1995; Black 2001; Bartle and Vass 2007; Coglianese and Mendelson 2010). In addition, the increasing prominence of private regulation in the food safety arena warrants a careful analysis of this phenomenon. Taking for granted that a *plurality* of public and private actors participate in food safety governance, this chapter aims at analysing the relationship between public and private food safety regulation to understand whether private regimes *complement* or rather *compete* with public regulation. Do private standards fill the gaps left by public regulation and in doing so protect consumers' health? Or do they rather play an adversarial role by displacing existing regulation or preventing new ones, signalling that private interests may be incompatible with public objectives? This chapter uses law and economics theory to answer these questions and analyse the incentives underlying PFSS. The chapter's approach is mostly theoretical, however empirical evidence is offered, when available, to support theoretical claims.

The expansion of PFSS in agribusiness in the last decades has stimulated a fertile stream of literature. Scholars have analysed some of the reasons for the widespread adoption of PFSS and some of the implications for suppliers, concluding that such voluntary standards have evolved to become de facto mandatory for producers (Bush and Bain 2004; Henson 2007; Fuchs and Kalfagianni 2010). Other scholars have focused on the distributive effects of standards, especially on producers in developing countries, where PFSS may act as barriers to entry for small players (Otsuki, Wilson et al. 2001; Hatanaka, Bain et al. 2005; Chen, Yang et al. 2008). Others have examined the important questions of the legitimacy and public accountability of private initiatives (Fuchs, Kalfagianni et al. 2009; Curtin and Senden 2011). The analysis of the effectiveness of private standards in protecting consumers' health and the interaction between public and private food safety regulation deserves additional scrutiny. Some research illustrates the relationship between public and private regulation (Henson and Caswell 1999; Fagotto 2014) and frames it in the novel context of transnational governance (Konefal, Mascarenhas et al. 2005; Cafaggi 2011). More optimistic observers suggest that there is a trend of 'co-regulation' by public and private actors (Garcia Martinez, Fearne et al. 2007). Others examined the strategic use of standards and whether private initiatives constitute an attempt by the industry to pre-empt public regulation (Lutz, Lyon et al. 2000; McCluskey 2007; McCluskey and Winfree 2009). Understanding how the industry contributes to food safety governance is especially critical at a time when government resources are eroding and there is a tendency to delegate important public responsibilities to private actors (Freeman 2000; Freeman and Kolstad 2007). This chapter fills a gap in this literature by applying a law and an economics framework to the analysis of private food safety governance and its relationship with government regulation.

The chapter is organised as follows. Section 2 illustrates the functioning of private standards by focusing on the different actors operating in the food supply chain and their roles. Section 3 explores some of the weaknesses of public regulation and discusses how private standards can complement public approaches. Section 4 discusses whether private standards may be competing with government regulation. Section 5 explores whether limits in PFSS enforcement constitute a form of capture. Section 6 offers concluding remarks.

11.2   PRIVATE FOOD SAFETY AND THE SUPPLY CHAIN

Firms in agribusiness have developed a sophisticated system of private standards to ensure the safety and quality of their products. There are no official statistics describing the breadth of this phenomenon, but the reach of industry regulation might be comparable to that of government regulation. Research suggests that private auditors conduct more than 200 000 food safety audits across 100 countries every year (Lytton and McAllister 2014). The GlobalG.A.P. standard alone is implemented by 94 000 suppliers worldwide (Fuchs and Kalfagianni 2010).

Private standards were introduced by retailers and industry associations active at the end of the supply chain to control the behaviour of the actors operating upstream (producers, processors) by imposing on them safety and quality controls. Agrifood supply chains are 'buyer-driven' and dominated by a handful of large retailers and manufacturers who exercise significant power in the supply chain (Gereffi 1994; Fuchs, Kalfagianni et al. 2009). Given the power exercised by actors at the end of the chain, it should come as no surprise that private standards were first introduced as business-to-business standards by large *retail chains* to control the safety of own label goods (products carrying the retailer's label, such as fresh fruit or meat). Their reach gradually expanded to include major manufacturers including brands of the calibre of McDonald's, Nestlé and Coca-Cola.[4]

To clarify how PFSS operate, consider an oversimplified food supply chain (figure 11.1).

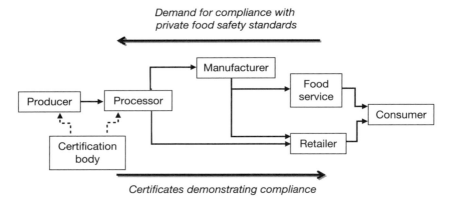

Figure 11.1　Private food safety in the supply chain

The first step is the producer (a farmer growing corn); then the food is processed in different ways by a food processor (a facility processing corn to create ingredients). Producers and processors are often referred to as 'suppliers' and they sell their products to 'buyers' (manufacturers, food service industry and retailers), who in turn commercialize foods to consumers. In order to protect their brand reputation and market standing, buyers require that their suppliers comply with privately developed food safety standards, as indicated by the top arrow in figure 11.1. Assurance that suppliers are in compliance is demonstrated through certificates, as shown by the bottom arrow in figure 11.1. Such certificates are issued by certification bodies (CBs) after they conduct facility audits.

Several actors contribute to the development and enforcement of private standards (figure 11.2).

Private standards are developed and administered by a scheme owner, which is generally backed by a large industry association. For example, the Safety Quality Food (SQF) standard is managed by the US-based Food Marketing Institute, and the BRC standard by the British Retail Consortium. Monitoring and enforcement of PFSS is carried out by CBs, which conduct audits on facilities and issue certificates to signal compliance. Certification bodies have to be verified and approved by scheme owners and their credentials evaluated by independent accreditation bodies, which are themselves accredited by a meta-regulator, the International Accreditation Forum. Scheme owners are in turn influenced by the meta-rules designed by the Global Food Safety Initiative (GFSI), an industry effort to establish equivalency among PFSS.[5] The GFSI

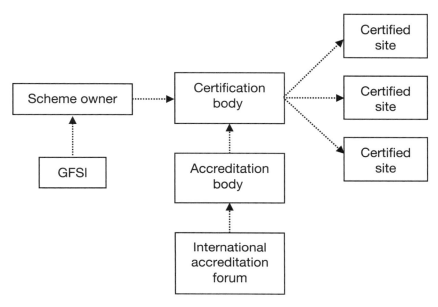

Figure 11.2   Actors in the food safety scheme

rules apply to all its recognized standards and trickle down to the actors participating in a scheme, in the form of requirements for auditors, CBs and technical specifications for accreditation bodies.

PFSS are characterised by:

1. the description of specific procedures and control points to minimise the penetration of risks into the food production process;
2. verification of compliance with the standard through internal documentation;
3. mechanisms of internal audit so that firms can self-monitor their compliance; and
4. external audits by third-party certifiers (Henson and Humphrey 2009).

Several factors contributed to the adoption of PFSS. Research shows that PFSS were introduced to protect retailers' reputations, to shield them from legal liability and to regain consumers' trust in the wake of foodborne outbreaks (Fulponi 2006; Havinga 2006). Buyers at the end of the supply chain needed a way to control the safety and predictability of the products they received and reduce transaction costs and information asymmetries associated with such controls (Henson and Northen 1998; Holleran, Bredahl et al. 1999; Deaton 2004). Legislative changes in response to the Bovine Spongiform Encephalopathy (BSE) crisis have emphasized the responsibility of the actors at the end of the supply chain. In the UK, the 1990 Food Safety Act introduced a due diligence defence, creating incentives for buyers to control the previous steps in their supply chains through PFSS (Hobbs, Fearne et al. 2002; Marsden 2010). Finally, global food trade has intensified, enabling buyers to source foods from cheaper markets and expand product availability to customers (Hooker 1999; WTO 2011). Albeit convenient, this trend also increases the chances of contamination, which called for private mechanisms to ensure safety across borders (Buzby 2003; Bush and Bain 2004; Gereffi and Sturgeon 2005).

11.3   DO PFFS 'FILL IN' FOR GOVERNMENT REGULATION?

Private food safety standards ensure the safety and predictability of foods and also have important public implications. Through PFSS, retailers and manufacturers provide safe foods to consumers, a critical public good, and one that is shared by the industry and government alike (Havinga 2006). Research investigating private regulation suggests that for private initiatives to increase consumers' welfare there has to be a 'strong natural coincidence' between public and private interest (Gunningham and Rees 1997). When we consider private food safety initiatives, it is beyond doubt that there is an alignment of public and private interests to provide food safety.

Private actors have powerful incentives to achieve food safety because the economic repercussions of foodborne outbreaks can be devastating. Research shows that firms involved in major meat and poultry recalls suffered significant shareholder losses (Thomsen and McKenzie 2001) and ready-to-eat meat brands involved in a recall suffered a 22 per cent decline in sales (Thomsen, Shiptsova et al. 2006). There can be long-term repercussions to foodborne outbreaks. The BSE crisis curbed consumer demand for meat in the UK, with a long term effect of a 4.5 per cent reduction (Burton and Young 1996). Finally, outbreaks can reverberate on entire food sectors or be attributed to the wrong food vehicle, with negative externalities also for firms whose products are safe. A 2008 outbreak of salmonella in the US was blamed on tomatoes, costing the industry an estimated $200million, while the real culprits were jalapeno and serrano peppers usually consumed with tomatoes (Maki 2009). The 2011 E. coli outbreak that ravaged Germany and other northern European countries was erroneously attributed to cucumbers from Spain, which resulted in the Spanish fresh produce industry losing 200 million euros per week.[6] It was later discovered that the source of the deadly outbreak were organic fenugreek seeds from Egypt (EFSA 2011). At times perfectly safe foods are destroyed to prevent contagion or producers suffer losses in sales because consumers stop purchasing certain categories of foods altogether (Marsh, Schroeder et al. 2004). Outbreaks have *systemic effects* on the industry. This makes food safety an industry-wide objective, creating incentives not only to control a firm's own supply chain for safety and quality, but also to exert *peer-to-peer pressure* to promote general safety, for example by enforcing stringent standards through networks of business associations. Initiatives like the GFSI are evidence of the sustained private efforts to promote food safety practices and create a culture of safety among the industry.

Not only is there a convergence of public and private interests in protecting consumers' health, but PFSS may even be covering for government in areas where public agencies are lacking, suggesting that there may be some complementarity between public and private initiatives (Fagotto 2014). Public food safety regulation presents several vulnerabilities, which can be attributed to institutional fragmentation, the international dimension of food safety, and poor enforcement. Consider first the level of *fragmentation* of domestic food safety systems. In the US, food safety responsibilities are shared by two agencies: the US Department of Agriculture (USDA), in charge of supervising meat, poultry and egg products (bizarrely, whole eggs are regulated by the FDA) and the Food and Drug Administration (FDA), in charge of all other foods. The two federal agencies have very different enforcement strategies. Whereas the USDA relies on thousands of inspectors to visually examine animal carcasses at meat processing facilities, the FDA uses sporadic inspections, every three years for facilities considered high-risk, and every five years for non-high-risk ones.[7] Responsibilities are also shared with 15 other agencies at the federal level, including the Centers for Disease Control and Prevention, the Environmental Protection Agency, and the Federal Trade Commission. Finally, state and local authorities also partake in food safety and play a particularly important role when it comes to inspections and emergency response. With so many actors sharing food safety responsibilities, it is not always clear which agency is in charge of which foods, especially for foods made of ingredients that are regulated by separate agencies, and the system has been criticized for its balkanisation (HLR 2007; Smith De Waal 2007).

A similar division can be observed in the EU, where EU institutions and national-level agencies share responsibilities in food safety. European food scares played an important role in shaping the EU food policy and institutions and a coherent food safety regulatory framework was put in place after the BSE crisis erupted in the UK (Vos 2000; Knowles, Moody et al. 2007). That crisis exposed the fragility not only of the UK food system, but also the EU one, which had an incoherent and piecemeal approach to food safety, dictated more by the necessity to facilitate food trade than to protect consumers' health (Alemanno 2007). This prompted a sweeping reform and the passage of Regulation (EC) No 178/2002. The EU General Food Law emphasized the importance of risk analysis and risk management to control food safety risks and ruled that the two functions should remain separated. It also established the creation of the European Food Safety Authority (EFSA), a body in charge of risk analysis and coordination with national food safety authorities. Food safety responsibility was transferred from the DG Agriculture to the DG Health and Consumers, in charge of protecting consumers' health. Also numerous member states created national food safety authorities and separated risk assessment and risk management functions in their domestic regulatory frameworks.[8] In this complex ecosystem, roles and responsibilities are not always clear. For example, whereas national authorities are responsible in case of an outbreak, the EU Commission has the prerogative to assume special emergency powers. This arrangement, as well as the division of responsibilities at the federal and state level in Germany, generated confusion and criticisms in the way the 2011 EHEC outbreak was handled by public authorities.[9]

Second, at the international level, one can observe not only a similar level of fragmentation, but also areas that are out of regulators' reach, leaving concrete vacuums in governance. Internationally, several multilateral bodies are involved in food safety governance. The World Trade Organization (WTO) provides a food safety framework for its member states. Specifically, the Agreement on Sanitary and Phytosanitary Measures (SPS) establishes a series of guidelines for member states' food safety legislation to ensure that national food safety rules do not become an unjustified barrier to international trade (Alemanno 2007). The SPS Agreement establishes that national food safety regulations should be based on science and risk assessment and should not be used arbitrarily as a protectionist measure. The Agreement also encourages member countries to base their food safety laws on international standards so as to favour harmonization and to participate in the development of such standards.

The World Health Organization (WHO) does not itself issue international regulations on food safety, but it indicates the Codex Alimentarius

Commission (Codex) as the principal intergovernmental body in charge of food safety. Codex, a body founded by the Food and Agriculture Organization (FAO) and the WHO, has elaborated hundreds of international standards and guidelines. Although Codex standards are not legally binding, they constitute a benchmark against which national regulations are evaluated and are used by the WTO in settling international food safety disputes (FAO/WHO 2006). Even if merely recommendatory, Codex standards are *de facto* mandatory for WTO members and serve as guidance to domestic food safety regulation. Governments have incentives to follow Codex standards to avoid trade disputes with other countries, suggesting that Codex serves more as a trade instrument than as a genuine food safety tool (Alemanno 2007). In sum, each government adopts its own food safety rules and, aside from the common framework offered by Codex, there is not a body of uniform and consolidated international food safety regulation. This creates significant inconsistencies, as a product that is safe for consumption in one country may be deemed unfit in another. The fungicide carbendazim was found in Brazilian orange juice that is commercialised in the US under American labels. The fungicide is legal in Brazil, but in the US it is not approved for use in citrus.[10] Recently, the FDA expressed concerns with the possible association between the use of wooden boards to age artisanal cheese and contamination with listeria, stimulating an intense debate among domestic and international cheese producers.[11] Since each country issues its own food safety rules, it is up to producers that seek to export as well as importers to make sure that the product in question complies with the requirements of the countries in which it will be consumed (Bamberger and Guzman 2009). Inevitably, identifying the relevant regulatory framework and adjusting production to meet the demands of different countries imposes high compliance costs on the industry, especially for less sophisticated players who lack the capacity to seek out and interpret the relevant regulatory requirements (Aruoma 2006; Yapp and Fairman 2006).

In the absence of a common food safety regulation governing foods that are globally traded, food import safety poses novel and significant challenges to which governments are only starting to respond (Coglianese, Finkel et al. 2009). Foods may originate from countries that have weak food safety rules, poor enforcement systems and limited food safety culture within the industry. Besides the egregious case of melamine contamination in milk, Chinese exports tend to present high levels of pesticides which causes concern to countries at the receiving end (Gale and Buzby 2009). Importing countries have devised a variety of responses to ensure import safety. Some legal systems validate ex-ante the food safety controls of exporting countries by establishing equivalency among food safety systems (Hooker 1999; Alemanno 2009), others, like the US system, rely more heavily on controls of imports at the border (Buzby 2003). Yet given the impossibility of inspecting all incoming foods, import safety measures should focus on supporting the *regulatory capacity* of exporters, a strategy that is likely to bear fruit only in the long run, leaving the present challenges of import safety unresolved.

Third, consider the limits in public enforcement and how these are compounded by the international dimension. Food safety regulations that prescribe performance standards are enforced through a network of inspectors and their effectiveness relies on a reliable inspection procedure and on a system of sanctions for those who evade compliance (Starbird 2000). Yet departments that carry out inspections appear under-staffed and under-resourced. In the US, for example, from 2004 to 2008, over 50 per cent of facilities under FDA authority were never inspected, a fact that can easily erode confidence in the government's ability to ensure safety (Department of Health and Human Services 2010). Enforcement efforts are further complicated at the international level, where governments are met with *jurisdictional boundaries* and with the resistance of exporting countries. A reform in US food safety regulation has strengthened international collaboration and introduced foreign branches of the FDA to perform facility inspections locally (Fagotto 2011). The reality of carrying out enforcement activities in other jurisdictions, however, remains daunting. When FDA inspectors sought to access Chinese factories implicated in the production of pet food contaminated with melamine, their visas were deliberately delayed by Chinese authorities, so when they were finally able to visit the facilities, one had been bulldozed and the other was empty (Lin 2013).

Consider now how private food safety standards may complement public regulation and address the problems of excessive fragmentation, international dimension and poor enforcement.

First, PFSS contain a clear and *consolidated set of requirements*, part of which build on internationally recognized HACCP standards as well as General Manufacturing Practices and ISO standards. This lowers compliance costs for regulatees because PFSS rules are available in a single, relatively simple document, so firms do not have to seek out regulations from different sources. Given that a standard applies not only domestically, but also internationally, producers know that compliance with a standard will satisfy the demands of *all* buyers that accept that standard, irrespective of their geographic location. In addition, private standards contain requirements, from allergen to traceability measures, that may even exceed public regulation, offering consumers protection in areas that are not yet regulated by government (Henson and Humphrey 2009).

Second, if we consider that products may originate from countries with inadequate food safety systems, private initiatives may provide a regulatory framework and incentives for compliance that the country of origin might not offer. Because of their transnational nature, PFSS can directly impact the behaviour of producers by building their management skills and food safety capacity, in spite of the vulnerabilities of their national food safety architecture. The ability to *intervene directly on producers* is a significant advantage over public regulation, which relies on lengthy negotiations among governments to allow access to foreign inspectors. This is an important area in which the industry complements the deficiencies of public enforcement across jurisdictional boundaries and offers controls where governments are still lagging behind.

Third, *compliance* with private standards is likely to be higher because of the frequency of private controls and, most importantly, because non-compliance could cost a firm its certificate and with it the ability to conduct business with buyers who require certified products. Since participation in food markets is conditional upon certification, suppliers have strong incentives to pass the audit and become certified (Fagotto 2014). Additionally, obtaining certification can significantly expand market opportunities for suppliers because any buyer accepting GFSI-recognized standards can purchase their products, an approach known as 'once certified, accepted everywhere'.[12] Incentives to become certified are only likely to increase, given that the number of buyers demanding compliance with GFSI-recognized standards is on the rise and that these buyers account for very powerful players in the food industry, including brands like Cargill, Ahold and Carrefour.[13] The enforcement of PFSS is conducted by CBs through annual facility audits and, in some cases, private controls can be more frequent than government inspections and may be able to detect risks that government is unaware of.

Private food safety standards are evidence that the industry is proactively focused on building its own capacity to manage food safety risks. The literature highlights the effectiveness of regulation that, rather than imposing prescriptive standards to stimulate reactive compliance, encourages the industry to participate in the design and management of regulatory controls (Coglianese and Nash 2001; Coglianese and Lazer 2003). Research has also found that, especially for smaller firms, regulation that emphasizes education improves compliance better than the traditional deterrence model (Fairman and Yapp 2005). Private food safety standards do precisely that by asking that facilities take charge of food safety and adopt management systems and HACCP plans, which are consolidated tools to promote food safety also endorsed in public food safety regulation (Pierson and Corlett 1992; Unnevehr and Jensen 1999; FAO/WHO 2006).

11.4   THE CASE FOR PFSS COMPETITION WITH PUBLIC REGULATION

A significant body of research argues that government regulation is put in place not to correct market failures, but rather to advance the private interests of regulated firms by, for example, influencing government to set up barriers to entry to competitors (Stigler 1971; Peltzman 1976; Becker 1983). Some scholars of private regulation warn that in the private sphere and in transnational settings, the risk that private regulation is designed to advance the industry's interests is even more acute (Braithwaite and Drahos 2000; Mattli and Woods 2009). Haufler suggests that private corporations can adopt different strategies vis-à-vis government regulation (Haufler 2003). The first are 'stonewalling strategies', where companies staunchly oppose regulation in their area. The second are 'national strategies', where companies oppose international regulation but favour domestic ones, with the expectation that the latter is easier to influence. The third are 'harmonization strategies', where private players favour international regulation as a way to reduce their costs of compliance with multiple regimes. Finally, corporations can opt for 'global self-regulatory strategies' in the hope to avoid not only domestic but also international regulation (Haufler 2003 p.231). Haufler observes a marked shift away from stonewalling and national strategies in favour of harmonization and especially private governance solutions. The reason for such a shift is defensive, as industry actors opt for private regulation in the hope to pre-empt government action and public regulation (Haufler 2003). There are several examples of cases where private regulation was adopted by government, which may support the view that private standards were set up to influence public regulation. Some firms reported that their animal welfare schemes were incorporated by government regulators, for example in Switzerland (Fulponi 2006). In numerous countries, included among them China, Mexico and Japan, national food safety standards were benchmarked on the EurepGAP standard (currently GlobalG.A.P.) for equivalency (Casey 2007) and the Brazilian government adopted milk standards that were developed by the private sector (Reardon and Farina 2002). A volume on private food law documents several instances in which private food safety rules were adopted by public regulators in the EU (Van Der Meulen 2011). In the US, a reform in food law introduced third-party audits to ensure import safety and Canadian regulators are exploring ways to leverage public inspections and private audits to avoid duplications (Fagotto 2011). As discussed earlier, standards are based on consolidated public food safety requirements and rather than prescribing the adoption of specific technologies, which could determine future regulatory choices, they generally mandate management systems, or process requirements, that may be reversed relatively easily. Rather than displacing government regulation, PFSS appear to operate in its shadow by facilitating compliance. In sum, there is hybridization between public and private food safety regulation yet there is no conclusive evidence on the effects and effectiveness of hybridization in protecting consumers.

Mattli and Woods offer a persuasive framework to analyse capture in global private regulation and argue that capture could result in regulation that sets barriers to entry for outsiders, or regulation that appears to be in the public interest, but is poorly enforced (Mattli and Woods 2009). First, whereas the industry appears to be able to influence global standard-setting in several domains thus limiting access for competitors (Büthe and Mattli 2011), this does not seem to apply in the case of PFSS. When considering whether PFSS constitute barriers to entry to competitors, one can observe that the contrary is happening. Private standards are advantageous also for competitors who do not require compliance because they generate *positive externalities* by raising general food safety levels in the industry, hence even retailers who might not buy in, can still enjoy enhanced food safety (Fagotto 2014).

11.5   CAPTURE BY POOR ENFORCEMENT

Private food safety standards may present a more subtle form of capture by setting up a promising regulatory framework that is poorly enforced, thus creating the appearance of good governance, but failing to meet regulatory goals (Mattli and Woods 2009). This form of capture – nominal regulation that is poorly enforced – is plausible because of limitations in third-party certification.

A nascent line of investigation focuses on the enforcement of PFSS to identify whether there are deficiencies that may lead to sub-optimal compliance, thus reducing PFSS ability to pursue the public interest. Research on third-party certification in other areas has focused on certifiers' role as gatekeepers (Kraakman 1986). Research on financial auditors concluded that since auditors are paid by those they are supposed to watch, they may be biased and favour clients over oversight duties (Prentice 2000; Bazerman, Loewenstein et al. 2002; Shapiro 2005). Audits in labour schemes present inconsistencies and gaps in auditors' skills

(O'Rourke 2003; Locke, Amengual et al. 2009; Locke 2013). Research on the role of third-party certification bodies in food safety is limited and identifies problems such as potential conflict of interest and gaps in auditor competencies (Powell, Erdozain et al. 2013; Lytton and McAllister 2014). Empirical research points to inconsistencies in audit findings and a pervasive 'checklist mentality' rather than a focus on overall food safety outcomes (Albersmeier, Schulze et al. 2009).

Consistent with other industries, the certification bodies that conduct food safety audits are selected and remunerated by the firms that seek certification, creating the risk of *conflict of interest*. Consequently, CBs may be too lenient with their auditees because these are their clients and a source of future business, given that CBs tend to have long lasting contracts with the firms they watch. The fact that the same CB, and often the same auditor within a CB, visit the same facility over time further increases the chances of capture by the auditee. Additionally, the market for certification is rather competitive and CBs may want to please their clients for fear that these may switch to other auditors. Opportunistic firms may seek less rigorous auditors to increase their chances of obtaining certification, a phenomenon known as 'audit tourism'. Certification bodies even used to be able to provide auditing and advisory services under the same roof, with 'firewalls' to avoid advising the same companies they audit.[14] In sum, the current structure for auditor selection and compensation is detrimental to the impartiality of third-party audits.

Auditor incompetence may also undermine confidence in third-party certification. Food safety outbreaks at facilities that had just been promoted by private auditors could be an indicator that auditors were not qualified to do the job. An egregious case involves Peanut Corporation of America, where the peanuts were contaminated with salmonella, sickening over 700 people and leading to the recall of over 2100 products containing peanuts originating from the facility.[15] The facility had been audited repeatedly and with positive results, but after the outbreak it emerged that one of the auditors was a specialist in fresh produce and was unaware of peanuts' susceptibility to salmonella.[16] It appears that whereas demand for certification is growing rapidly, there is not a congruous supply of skilled auditors because academic training in this field is lacking (Powell, Erdozain et al. 2013). The industry seems to be aware of this limitation and has instituted a special committee within the GFSI to focus on auditor competencies and to verify credentials.[17]

Finally, audits may not be an adequate tool to capture typical conditions at a facility and, most importantly, to generate incentives for consistent compliance. Audits last two days, happen at a yearly interval and are announced. The fact that *audits are scheduled in advance* gives the auditee a chance to prepare for the audit by adjusting compliance to the timing of the audit, for example by repairing defective machinery, cleaning the premises or filling records. This is why audits are not likely to capture the *typical behaviour* at an audited facility, which brings into question the reliability of the information generated by audits, on which certification decisions are based. Although the industry as a whole has a systemic interest in achieving high food safety levels, it would be erroneous to consider the industry as a monolith. Whereas some firms value food safety and their reputation, others may discount the effects of an outbreak or may just want to evade food safety compliance to cut on costs. Such firms are likely to prepare for the audit by improving compliance, only to return to their typical (lower) levels of compliance after they achieve certification, being aware that private controls will not occur until the following year. Industry monitoring lacks mechanisms to verify that the conditions found during an audit are also met during the interval between audits. The industry seems to be aware that announced audits may favour strategic behaviour and is gradually shifting towards an *unannounced audit* system. The BRC standard has introduced a voluntary unannounced audit programme for companies that wish to signal their superior food safety systems to clients. Some buyers, like the retail chain ASDA, have responded by asking that suppliers for ASDA brand products choose the BRC unannounced audit option.[18] The SQF standard has introduced one mandatory unannounced audit out of every three audits for all its certified facilities as a measure to stimulate consistent audit preparedness.[19]

Deficiencies in the way PFSS are enforced appear detrimental to food safety, yet it is unlikely that private initiatives constitute a form of capture by providing just 'cosmetic compliance' to prevent government regulation (Krawiec 2003). In particular, players active at the end of the supply chain are motivated by strong economic incentives to offer safe foods to consumers, yet the enforcement mechanisms they have put in place may not correct the behaviour of opportunistic suppliers and need to be improved to generate higher compliance.

11.6   CONCLUSION

This chapter highlights ambiguities in the interaction between public and private initiatives. On the one hand private standards show a strong identity with public interest objectives, making the pursuit of food safety a shared goal of public and private regulatory efforts. Firms with recognized brands could be seriously damaged by a foodborne outbreak in terms of revenue loss and compromised reputation. Outbreaks also have serious systemic effects on entire food sectors, making food safety a key industry objective. PFSS may even fill in for lacking government regulation in promoting food safety across borders. Government inspections across jurisdictional boundaries face serious obstacles and exporting countries may have rudimentary food safety systems. By intervening directly with producers, PFSS by-pass government and ensure safety irrespective of the food safety system of the food's country of origin. This may suggest that there is complementarity between public and private food safety efforts.

Yet one should not hastily conclude that PFSS should replace government regulation or that public food safety functions should be entrusted to the industry, for example by delegating inspection responsibilities to private auditors. Problems of conflict of interest, auditor incompetence and the announced nature of audits cast a shadow over private initiatives. Because they are selected and paid by firms seeking certification, auditors may be interested in protecting auditees and therefore lax in their controls. Announced audits incentivize strategic behaviour because firms may prepare to pass the audit by adjusting compliance. These deficiencies in private enforcement question the ability of PFSS to deliver food safety consistently, yet they are not sufficient to corroborate the view that standards compete with government regulation by providing just nominal protection.

In order to truly achieve complementarity and even collaboration in public/private food safety governance, the limitations in third-party certification should be corrected. Similarly, public regulators should use scepticism and should carefully verify the work of auditors and, in particular, audit results before incorporating PFSS elements in their toolkit. The industry is taking steps to reduce compliance costs through consolidation and harmonization and has introduced unannounced audits to improve the reliability of its controls. Given the alignment of public and private interests in the field, government should also collaborate with the industry to identify solutions to correct deficiencies in PFSS enforcement.

This important field of analysis would greatly benefit from a thorough investigation and categorization of varieties of public/private hybridization in food safety governance. Investigations on the political economy of the interaction between public and private regulation are lacking and could be an important contribution to the debate on the collaborative vs. competitive nature of the relationship. Finally, empirical research on the effects of incorporating private elements in public regulation would illuminate the effectiveness of public/private interactions in food safety.

NOTES

*   I am grateful to Alessandra Arcuri, Michael Faure, Archon Fung, Tetty Havinga, and to participants in the ECPR's Standing Group on Regulation and Governance Conference 2012 at the University of Exeter for valuable comments.

1. Source: www.cdc.gov/foodborneburden/2011-foodborne-estimates.html. Site accessed 24 July 2014.
2. Additional information on PFSS can be found at mygfsi.com/about-gfsi/gfsi-recognised-schemes.html. Site accessed 24 July 2014.
3. This chapter's terminology distinguishes between public and private regulation. Public regulation (also referred to as government regulation) is intended as regulation issued by institutions that derive their authority from a public mandate, such as national or international public agencies. Private regulation is designed and enforced by industry actors with no public mandate.
4. Source: http://mygfsi.com/gfsifiles/2013-05_What_is_GFSI_-_Internet.pdf. Site accessed 24 July 2014.
5. As of July 2014, ten PFSS were benchmarked for equivalency by the GFSI. Source: mygfsi.com/about-gfsi/gfsi-recognised-schemes.html. Site accessed 24 July 2014.
6. Giles Tremlett and Helen Pidd, 'Germany admits Spanish cucumbers are not to blame for E coli outbreak', *The Guardian*, 31 May 2011. Source: http://www.guardian.co.uk/uk/2011/may/31/e-coli-deaths-16-germany-sweden. Site accessed 24 July 2014.
7. This frequency of inspection was introduced by the 2010 Food Safety Modernization Act. Source: http://www.fda.gov/Food/GuidanceRegulation/FSMA/. Site accessed 24 July 2014.
8. See Gabriele Abels and Alexander Kobusch in this volume.
9. Source: http://www.regblog.org/2011/06/europes-e-coli-outbreak-the-eu-food-safety-regime-under-stress.html. Site accessed 24 July 2014.
10. Paul Kiernan and Betsy Mckay, 'Coke, Pepsi Attempt to Ease O.J. Fears', *The Wall Street Journal*, 13 January 2012, http://online.wsj.com/article/SB10001424052970204542404577156931248564436.html.
11. Sources: http://www.fda.gov/Food/NewsEvents/ConstituentUpdates/ucm400808.htm; http://www.theguardian.com/commentisfree/2014/jun/17/cheese-wood-boards-unsafe. Sites accessed 24 July 2014.
12. Source: http://mygfsi.com/communication/gfsi-general-presentation.html. Site accessed 24 July 2014.
13. Source: http://mygfsi.com/communication/gfsi-general-presentation.html. Site accessed 24 July 2014.
14. ISO/IEC 17065 standard is attempting to resolve this conflict of interest by completely separating the two lines of business as of 2015.
15. Source: www.cdc.gov/salmonella/typhimurium/update.html#outbreakinvestigation. Site accessed 24 July 2014.
16. Source: www.nytimes.com/2009/03/06/business/06food.html?pagewanted=all. Site accessed 24 July 2014. Even though auditor incompetence is often cited as a limitation of private food safety enforcement, this shortcoming is not exclusive to private instruments, as incompetent government inspectors exist as well.
17. Source: http://mygfsi.com/technical-resources/gfsi-auditor-competency-framework.html. Site accessed 24 July 2014.
18. Source: https://www.gov.uk/government/uploads/system/uploads/attachment_data/file/262372/fsn-asda-20131112.pdf. Site accessed 24 July 2014.
19. Source: www.sqfi.com/2014/01/06/sqf-becomes-first-internationally-accredited-third-party-assessment-program-to-require-unannounced-audits/. Site accessed 24 July 2014.

REFERENCES

Albersmeier, F., H. Schulze et al. (2009), 'The Reliability of Third-party Certification in the Food Chain: From Checklist to Risk Oriented Auditing', *Food Control*, 20, 927–935.

Alemanno, A. (2007), *Trade in Food: Regulatory and Judicial Approaches in the EC and the WTO*, London: Cameron May.

Alemanno, A. (2009), 'Solving the Problem of Scale: The European Approach to Import Safety and Security Concerns', in C. Coglianese, A.M. Finkel and D. Zaring, *Import Safety: Regulatory Governance in the Global Economy*, Philadelphia: University of Pennsylvania Press.

Aruoma, O.I. (2006), 'The Impact of Food Regulation on the Food Supply Chain', *Toxicology*, 221, 119–127.

Bamberger, K.A. and A.T. Guzman (2009), 'Importers as Regulators', in C. Coglianese, A.M. Finkel and D. Zaring, *Import Safety: Regulatory Governance in the Global Economy*, Philadelphia: University of Pennsylvania Press.

Bartle, I. and P. Vass (2007), 'Self-regulation within the Regulatory State: Towards a New Regulatory Paradigm?', *Public Administration*, 85(4), 885–905.

Bazerman, M.H., G. Loewenstein et al. (2002), 'Why Good Accountants Do Bad Audits', *Harvard Business Review*, 97–102.

Becker, G. (1983), 'A Theory of Competition among Pressure Groups for Political Influence', *Quarterly Journal of Economics*, 98, 371–400.

Black, J. (2001), 'Decentring Regulation: Understanding the Role of Regulation and Private Regulation in a Post-Regulatory World', *Current Legal Problems*, 54, 103–146.

Braithwaite, J. and P. Drahos (2000), *Global Business Regulation*, Cambridge UK/ New York: Cambridge University Press.

Burton, M. and T. Young (1996), 'The Impact of BSE on the Demand for Beef and Other Meats in Great Britain', *Applied Economics*, 28, 687–693.

Bush, L. and C. Bain (2004), 'New? Improved! The Transformation of the Global Agrifood System', *Rural Sociology*, 69(3), 321–346.

Büthe, T. and W. Mattli (2011), *The New Global Rulers: The Privatization of Regulation in the World Economy*, Princeton NJ: Princeton University Press.

Buzby, J.C. (ed.) (2003), *International Trade and Food Safety: Economic Theory and Case Studies. USDA Agricultural Economic Report No. 828*, Washington DC: US Department of Agriculture.

Cafaggi, F. (2011), 'New Foundations of Transnational Private Regulation', *Journal of Law and Society*, 38(1), 20–49.

Casey, D. (2007), 'Private Food Safety and Quality Standards and the WTO', *University College Dublin Law Review*, 65(7).

Chen, C., J. Yang et al. (2008), 'Measuring the Effect of Food Safety Standards on China's Agricultural Exports', *Review of World Economics*, 144(1), 83–106.

Coglianese, C., A.M. Finkel et al. (2009), *Import Safety: Regulatory Governance in the Global Economy*, Philadelphia: University of Pennsylvania Press.

Coglianese, C. and D. Lazer (2003), 'Management-Based Regulation: Prescribing Private Management to Achieve Public Goals', *Law and Society Review*, 37, 691–730.

Coglianese, C. and E. Mendelson (2010), 'Meta-Regulation and Self-Regulation', in R. Baldwin, M. Cave and M. Lodge, *The Oxford Handbook of Regulation*, Oxford: Oxford University Press.

Coglianese, C. and J. Nash (2001), *Regulating from the Inside: Can Environmental Management Systems Achieve Policy Goals?*, Washington DC: Resources for the Future.

Curtin, D. and L. Senden (2011), 'Public Accountability of Transnational Private Regulation: Chimera or Reality?', *Journal of Law and Society*, 38(1), 163–188.

Deaton, B.J. (2004), 'A Theoretical Framework for Examining the Role of Third-party Certifiers', *Food Control*, 15, 615–619.

Department of Health and Human Services, O. o. I. G. (2010), *FDA Inspections of Domestic Food Facilities*.

EFSA (2011), *Tracing Seeds, in Particular Fenugreek (Trigonella Foenum-Graecum) Seeds, in Relation to the Shiga Toxin-Producing E. coli (STEC) O104:H4 2011 Outbreaks in Germany and France*, Parma, Italy.

EFSA and ECDC (2011), 'European Union Summary Report on Trends and Sources of Zoonoses, Zoonotic Agents and Food-borne Outbreaks in 2009', *EFSA Journal*, 9(3).

Fagotto, E. (2011), 'Governing a Global Food Supply: How the 2010 FDA Food Safety Modernization Act Promises to Strengthen Import Safety in the US', *Erasmus Law Review*, 3(4), 257–273.

Fagotto, E. (2014), 'Private Roles in Food Safety Provision: The Law and Economics of Private Food Safety', *European Journal of Law and Economics*, 37(1), 83–109.

Fairman, R. and C. Yapp (2005), 'Enforced Self-Regulation, Prescription, and Conceptions of Compliance within Small Businesses: The Impact of Enforcement', *Law & Policy*, 27(4), 491–519.

FAO/WHO (2006), 'FAO/WHO Guidance to Governments on the Application of HACCP in Small and/or Less-developed Food Businesses', FAO Food and Nutrition Paper 86, Rome: FAO.

FAO/WHO (2006), *Understanding the Codex Alimentarius*, Rome: Joint FAO/WHO Food Standards Programme.

Freeman, J. (2000), 'The Private Role in Public Governance', *New York University Law Review*, 75, 543.

Freeman, J. and C.D. Kolstad (2007), *Moving to Markets in Environmental Regulation: Lessons from Twenty Years of Experience*, Oxford, UK and New York, NY: Oxford University Press.

Fuchs, D. and A. Kalfagianni (2010), 'The Causes and Consequences of Private Food Governance', *Business and Politics*, 12(3), 1–36.

Fuchs, D., A. Kalfagianni et al. (2009), 'Retail Power, Private Standards, and Sustainability in the Global Food System', in J. Clapp and D. Fuchs, *Corporate Power in Global Agrifood Governance*, Cambridge, MA and London, UK: MIT Press, pp. 29–59.

Fuchs, D., A. Kalfagianni et al. (2009), 'Actors in Private Food Governance: The Legitimacy of Retail Standards and Multistakeholder Initiatives with Civil Society Participation', *Agriculture and Human Values*, DOI 10.1007/s10460-009-9236-3.

Fulponi, L. (2006), 'Private Voluntary Standards in the Food System: The Perspective of Major Food Retailers in OECD Countries', *Food Policy*, 31, 1–13.

Gale, F. and J.C. Buzby (2009), 'Imports from China and Food Safety Issues', UER Service, Washington DC, *Economic Information Bulletin*, 52.

Garcia Martinez, M., A. Fearne et al. (2007), 'Co-regulation as a Possible Model for Food Safety Governance: Opportunities for Public-Private Partnerships', *Food Policy*, 32, 299–314.

Gereffi, G. (1994), *Commodity Chains and Global Capitalism*, Westport: Greenwood Press.

Gereffi, G. and T. Sturgeon (2005), 'The Governance of Global Value Chains', *Review of International Political Economy*, 12(1), 78–104.

Gunningham, N. and J. Rees (1997), 'Industry Self-Regulation: An Institutional Perspective', *Law & Policy*, 19(4), 363–414.

Hatanaka, M., C. Bain et al. (2005), 'Third-party Certification in the Global Agrifood System', *Food Policy*, 30, 354–369.

Haufler, V. (2003), 'Globalization and Industry Self-Regulation', in M. Kahler and D.A. Lake, *Governance in a Global Economy*, Princeton: Princeton University Press, pp. 226–252.

Havinga, T. (2006), 'Private Regulation of Food Safety by Supermarkets', *Law & Policy*, 28(4), 515–533.

Henson, S. (2007), 'The Role of Public and Private Standards in Regulating International Food Markets', *Journal of International Agricultural Trade and Development*, 4(1), 63–81.

Henson, S. and J. Caswell (1999), 'Food Safety Regulation: An Overview of Contemporary Issues', *Food Policy*, 2, 589–603.

Henson, S. and J. Humphrey (2009), *The Impact of Private Food Safety Standards*, FAO/WHO.

Henson, S. and J. Northen (1998), 'Economic Determinants of Food Safety Controls in Supply of Retailer Own-Branded Products in United Kingdom', *Agribusiness*, 14(2), 113–126.

HLR (2007), 'Reforming the Food Safety System: What if Consolidation isn't Enough?', *Harvard Law Review*, 120(5), 1345–1366.

Hobbs, J.E., A. Fearne et al. (2002), 'Incentive Structures for Food Safety and Quality Assurance: An International Comparison', *Food Control*, 13, 77–81.

Holleran, E., M.E. Bredahl et al. (1999), 'Private Incentives for Adopting Food Safety and Quality Assurance', *Food Policy*, 24(6), 669–683.

Hooker, N.H. (1999), 'Food Safety Regulation and Trade in Food Products', *Food Policy*, 24, 653–668.

Jones, K., N. Patel et al. (2008), 'Global Trends in Emerging Infectious Diseases', *Nature*, 451(7181), 990–993.

Knowles, T., R. Moody et al. (2007), 'European Food Scares and Their Impact on EU Food Policy', *British Food Journal*, 109(1), 43–67.

Konefal, J., M. Mascarenhas et al. (2005), 'Governance in the Global Agrofood System: Backlighting the Role of Transnational Supermarket Chains', *Agriculture and Human Values*, 22, 291–302.

Kraakman, R.H. (1986), 'Gatekeepers: The Anatomy of a Third-Party Enforcement Strategy', *Journal of Law, Economics & Organization*, 2(1), 53–104.

Krawiec, K.D. (2003), 'Cosmetic Compliance and the Failure of Negotiated Governance', *Washington University Law Quarterly*, 81, 487–544.

Lin, C.-F. (2013), *Public-Private Regime Interactions in Global Food Safety Governance*, Comparative Research in Law and Political Economy, Toronto: Osgoode Hall Law School, York University.

Locke, R.M. (2013), *The Promise and Limits of Private Power: Promoting Labor Standards in a Global Economy*, New York: Cambridge University Press.

Locke, R.M., M. Amengual et al. (2009), 'Virtue out of Necessity? Compliance, Commitment, and the Improvement of Labor Conditions in Global Supply Chains', *Politics Society*, 37, 319.

Lutz, S., T.P. Lyon et al. (2000), 'Quality Leadership when Regulatory Standards are Forthcoming', *Journal of Industrial Economics*, 48, 331–348.

Lytton, T.D. and L.K. McAllister (2014), 'Oversight in Private Food Safety Auditing: Addressing Auditor Conflict of Interest', *Wisconsin Law Review*, 289.

Maki, D.G. (2009), 'Coming to Grips with Foodborne Infection – Peanut Butter, Peppers, and Nationwide Salmonella Outbreaks', *New England Journal of Medicine*, 360(10), 949–953.

Marsden, T. (ed.) (2010), *The New Regulation and Governance of Food*, New York: Routledge.

Marsh, T.L., T.C. Schroeder et al. (2004), 'Impacts of Meat Product Recalls on Consumer Demand in the US', *Applied Economics*, 36(9), 897–909.

Masson-Matthee, M. (2007), *The Codex Alimentarius Commission and Its Standards*, The Hague: TMC Asser Press.

Mattli, W. and N. Woods (2009), *The Politics of Global Regulation*, Princeton: Princeton University Press.

McCluskey, J.J. (2007), 'Public and Private Food Quality Standards: Recent Trends and Strategic Incentives', in J.F.M. Swinnen, *Global Supply Chains, Standards, and the Poor*, Wallingford: CABI.

McCluskey, J.J. and J.A. Winfree (2009), 'Pre-Empting Public Regulation with Private Food Quality Standards', *European Review of Agricultural Economics*, 36(4), 525–539.

O'Rourke, D. (2003), 'Outsourcing Regulation: Analyzing Nongovernmental Systems of Labor Standards and Monitoring', *Policy Studies Journal*, 31(1), 1–29.

Ogus, A. (1995), 'Rethinking Self-Regulation', *Oxford Journal of Legal Studies*, 15(1), 97–108.

Otsuki, T., J.S. Wilson et al. (2001), 'Saving Two in a Billion: Quantifying the Trade Effect of European Food Safety Standards on African Exports', *Food Policy*, 26, 495–514.

Peltzman, S. (1976), 'Toward a More General Theory of Regulation', *Journal of Law and Economics*, 19(2), 211–240.

Pierson, M.D. and J.D.A. Corlett (eds) (1992), *HACCP: Principles and Applications*, New York: Van Nostrand Reinhold.

Powell, D., M.S. Erdozain et al. (2013), 'Audits and Inspections are Never Enough: A Critique to Enhance Food Safety', *Food Control*, 30(2), 686–691.

Prentice, R.A. (2000), 'The SEC and MDP: Implications of the Self-Serving Bias for Independent Auditing', *OHIO ST. L. J.*, 61, 1597–1664.

Reardon, T. and E. Farina (2002), 'The Rise of Private Food Quality and Safety Standards: Illustrations from Brazil', *International Food and Agribusiness Management Review*, 4, 413–421.

Scott, C., F. Cafaggi et al. (2011), 'The Conceptual and Constitutional Challenge of Transnational Private Regulation', *Journal of Law and Society*, 38(1), 1–19.

Shapiro, A. (2005), 'Who Pays the Auditor Calls the Tune? Auditing Regulation and Clients' Incentives', *Seton Hall L. Rev.*, 35, 1029–1095.

Smith De Waal, C. (2007), 'Food Safety and Security: What Tragedy Teaches Us about Our 100-Year-Old Food Laws', *Vanderbuilt Journal of Transnational Law*, 40, 921.

Starbird, A.S. (2000), 'Designing Food Safety Regulations: The Effect of Inspection

Policy and Penalties for Noncompliance on Food Processor Behavior', *Journal of Agricultural and Resource Economics*, 25(2), 616–635.

Stigler, G.J. (1971), 'The Theory of Economic Regulation', *Bell Joural of Economics and Management Science*, 2(1), 3–21.

Thomsen, M.R. and A.M. McKenzie (2001), 'Market Incentives for Safe Foods: An Examination of Shareholder Losses from Meat and Poultry Recalls', *American Journal of Agricultural Economics*, 83(3), 526–538.

Thomsen, M.R., R. Shiptsova et al. (2006), 'Sales Responses to Recalls for Listeria Monocytogenes: Evidence from Branded Ready-to-Eat Meats', *Review of Agricultural Economics*, 28(4), 482–493.

Unnevehr, L.J. and H.H. Jensen (1999), 'The Economic Implications of Using HACCP as a Food Safety Regulatory Standard', *Food Policy*, 24(6), 625–635.

Van Der Meulen, B. (ed.) (2011), *Private Food Law*, Wageningen: Wageningen Academic Publishers.

Vos, E. (2000), 'EU Food Safety Regulation in the Aftermath of the BSE Crisis', *Journal of Consumer Policy*, 23, 227–255.

WTO (2011), *International Trade Statistics 2011*, Geneva: WTO.

Yapp, C. and R. Fairman (2006), 'Factors Affecting Food Safety Compliance within Small and Medium-sized Enterprises: Implications for Regulatory and Enforcement Strategies', *Food Control*, 17(1), 42–51.

12. Between public and private requirements: Challenges and opportunities for the export of tropical fruits from developing countries to the EU

Vanessa Constant Laforce

12.1 INTRODUCTION

The export of tropical fruits from developing countries (DCs) to the European Union (EU) offers significant economic and social gains. Food scares over the last two decades in industrialised countries have led to increasingly stringent food safety regulations. Consumers' concerns about the safety and quality of food have also influenced the private sector, which has developed numerous standards for imported fruits sold in supermarkets. In addition to EU regulations, developing countries (DCs) have also to comply with the evolving 'voluntary' requirements imposed by private companies in order to participate in value chains. Consequently, the export of tropical fruits from DCs are affected by food safety regulations and standards imposed by both EU governmental and non-governmental actors. With food safety being a top priority for both the public and private sectors, there is a need to examine the development of these requirements as applied to tropical fruits. Therefore, this chapter critically analyses, from a legal perspective, the issues of exporting tropical fruits to the EU market.

Meeting food safety standards imposed by developed countries is an important issue for developing countries (DCs) which export food products to these markets. The strictness of the standards can affect the ability of DCs to access developed countries' markets and ultimately restricts their effective participation in international trade. Using the example of tropical fruits, this chapter will highlight the difficulties that DCs are facing due to the variety of food safety standards established within the EU market. The production and export of tropical fresh fruits from DCs to the EU has grown rapidly during the past decade in response to the high consumer demand for fresh produce, variety and 'healthiness' (Jaffee et al. 2005, 317). In light of the accelerated year-round demand for the delivery of fresh produce, international trade in fresh fruits is a 'multibillion-dollar business' (FAO website), which is particularly important for DCs' foreign exchange and rural employment (Perry 2008, 7). However, global trade of tropical fresh fruits represents risks to human health and the environment as a result of the use of toxic plant protection products (PPP). PPPs, more commonly known as pesticides, are important for the commercial production of these products but leave residues in and on food, which have a serious impact on both human health and the environment. This has led to the imposition of new legislation and the reinforcement of control systems within the EU, which must also take into account the international obligations laid down in the World Trade Organisation's (WTO) Sanitary and Phytosanitary Agreement (the SPS Agreement) and the international food safety standards contained in the Codex Alimentarius Commission (Codex) (Roberts et al. 2005, 470).

In parallel with EU regulatory developments, the private sector has rapidly developed its own quality and safety standards, based on a combination of international and national regulations for pesticides and other food safety standards. One such example is the GlobalG.A.P. system. GlobalG.A.P. is examined in this chapter as it is considered an important standard affecting horticultural exports to the EU (UNCTAD 2007, 19). GlobalG.A.P. is an international private sector organisation that covers both food safety and non-food safety issues, and includes, for instance, environmental protection requirements (GlobalG.A.P. website). Food safety has become a top priority for the private sector, and therefore it is understood that private standards are becoming the 'predominant drivers of agri-food systems' (Henson et al. 2005, 242).

Both standards and regulations seek to ensure public health and safety in relation to food by outlining how food should be produced, processed and delivered to the consumer (Fulponi 2006, 2). They can also have an important impact on international trade by ensuring consumer's confidence in imported food and thereby increasing economic growth (DFID 2001). This is why their position within the governance structure of the food system is considered significant (Fulponi 2006, 2). However, despite having the same objective, private standards and public regulations in food safety differ from each other. Regulations, passed by the Council of the EU and the European Parliament, constitute legal acts of the EU and, as such, are an example of hard law. These are defined as having 'general application, (. . .) binding in (their) entirety and directly applicable in all Member States'.[1] Accordingly, EU regulations are legally enforceable throughout the EU. In contrast, standards have no legally binding force and therefore could be considered 'soft law'. The WTO defines a standard as being a 'document approved by a recognized body, that provides, for common and repeated use, rules, guidelines or characteristics for products or related processes and production methods, with which compliance is not mandatory'.[2]

Consequently, if DCs want to export tropical fruits to the EU market, they must comply with public requirements while being free to observe those imposed by private companies. However, in light of the high proportion of fresh fruits sold in supermarkets, retailers have become 'increasingly powerful' actors in the food chain (Havinga 2006, 528). Dependent suppliers have little or no option but to comply if they want to participate effectively in value chains. Therefore, it has been observed that private standards can be de facto compulsory for suppliers (WTO 2007b). Against this background, this chapter analyses the issues of exporting tropical fruits to the EU market. The chapter is organised in the following manner. It begins with a brief overview on the issue of pesticide residues in DCs. Then, the chapter will examine respectively the EU regulations and GlobalG.A.P. requirements for pesticides and their residues. Finally, the chapter will highlight the implications of these requirements for tropical fruits exports and will then provide a conclusion.

12.2   BACKGROUND

DCs are the main producers and exporters of fresh tropical fruits around the world. These products account for about 98 per cent of total production and are exported mainly to developed countries, representing around 80 per cent of global import trade (FAO website). It is widely recognised that DCs are heavily dependent on trade in tropical products that forms the backbone of their economies and accounts for the 'bulk' of their export earnings (Perry 2008, 7). These products provide opportunities for poverty alleviation, rural development and export diversification (UNCTAD 2007). Mangoes, pineapples, papayas, and avocados are the main tropical fruits produced worldwide and account for about '75 per cent of global fresh tropical fruit production' (FAO 2003). The Caribbean and Latin America are among the most important tropical fresh fruits producing regions, accounting for 32 per cent of global production, and export largely to the EU (European Commission 2005).

Given this context, there is a need for farmers in DCs to maintain successful production of tropical food products while combating significant tropical fruits pests, which damage both the quantity and quality of the crops. The use of agrochemicals is considered the easiest way for DCs to protect their crops and thus increase the production of food (Carvalho 2006, 689). Therefore, pesticides are applied in very high amounts in small farms and industrial plantations (Carvalho 2006, 688). Overuse of pesticides or the abuse or misuse of these highly toxic PPPs can seriously contaminate soils, water, and fruits, with grave human health risks (Carvalho 2006, 688).

It must be noted that the use of agrochemicals as a way to improve food security is used in both developed and DCs. However, in light of consumers' concerns over pesticide residues, developed countries have chosen to move towards more natural pest control products that are more expensive, but are deemed to be more ecologically friendly than chemical pesticides (Carvalho 2006, 689). In contrast, most DCs cannot afford the use of such alternative PPPs, due mainly to their limited access to foreign currency (Ecobichon 2001, 28). Farmers, in particular, use cheap chemicals like DDT.[3] Such chemicals are cheap because their patents have expired and/or because they are offered for use by developed countries, where these products are no longer used (Carvalho 2006, 689). The issue of high pesticide residues in DCs is often linked to the lack of farmers' training and awareness of their toxic effects (PAN UK 1998). Moreover, there is the problem of pesticide containers with missing or damaged labels. Farmers are also using products provided with complex instructions that are frequently written in a foreign language (PAN UK 1998). These problems are particularly common for users of pesticides on small farms that provide the bulk of the country's commodities exports, but who have poor reading and writing skills. These farmers cannot rely on their own governments, who usually just implement a basic SPS control system. Therefore, these farmers are unable to control health and safety practices with regard to pesticide application, or to check the incidence of pesticide residues (PAN UK 1998). The EU is aware of this situation and this gives rise to concerns for the safety of tropical fresh fruits produced in these countries for international exports.

12.3   PUBLIC REGULATIONS: THE EU CONTROL OF PESTICIDES AND THEIR RESIDUES IN FRESH FRUITS

The EU has enacted important provisions governing the use of pesticides in agriculture and regulating pesticide residue levels in food. While recognising the necessity of using PPP to ensure food security, Regulation (EC) No 1107/2009 establishes the rules regarding 'the authorisation of plant protection products in commercial form, for their placing on the market, use and control within the EU'.[4] It also provides rules for the approval of active substances, safeners and synergists contained in PPPs.[5] The aim of the regulation is to ensure 'a high level of protection of human, animal health and the environment (. . .) while improving agricultural production'.[6] The regulation seeks to do so by facilitating the identification of PPPs and substances that 'do not have any harmful effect on human or animal health or any unacceptable effects on the environment'.[7] Accordingly, the regulation provides that 'a [PPP] shall not be placed on the market or used unless it has been authorised'.[8] Despite the fact that the authorisation of PPPs is still the responsibility of individual EU Member States, in order to be approved the product must comply with the authorisation conditions as detailed in Article 29 of the regulation.

The use of pesticides inevitably leaves residues in treated food products and it is impossible to ensure that food is 100 per cent free of pesticides. Consequently, in 2005, an EU regulation was enacted to control pesticide residue levels and to guarantee human health safety.[9] This regulation seeks to ensure acceptable levels of residues at the EU level in, or on, agri-food products for human health, by establishing a maximum residue level (MRL) of pesticides legally permitted in food commodities.[10] The regulation requires that setting the level of pesticide residues in food must be consistent with good agricultural practice (GAP) and the 'Acceptable Daily Intake'.[11] This is necessary in order to fully protect all categories of consumers, and particularly the more vulnerable such as the unborn and children.[12] Shaw and Vannoort pointed out in 2002 that GAP occurs when pesticides are applied to fruits and vegetables at the right time and in conformity with the directions on the label, and they believe that this process ensures that MRLs are not exceeded (Shaw et al. 2002, 222).

The regulation separates 'definitive' MRLs tolerances, established at EU level, from 'temporary' but mandatory harmonised MRLs tolerances, referring to those levels that still need to be considered.[13] These tolerances are science-based and established in consultation with the European Food Safety Authority (EFSA), which was established in 2002 as an independent scientific point of reference in risk assessment.[14] The EFSA's Panel on PPPs and their residues plays a key role in the control of pesticides. It provides scientific advice and opinions on pesticides residues and their potential danger to consumers' health to the European Commission. This support from the EFSA is based on scientific information and data that are important for the adoption and implementation of effective legislation and policies.

The regulation applies to products listed in its Annex I. MRLs for those products are specified in Annexes II and III of the regulation, with the default MRL being 0.01 mg/kg.[15] When the MRL is exceeded, food products cannot enter the EU market.[16] However, it must be noted that, despite taking into account scientific data to assess the risks of residues on consumer health, MRLs are not a toxicology parameter (Van der Meulen et al. 2008, 325). Rather, MRLs are considered to be an indication of the misuse of a pesticide and not an actual risk to human health (WTO 2005b). Given this, there is no guarantee that a fruit that contains pesticide residues over the established maximum level will represent a real danger for the consumer. This is particularly so if the product is only rarely consumed by an individual. Indeed, people living in the same country and region do not have the same dietary habits. Furthermore, some people will not be affected by residues either way. Despite this, when such an excess over the MRL index is identified, the EU Member States' authorities are informed, through the Rapid Alert System for Food and Feed (RASFF) whenever there is an immediate threat to consumer safety and health (WTO 2005b).[17] Such action can affect exporters when food products consignments are rejected at the border or when products are withdrawn from the importer's market (RASFF 2009).

12.4   THE PRIVATE SECTOR: THE GLOBALG.A.P. REQUIREMENTS FOR PESTICIDES AND THEIR RESIDUES

In parallel with EU legislation, GlobalG.A.P. has developed a system of rules in relation to the import of fresh fruits. Described as a 'satellite navigation system' (GlobalG.A.P. website), GlobalG.A.P. was originally created by European retailers in 1997 as EurepGAP[18] and now comprises many large companies worldwide (Lang, 2006, 32). The organisation seeks to change growers' attitudes towards food production by imposing a performance standard, with defined criteria to follow, in order to render production processes safe (Yudin 2008, 2). Accordingly, the organisation applies one standard, the Integrated Farm Assurance Standard (IFA), which is a pre-farm gate standard that addresses the entire agricultural production process of the product (GlobalG.A.P. 2011a).

GlobalG.A.P.'s requirements are referred to as Control Points and Compliance Criteria (CPCC). CPCC pertaining to the production of fresh fruits and vegetables encompass a mix of food safety, environmental and social standards. They include 'intensive employee training, meticulous record keeping, frequent management reassessments of work methods and results, and annual on-farm inspections of work methods and paperwork by external auditors' (Yudin 2008, 2). Each requirement is ranked into three levels of importance, leaving farmers with limited flexibility on some of them. These are the 'major musts', which are the mandatory control points, the 'minor musts' and lastly the 'recommendations' which are not compulsory. In order to obtain and maintain a GlobalG.A.P. certification, fresh fruits producers must comply with all major requirements and must meet at least 95 per cent of the minor requirements (GlobalG.A.P. 2011a). Failure to respect these requirements will result in GlobalG.A.P. certification being denied or suspended.

In order to participate in the GlobalG.A.P. market, DCs exporting tropical fruits have to meet the organisation's CPCC in relation to pesticides. These requirements are usually in line with the EU legislation but some of them can be identified as extending beyond public controls (Lee 2006, 31). One example is the 'major must' GlobalG.A.P. control point prohibiting the use of PPPs that has been banned by the EU on crops destined for sale in the EU (GlobalG.A.P. 2009). Such control imposes requirements on DCs, additional to those set out by EU Regulation 396/2005. The latter does not prohibit the use of banned pesticides in DCs on crops destined for the EU market. The regulation indicates that the usage of these pesticides could have been unauthorised in the EU for reasons other than public health reasons.

Consequently, imported food products containing residues from banned pesticides are allowed to enter the EU market if they meet the set MRLs.[19] Accordingly, when farmers in third world countries use unauthorised crop protection, traders can request an 'import tolerance' for the food product exported.[20] It can be argued that such a possibility reflects the contrasting climatic conditions between the EU and some DCs. This is particularly important for DCs that want to export tropical fruits that are not produced within the EU. Citing environmental concerns, the EU can ban a PPP that DCs use to destroy tropical crop-damaging pests that are not found in temperate zones.

Another example is the GlobalG.A.P. compulsory requirement from the producer or the producer's customer to conduct an annual or more frequent analysis of PPP residues in all products (GlobalG.A.P. 2007). While such a self-testing requirement by the producer is not established by the EU legislation, it is pointed out that testing of such residues is costly and cannot be avoided, even when the risk is minor and no chemical PPPs have been used (Mattson 2009, 15). Such requirements from GlobalG.A.P. are considered 'very premature' (Lee 2006, 32). They impose far higher costs for analysis on farmers who have shifted from a monocropping farming pattern to a mixed food crop system for organic production, which is currently in high demand (Mattson 2009, 15). By growing organic fresh fruits, DCs contribute considerably to biodiversity, since organic agriculture should not involve the use of toxic chemical inputs. However, it seems that GlobalG.A.P., which claims to respond to public concerns on environmental protection, favours monocropping which tends to attract less diseases and pests but causes significant damage to agri-biodiversity (Mattson 2009, 15).

GlobalG.A.P. published a revised version of the IFA standard in March 2011 that became obligatory from January 2012. The previous CPCC prohibiting the use of EU-banned PPPs has been removed from the new IFA. In addition, GlobalG.A.P. has maintained the self-testing requirement but has clarified its process. It only obliges producers who apply PPPs to assess annually the risk associated with their use in order to ensure compliance with the MRLs set by the importing country (GlobalG.A.P. 2011b). Thus, producers of organic products are exempt from this requirement. Depending on the assessment results, producers must also provide evidence of PPP residue analysis that must be done in accordance with the GlobalG.A.P. guidelines. It is clear that these requirements will help DCs to meet the legal EU MRLs. However, they still exceed EU legislation, which does not require the importing country to perform such a risk assessment. The control of MRLs must be carried out using the established national programmes of the EU Member States that import products from third countries.[21] Consequently, these strict requirements will continue to penalise users of PPPs.

12.5   THE IMPLICATIONS FOR TROPICAL FRUIT EXPORTS

It is apparent that both public and private standards pursue legitimate and well-founded objectives by seeking to ensure food safety for the public (Broberg 2009, 7). However, the MRL for pesticides is seen as a 'potentially major threat to the future development of trade' in non-traditional fruits (Henson et al. 2005, 38). It must be noted that when pesticides residues exceed EU MRLs, consignments can be detained, rejected or even destroyed by the EU Member States' authorities (Lee 2006, 24). The country or the supplier can be prohibited from the market, with a risk of a temporary or permanent ban on exports being imposed (Lee 2006, 24). DCs are also affected by the occasional changes in MRLs, which can occur to prevent violations within the EU. An example of this occurred in 2001 when the EU imposed a significant reduction in the MRL for ethephon, a pesticide generally used for de-greening pineapples (Gogoe 2001). In particular, Ghana had two shiploads of pineapples refused entry to the EU for violating the MRL value for ethephon, as it was unaware of the changes that had been made (Graffham 2006, 18). The rejected fruits met the old MRL. As such, the consignments would have been accepted if they had arrived at the EU border a few days earlier (Graffham 2006, 17). It is clear that issues arising from violations of MRLs could damage the reputation of the exporting country, the supplier and the importer. This could also affect customer confidence. Caribbean and Latin American suppliers of tropical fresh fruits may, as a consequence, lose EU market buyers and may even risk being excluded from the EU market altogether (Lee 2006, 24). With their reputation at stake, DCs willing to participate in the value chain must comply with private standards for food safety and good production practices imposed by corporate buyers. However, private standards, by imposing additional requirements, with their additional financial burden, can increase trade barriers and therefore 'decrease market size or limit the number of firms participating' (Reardon et al. 2002, 417).

In June 2005, Saint Vincent and the Grenadines raised complaints at the WTO SPS Committee meeting about the SPS requirements imposed by the then EurepGAP (now GlobalG.A.P.) for exporting bananas and various fresh fruits and vegetables to supermarkets in the United Kingdom (UK). In their view, the requirements were higher than those provided by the UK government, hence restricting international trade (WTO 2005a, 16). From the viewpoint of DCs, private standards schemes present numerous challenges to small vulnerable economies (WTO 2007a).

Since then, the WTO SPS Committee has continued the discussion about the issue of private standards in regular meetings. In addition, an ad hoc working group of 30 interested WTO Members, including the EU, was formed. A number of countries from the working group highlighted a few opportunities for trade created by private standards. They are of the view that private standards can facilitate compliance with official requirements, and help improve the quality and safety of products (WTO 2009b; 2009d). However, most WTO Members reiterate the negative impacts of private food standards on the export of their products (WTO 2009a).

In the case of GlobalG.A.P. standards, DCs point out that they are more stringent and exceed those applied by international standards such as those established by Codex,[22] which is one of the SPS's 'three sisters'[23] (Van der Meulen et al. 2008, 471). For example, DCs indicate that GlobalG.A.P. requires stricter monitoring and implementation mechanisms, and establishes lower MRLs than Codex (WTO 2009c; 2009d). In addition, DCs point out that GlobalG.A.P. standards exceed official national and import regulatory requirements for tropical fruits. For instance, they 'treat in more detail some aspects of the banana growing process from sprouting of the plant up to the stage of processing for marketing'(WTO 2009c). DCs argue that overall, private standards restrict market access to the EU for their tropical fruits 'due to the rejection of goods and the increased cost of production and export processes' (WTO 2009b). The compliance cost with GlobalG.A.P. is variable and, in some cases, double that of compliance with official standards (WTO 2009c). For example, it ranges from EUR 1550 to EUR 3600 a year for Costa Rica (WTO 2009c). This particularly affects smallholders who provide the major part of tropical fruits for exports. They often lack the necessary financial and technical resources to meet the demanding standards, or to carry out the costly conformity assessments. This has resulted in the exclusion of some smallholders from the supply chain (WTO 2009d).

The concerns raised by Saint Vincent and the Grenadines have not yet, at the time of writing, been resolved. Nevertheless, in order to deal with the identified negative effects of private SPS standards on agri-food exports, the working group has considered twelve possible actions for the SPS Committee and the WTO Members (WTO 2010). The working group invited the SPS Committee to endorse six of these proposed actions upon which the Members reached an agreement. Firstly, they proposed that a clear definition of 'SPS-related private standards' should be developed by the SPS Committee, which should then limit any discussions to these. The second action suggests that the SPS Committee and the international standards, namely Codex, the World Organization for Animal Health and the International Plant Protection Convention, exchange information about their work in the area. Thirdly, the group agreed that the Secretariat should inform the SPS Committee about relevant developments in other WTO forums linked to SPS issues. Fourthly, the working group recommends that Members communicate with the entities in their countries involved in private SPS standards. They should regularly exchange information about private SPS standards and about their own work on this issue. This action would help these private sector bodies understand the issues raised in the SPS Committee and the importance of rules established by the aforementioned international standards. The fifth action proposes that the SPS Committee works closely with the abovementioned international standards in order to 'provide further clarity on this issue and promote the use of international standards'. Lastly, it is proposed that Members exchange information related to private SPS standards, in order to improve their understanding and awareness on how 'these compare or relate to international standards and governmental regulations' (WTO 2011a). The implementation of the last proposed action has led to different opinions among the participants of the working group. Some Members, such as the EU and the United States, believe that this action should not be part of the SPS Committee discussions (WTO 2011b). Consequently, in March 2011, the SPS Committee agreed only on the first five actions. The sixth proposed action, and the other action proposals on which the working group could not reach an agreement, are still, at the time of writing, under discussion (WTO 2011b).

12.6 CONCLUSION

The EU SPS measures are important requirements for the importation of tropical fruit products from DCs. While the focus in the EU is to maintain a low level of health risks related to food consumption, the main concern generally within DCs is food security (Achterbosch et al. 2002, 6). DCs are trying to ensure food productivity in tropical climatic conditions conducive to the spread of crop pests and plant diseases. This chapter analysed the issues of exporting tropical fresh fruits to the EU market. The SPS requirements imposed by both private and public groups pose significant challenges for DCs. However, it is clear from the discussions in the WTO SPS Committee that the increasing role of private standards in international trade is the main issue for DCs and it has thus become a top priority for DCs. The system of rules imposed by GlobalG.A.P. is widely criticised by DCs who argue that they exceed official import requirements. In the case of pesticides use and residues, GlobalG.A.P. complements public controls by imposing higher and wider requirements than EU legislation. Implementing these requirements creates excessive financial costs for producers and exporters who lack the administrative, technical, financial and scientific capacity (Jaffee et al. 2004, 3). Hence, private standards are significant barriers to DCs' exports and undermine their competitive position.

Since 2005, the WTO SPS Committee has become an important forum for DCs to discuss these issues. Arguably, the substantial amount of work undertaken in the SPS Committee and the ad hoc working group has influenced the private sectors. In 2011, GlobalG.A.P. issued a new IFA amending the strict requirements concerning MRLs. However, the organisation raises a reminder that while it does not replace current EU legislation, it sets a minimum level of compliance in case of inexistent legislation or where existing laws are not strict enough (GlobalG.A.P. 2011a). Accordingly, the new pesticide MRLs requirements set by GlobalG.A.P. remain stricter than EU legislation.

DCs have a comparative advantage in producing tropical fruits, and improving their food safety performance should, therefore, be prioritised. In order to comply with private standards they will need focused improvements in their industry standards, with appropriate investment and key staff training. However, these improvements need to be made with the support of governmental regulatory reforms. These actions will help producers and exporters in DCs to meet the required standards and improve the safety and quality of their products. In the long term, this should help the EU private sector and improve the level of consumer trust in the ability of DCs to produce safe food that meets both SPS regulations and standards. Consequently, DCs' ability to comply with complex and costly standards will depend on the strategic decisions made by their governments and their ability to obtain strategic investment funds, as well as the actions adopted by the WTO.

NOTES

1. Article 288 TFEU.
2. Definition provided by the WTO in Annex 1, para 2 of the Agreement on Technical Barriers to Trade.
3. Dichlorodiphenyltrichloroethane.
4. Article 1(1) of Regulation (EC) No 1107/2009.
5. Article 1(2) of Regulation No 1107/2009.
6. Article 1(3) of Regulation No 1107/2009.
7. Preamble 8 of Regulation No 1107/2009.
8. Article 28 of Regulation No 1107/2009.
9. Regulation No 396/2005.
10. Article 3 (2)(d) of Regulation No 396/2005.
11. Article 3 (2)(d) of Regulation No 396/2005.
12. Article 3 (2)(d) of Regulation No 396/2005.
13. Article 22(1) of Regulation No 396/2005.
14. Recital 34 Regulation (EC) No 178/2002.
15. Article 18(1)(b) of Regulation (EC) No 396/2005.
16. Article 18 of Regulation No 396/2005.
17. Established under Article 50 of Regulation (EC) 178/2002.
18. Euro-Retailer Produce Working Group.
19. Article 3(g) of Regulation No 396/2005.
20. Article 3(g) of Regulation No 396/2005 states that 'import tolerance' means an MRL set for imported products to meet the needs of international trade.
21. Article 26 of Regulation No 396/2005.
22. Codex is a set of rules created in the 1960s by the World Health Organisation and the Food Agricultural Organisation, in order to ensure consumer's health and fair practices in international food trade.
23. The other two being the International Office of Epizootics, for animal health and zoonoses, and the International Plant Protection Convention, for plant health.

REFERENCES

Achterbosch, T. and F. Van Tongeren (2002), 'Food safety measures and developing countries: literature overview', LEI Agricultural Economics Research Institute, Working Paper, March 2002.

Broberg, M. (2009), 'European food safety regulation and the developing countries: regulatory problems and possibilities', DIIS Working Paper.

Carvalho, F.P. (2006), 'Agriculture, pesticides, food security and food safety', *Environmental Science and Policy*, 9, 685–692.

Consolidated versions of the Treaty on European Union and the Treaty on the Functioning of the European Union, OJ C 83 of 30.3.2010.

Department for International Development (2001), 'Standards as barriers to trade: issues for development', DFID Background Briefing, London: Department for International Development.

Ecobichon, D.J. (2001), 'Pesticide use in developing countries', *Toxicology*, 160, 27–33.

European Commission White Paper (2005), 'Opening the door to development: developing country access to EU markets 1999–2003', Brussels, 23 May.

Food and Agricultural Organization of the United Nations (FAO), 'Food safety and quality: "fresh fruits and vegetables"'. Online. Available from: http://www.fao.org/ag/agn/agns/foodproducts_fresh_en.asp. (Accessed 26/08/2011).

Food and Agricultural Organization of the United Nations (FAO) (2003), 'Medium-term prospects for agricultural commodities, projections to the year 2010', Rome: FAO. Online. Available from: http://www.fao.org/docrep/006/y5143e/y5143e1a.htm (Accessed 26/08/2011).

Fulponi, L. (2006), 'Private voluntary standards in the food system: the perspective of major retailers in OECD countries', *Food Policy*, 31, 1–13.

GlobalG.A.P. (2007), 'Control points and compliance criteria – integrated farm assurance, fruits and vegetables'.

GlobalG.A.P. (2009), 'Control points and compliance criteria – integrated farm assurance, crops base'.

GlobalG.A.P. (2011a), 'General regulations: integrated farm assurance introduction', GlobalG.A.P. website. Online. Available from: http://www.globalgap.org/cms/front_content.php?idcat=3. (Accessed 15/05/2010).

GlobalG.A.P. (2011b), 'Control points and compliance criteria – integrated farm assurance, crops base'.

Gogoe, S., A. Dekpor and S. Williamson (2001), 'Prickly issues for pineapple pesticides', *Journal of Pesticide Action Network UK*, Pesticide News No. 54, 4–5. Online. Available from: http://www.pan-uk.org/pestnews/Issue/pn54/pn54p4.htm (accessed 12/12/2010).

Graffham, A. (2006), 'EU legal requirements for imports of fruits and vegetables (a suppliers guide)', *Fresh Insights* no. 1, DFID/IIED/NRI.

Havinga, T. (2006), 'Private regulation of food safety by supermarkets', *Law & Policy*, 28, 515–533.

Henson, S. and S. Jaffee (2005), 'Jamaica's trade in ethnic foods and other niche products: the impact of food safety and plant health standards', The International Bank for Reconstruction and Development/The World Bank.

Henson, S. and T. Reardon (2005), 'Private agri-food standards: implications for food policy and the agri-food system', *Food Policy*, 30, 241–253.

Jaffee, S. and S. Henson (2004), 'Standards and agro-food exports from developing countries: rebalancing the debate', World Bank Policy Research Working Paper 3348, June 2004.

Jaffee, S. and O. Masakure (2005), 'Strategic use of private standards to enhance international competitiveness: vegetable exports from Kenya and elsewhere', *Food Policy*, 30, 316–333.

Lee, G.C.-H. (2006), *Private Food Standards and their Impacts on Developing Countries*, Brussels: European Commission, DG Trade Unit G2.

Mattson, E. (2009), *Comparative Study on the GLOBALG.A.P. Fruit and Vegetables Standard and the EU Organic Agriculture Regulation*, Geneva: UNCTAD.

Perry, S. (2008), 'Tropical and diversification products, strategic options for developing countries', Issue paper No. 11, ICTSD Programme on Agricultural Trade and Sustainable Development.

Pesticides Action Network UK (1998), 'Pesticide residues in food', Pest management note n° 8, November 1998.

Rapid Alert System for Food and Feed (2009), *Annual Report 2009*.

Reardon, T. and E. Farina (2002), 'The rise of private food quality and safety standards: illustrations from Brazil', *International Food and Agribusiness Management Review*, 4, 413–421.

Regulation (EC) No 178/2002 of the European Parliament and of the Council of 28 January 2002 laying down the general principles and requirements of food law, establishing the European Food Safety Authority and laying down procedures in matters of food safety, OJ L 31, 1.02.2002.

Regulation (EC) No 396/2005 of the European Parliament and of the Council of 23 February 2005 on maximum residue levels of pesticides in or on food and feed of plant and animal origin and amending Council Directive 91/414/EEC, OJ L 70, 16.3.2005.

Regulation (EC) No 1107/2009 of the European Parliament and of the Council of 21 October 2009 concerning the placing of plant protection on the market and repealing Council Directives 79/117/EEC and 91/414/EEC, OJ L, 24.11.2009.

Roberts, D. and L. Unnevehr (2005), 'Resolving trade disputes arising from trends in food safety regulation: the role of the multilateral governance framework', *World Trade Review*, 4, 469–497.

Shaw, I., and R. Vannoort (2002), 'Pesticides', in D.H. Watson (ed.), *Food Chemical Safety, Vol 1: Contaminants*, Cambridge: Woodhead Publishing Ltd.

UNCTAD (2007), 'Food Safety and Environmental Requirements in Export Markets – Friend or Foe for Producers of Fruit and Vegetables in Asian Developing Countries?', UNCTAD/DITC/TED/2006/8, United Nations Publication.

Van der Meulen, B. and M. Van der Velde (2008), *European Food Law Handbook*, Wageningen: Wageningen Academic Publishers.

WTO (2005a), Meeting held on 29–30 June 2005, G/SPS/R/37/Rev.1, 18 August.

WTO (2005b), 'Questions and answers on the procedure to obtain import tolerances and the inclusion of active substances for plant protection uses in the European Communities list', Communication from the European Communities, G/SPS/GEN/557, 29 March.

WTO (2007a), 'Private industry standards', Communication from Saint Vincent and the Grenadines, G/SPS/GEN/766, 28 February.

WTO (2007b), 'Private voluntary standards and developing countries market access: preliminary results', Communication from OECD, G/SPS/GEN/763, 27 February.

WTO (2009a), 'Effects of SPS-related private standards – compilation of replies', G/SPS/GEN/932/Rev.1, 10 December.

WTO (2009b), 'Questionnaire on SPS-related private standards: Dominican Republic', 24 April.

WTO (2009c) 'Questionnaire on SPS-related private standards: Costa Rica', 24 April.

WTO (2009d) 'Questionnaire on SPS-related private standards: Colombia', 20 February.

WTO (2010), 'Possible actions for the SPS committee regarding SPS-related private standards', G/SPS/W/247/Rev.3, 11 October.

WTO (2011a), 'Report of the ad hoc working group on SPS-related private standards to the SPS Committee', G/SPS/W/256, 3 March.

WTO (2011b), 'Summary of the meeting of 30–31 March 2011', G/SPS/R/62, 27 May.

Yudin, R.C. and K.R. Schneider (2008), 'European Food Safety Certification – The "GlobalG.A.P." Standard and its Accredited Certification Program', FSHN 0801, Institute of Food and Agricultural Sciences (IFAS), Gainesville: University of Florida.

13. The meta-governance of co-regulation: Safeguarding the quality of Dutch eggs

Haiko van der Voort

13.1 INTRODUCTION

In times of budget cuts and 'regulatory governance' philosophies, public regulators keep a keen eye on private systems, in an attempt to safeguard the quality and safety of products.

This may explain the popularity of co-regulation. The concept encompasses a variety of arrangements in which regulations are specified, administered and enforced by a combination of the state and the regulated organizations (Bartle and Vass 2005; Garcia Martinez et al. 2007; 2013). Relying on these private systems would probably save valuable inspection capacity and maintain quality and safety at an acceptable level.

Co-regulation also requires many coordination efforts between government, industry and third parties. Broadly defined, they serve common values (such as safety, quality, sustainability), but with different purposes and methods. The literature on (self-)regulation describes tensions between public regulators ('government') on the one hand and private regulatees ('self-regulating industry') on the other. Much of this literature looks at coordination from a public perspective. It seems to aim at making self-regulation suitable for government purposes. The authors find plenty of incompatibilities. Industry would tend to serve its own interests rather than public values (Gunningham and Rees 1997; Grabosky 1995; Bartle and Vass 2005; Hutter 2006), and an emphasis on efficiency would compromize the effectiveness of self-regulation (Rametsteiner and Simula 2002). A lack of commitment would result in symbolic self-regulation (King and Lenox 2000; O'Rourke 2003; Power 2003; De Marzo et al. 2005).

The incompatibilities will result in a dynamic game between the actors involved. However, literature on the dynamics of co-regulation is surprisingly rare (examples are Howlett and Rayner 2004; Barkay 2009). In this chapter, the dynamics of co-regulation are analysed by using the well-known concepts of 'governance' and 'meta-governance'. 'Governance' refers to the dynamic game of co-regulation, while 'meta-governance' refers to how the rules of such a game are created.

The main question is how introducing this 'metalevel' in an analysis may help in understanding the dynamics of co-regulation. This question will be addressed using a case study of a specific co-regulation arrangement for maintaining the quality of Dutch eggs. In the next section, a typology of theoretical governance approaches will be provided. In section 13.3 two interpretations of 'meta-governance' will be given. The Dutch eggs case will be discussed in sections 13.4, 13.5 and 13.6. The chapter concludes with a reflection on this co-regulation effort and on the way the concept of meta-governance has enriched our understanding (section 13.7).

13.2   CO-REGULATION AS GOVERNANCE

Much of the literature on regulation distinguishes 'government' and 'industry'. Government, then, is assumed to be the regulator, and industry the regulated.

13.2.1   Co-Regulation: Three Domains of Actors

However, in the case of co-regulation, public regulators are not the only organizations defining standards for the 'industries'. The industry is also defining standards for themselves. Moreover, lots of other organizations, such as banks, insurance companies, or NGOs are also doing the same thing, but in a different way (Gunningham and Grabosky 1998; Hutter 2006). In some cases, these third parties are explicitly invited to participate in co-regulation. A common form of this is 'third party certification', where certification bodies do inspection work according to schemes co-written by government and industry, but also in accordance with the standards of accreditation bodies. Co-regulation in this way involves three categories of actors who have a specific regulatory role. Government has legal authority to regulate, the industry has taken the initiative to regulate itself, and the certification- and accreditation-bodies – referred to as private regulators[1] – are hired by the regulated industry to actually perform the inspections. They have their own methodology that is institutionalized in international standards and can be seen as the terms for providing their services (i.e. Barnett and Finnemore 2004; Schepel 2005). In co-regulation the actors involved coordinate their inspection activities – such as monitoring and sanctioning – to safeguard shared values, like safety and quality. Figure 13.1 shows my idea of co-regulation.

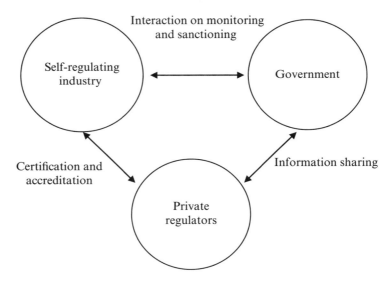

Figure 13.1   Co-regulation

Government and industries agree to coordinate their inspection activities. The private regulators are involved through a contract with the regulated industries to offer their services. In some cases, government and private regulators agree to share the information that results from their activities.

Figure 13.1 does not represent actors, but categories (or 'domains') of actors with specific interests, roles and responsibilities regarding regulation. Government (in this context) has regulation as their legal task, the (self-regulatory) industry has instrumental motives for its (self-)regulation, whereas the private regulators have a commercial interest. These private regulators have their own distinct technical standards for their inspections which may differ from those of the other actors, and to which I will refer later in this chapter.

13.2.2 Co-regulation as Governance

Co-regulation requires interaction between government, industry and private regulators. All domains can be seen as relatively autonomous rule systems. Government develops and enforces laws and regulations, on the basis of a democratic system. Private regulators develop and use rules for standardization, on the basis of international bargaining processes between industries and (sometimes) governments. Self-regulating industries develop their rules based on bargaining processes within their own ranks. So the different rules, no matter in which domain they are developed, are the results of heavy investments in procedures and bargaining processes. The institutional settings in which these investments are made differ per domain. Despite these differences, they all have their source of legitimacy. This makes it hard to resolve conflicts between rules of different domains.

This perspective on co-regulation fits the current writings on 'governance'. 'Governance' reflects the insight that (government) policy is made and implemented in horizontal settings: complex sets of interactions between mutually dependent but relatively autonomous public and private parties. Steering by a single actor is hard in this context. This is mainly due to the variety of actors, their mutual dependencies, and the dynamics of the context in which steering happens (Koppenjan et al. 2009; De Bruijn and Ten Heuvelhof 2008). Because of these complicating factors, steering is best understood as a variety of steering efforts by various actors, which is referred to as 'governance' (Kooiman 1993; Pierre 2000). The increased acknowledgement of the complicating factors for steering is often presented as a shift from 'government' to 'governance'. 'Government', then, refers to a (public) hierarchical actor who has exclusive steering abilities, while 'governance' stresses patterns of steering efforts by various actors. This is useful when studying co-regulation, as 'governance' allows for various perspectives on cooperation between public and private parties. Co-regulation is not just about the use of private quality systems by government, but also cooperation with government by private parties.

The sets of actors involved in 'governance' are often referred to as 'governance networks' (Kooiman 2003; Kooiman and Jentoft 2009) or 'regulatory networks' (Parker and Nielsen 2009). Networks stress variety and interdependence between actors and imply rules of mutual adjustment and proportionality. These networks may cut across existing territorial, administrative and functional boundaries (Castells 1996; Rhodes 1997; Kickert, Klijn and Koppenjan 1997).[2]

Applying this concept to my conception of co-regulation is helpful because both governance and co-regulation imply horizontal interaction. Framing co-regulatory interactions as governance, however, doesn't contribute much to an explanation of the dynamics of co-regulation. Yes, there are interaction and steering efforts all over the place. However, they tend to be too fluent to grasp. To understand dynamics we need to find patterns in interaction. For this, a look at the organization of these interactions rather than the interactions themselves may be helpful. However, this organization is a subject of interaction between the different domains itself. This way, an analysis of the dynamics of co-regulation should be done at some meta-level (interactions on interactions). This could be achieved with the help of the concept 'meta-governance'.

13.3   THE DYNAMICS OF CO-REGULATION: META-GOVERNANCE?

Co-regulation implies interactions between public and private regulators, which will tend to happen on a regular basis. In order to understand the dynamics of co-regulation, one needs to discuss how these interaction-patterns are influenced. The concept of 'meta-governance' might help for this. This concept is referred to as the 'governance of governance' (Jessop 2002, 2004). I distinguish two schools of 'meta-governance'.

13.3.1   Meta-Governance as Design

Some scholars describe meta-governance as deliberate design. They acknowledge complexities of horizontal interaction, such as the lack of authority of a single actor to impose their will on others. They see a way out in 'meta-governance' as the deliberate (re)design of rules, standards and habits of actors (Sörensen and Torfing 2007, 175; Jessop 2003; Klijn and Edelenbos 2007). As such, they see meta-governance as a form of institutional design. This way 'design' implies active and deliberate meta-governance, applied to a specific and definable 'governance network'. Triantafillou (2007) speaks in this connection of 'network formation'. A specific form of institutional design is a design of an interaction process between (public and private) actors about a specific problem. This is called 'process architecture' or 'process design' (De Bruijn et al. 2002; Klijn and Edelenbos 2007). An example of institutional design is the (ill-fated) 'roadmap to peace' about the Israeli-Palestinian conflicts. It was proposed in 2005 by outside authorities (the United States, the European Union, Russia and the United Nations) and contains rules for interaction between the countries involved. The majority of the rules are not about the negotiations themselves, but the way the negotiations should be organized, including, for instance, an agenda and rules about closure of decision making.

13.3.2   Meta-Governance as an Emergent Phenomenon

Other scholars see meta-governors as more involved in governance processes. They participate, more than designers, in the interactions themselves. That is why Sörensen and Torfing (2007, 181) distinguish hands-off (designing) and hands-on (participating) types of meta-governance. Examples of this hands-on type are formulating (public) policy, knowledge sharing, and providing (organizational) capacity (Whitehead 2003; Sörensen and Torfing 2007, 176).

This 'meta-governance as an emergent phenomenon' suggests a more horizontal relation between meta-governors and other actors. Some even do not define a specific meta-governor (for example Kooiman and Jentoft 2009). O'Toole (2007) writes:

> Public authorities may not be the only ones working at the meta-level. In fact, it becomes an empirical question as to whether public authorities are at all involved at the meta-level; an alternative might be that other social actors sometimes set the basic rules of the game that ultimately (at another level of action) produces outputs and outcomes.

An important suggestion from this quote is that there may be several meta-governors. This in turn suggests that meta-governance does not have to be intentional. It may be that the outcome of meta-governance cannot be linked to the purposes of a single actor, but may be a result of several interventions from several actors who sometimes operate at some 'meta-level'. In this way, meta-governance is an emergent, not a deliberate, activity. The current European Union, for example, is not a result of a deliberate design. Its origin may be a design, but in the course of time fundamental changes in aims and the number of member states took place. These changes are about the organization of interaction among member states. They are the result of bargaining in a more horizontal context, without an explicit meta-governor.

There is another issue about the deliberate school. Until now, the ideas on meta-governance suggest a relatively well-determinable 'governance-system'. This makes it possible to change systems deliberately. An important criticism of this literature is that it is rather deterministic. It is quite optimistic about the ability to steer social interaction (Kelly 2006), so it is not so much about the 'governance' of 'governance', as well as about the 'government' of 'governance'. Several – mainly post-modernist – thinkers have tried to avoid this supposed pitfall. They assume 'self referentiality', the unavoidability that actors define the world – and its institutions – and their own place in it themselves (see for instance Foucault 1991; Jessop 2003; Dean 2010). This way any actor may frame the governance system in its own way. There is no authoritative central definition of a governance system. Definitions are dispersed over the system, as are definitions of interventions in the system.

The two perspectives on meta-governance are summarized in table 13.1. It takes the different ideas on meta-governance to extremes. I call them 'government of governance', which stands for intentionally and

Table 13.1   Two perspectives on meta-governance

	Design: 'government of governance'	Emergent: 'governance of governance'
Meta-governor	One actor	More actors
Meta-governance interventions	Deliberate	Emergent
Framing governance system	Centric	Dispersed

holistically regulated interactions, and 'governance of governance', which are interaction patterns determining interaction patterns. The first suggests some design of governance systems, the latter management efforts within governance systems.[3]

As 'governance' of co-regulation is framed as the interactions between government, self-regulatory industries and private regulators, 'meta-governance' is the 'governance' of these interactions. It deals with organization of co-regulation. The discussion on 'meta-governance' questions the dynamics of co-regulation quite explicitly. It questions whether the organization is made up by some 'meta-governor' or whether it is an emerging phenomenon.

13.4   SAFEGUARDING THE QUALITY OF EGGS BY CO-REGULATION: A DUTCH STORY

In order to answer the main question, namely how meta-governance may help us understand dynamics of co-regulation, a case study of a specific co-regulation effort was conducted. The information for the case study is taken from a desk study and 22 semi-structured interviews with managers and inspectors from government, industry, and private regulators.

The case is an example of a deliberate attempt at institutional design by the government, using a centric frame of the governance system. It was the intention to 'govern governance'. I was in particular interested in the effects of the process on the design-as-intended and the design-as-realized. Who was the governor after all? Whose interventions mattered and which definition was dominant?

I start with a brief description of the three domains involved, followed by a description of 'governance' as intended according to the design. Subsequently, I describe the process as it has been 'running' until now.

This process comprises both the introduction of the design and the design-in-action.

The policy trend of involving all kinds of self-regulation efforts in regulatory arrangements hasn't bypassed the Netherlands. Following an authoritative policy vision in 2005,[4] all Dutch ministries and inspectorates have formulated strategic plans to be more selective in their regulatory efforts, conduct risk analyses, and investigate whether private self-regulatory programmes could be an input for such risk analyses. The main goals are the reduction of the regulatory burden for industries and to increase the efficiency of regulation, by targeting, among others, regulatory efforts aimed at the 'bad apples'.

All ministries have developed strategies in their own style. The Dutch Ministry of Agriculture has adopted 'Toezicht op Controle' ('Oversight of Controls', TOC from now on), a policy framework that outlines institutional requirements for cooperation with industries and their self-regulatory bodies.[5]

The policy framework is quite an elaborative document. It attempts to bring order in the relations and interactions between public and private inspectorates and industry. It stresses the final responsibility of government for the quality of regulation and oversight and the extra efforts this implies for industries, like necessary coordination with public and private inspectorates and auditors (TOC, p.13). Moreover, the government formulates requirements for the organization and functioning of the bodies that carry out the audits (TOC, p.8).

Once the TOC programme was established, the ministry tried to stimulate sectors to develop cooperation modes on the basis of it. The first sector that did so was the poultry sector. The potential reduction of inspections would save considerable time and money for the industry. The already existing privately owned quality system *IKB ei*[6] would be suitable for TOC.

13.5 ABOUT A SIMPLE EGG: THREE DOMAINS

The key players in this regulatory effort are government, industry, and private regulators. They have their own roles and are committed to different rules.

13.5.1 Industry: 1200 Farmers Represented in Public-Private Bodies

Within the value chain, the poultry farmers buy the chickens and sell their eggs to trading companies. These poultry farms are usually relatively small companies. They are organized in two associations: the NOP (Dutch poultry farmers' organization) and the NVP (Dutch poultry farmers' labour union). The entire chain is represented in the *Productschap voor Pluimveehouders en Eieren* (Commodity Board for Poultry Farmers and Eggs; PPE). This is a hybrid form of the public and the private. It has public regulatory authority for technical issues, such as the registration of chickens and the management of the salmonella bacteria problem. At the same time, because of its unique position amidst the entire chain, it tends to represent the industry in discussions with government.

The poultry sector has its own voluntary arrangement: IKB ei. This is managed by the PPE. It has its own third party certification system to safeguard the quality of eggs and animal welfare. Around 800 out of 1200 companies use this system. The international market is a major incentive to adopt the quality system, for a considerable amount of Dutch eggs are exported. An internationally recognized quality system is vital for future sales.

13.5.2   Government: Two Ministries, Three Inspectorates

Most of the public regulations on the sector are about hygiene in the production process and the products, animal welfare, and ensuring that the correct information is provided on the eggs (using a stamp). Several inspectorates are involved in enforcing these regulations.

The *Algemene Inspectie Dienst* (General Inspection Service; AID) selectively controls for animal welfare. The standards for these inspections are provided by the Dutch *Legkippenbesluit 2003*. The inspections are paid for by the government. The AID has the authority to apply criminal law in case of serious violations.

The *Voedsel en Waren Autoriteit* (Food and Consumer Product Safety Authority, VWA) provides certificates for exporting eggs and pays random inspection visits to every company that wants to export its products. The VWA also mandates inspection authorities for hygiene standards to the *Controlebureau voor Pluimvee, Eieren en Eiproducten* (Inspection Office for Poultry, Eggs and Egg Products; CPE).[7]

The CPE controls several issues, mandated by government. The standards are derived from national regulations on hygiene and European directives.[8] The latter are concerned with stamping the eggs. The stamp encodes the housing system of the chickens (e.g. their space and treatment), the country and the stable the eggs come from, and the production date of the egg. Inspections by the CPE are paid for by the inspectees, in accordance with Dutch guidelines for inspections by semi-public bodies.[9]

13.5.3 Private Regulators: Two Certification Bodies and an Accreditation Body

Quality standards are also provided by a 'third party certification system' – the private regulator – comprised of two certification bodies and the national accreditation body RvA (Accreditation Council), assigned by the Dutch government. The quality system, its schemes and the certification bodies are all accredited by the RvA, applying recognized international standards. IKB ei strives for accreditation for product certification (NEN EN45011 Guide 65).

The standards the RvA uses for product certification concern methodological issues, such as the way a certification body can measure quality aspects and whether and how these methods are written down in schemes. The RvA also sets standards for the interaction between actors. They usually deal with the organization of the quality system, as follows:

1. standards should be administered by a Board of Experts, wherein the sector is represented;
2. inspection and assessment should be institutionally separated; and
3. inspection and judgement should be done by independent certification bodies, which operate in a market setting.

Certification bodies announce their audit visits beforehand and get paid by the auditees, which are in fact their customers. Because the number of farmers in the poultry sector is limited, there are only two certification bodies.

The private regulators try to provide added value to the regulators, as the regulators are their customers. The accreditation body serves this market by providing and applying international standards, and is paid for these services. This way the accreditation body has a monopoly, for it is the only organization allowed to perform these activities.[10]

13.6 TOC IN ACTION: THE DYNAMICS OF CO-REGULATION

Now that the three domains have been explained and the scene for 'governance' has been set, it is time to see how the model works in practice. In this section I describe the dynamics of the adoption and execution of TOC.

13.6.1   TOC in Practice

The poultry sector applied for a TOC arrangement after the system has been approved. The main consequences of application of TOC to IKB ei are threefold:

1. The CPE and AID stop inspecting for most of the regulations they are supposed to enforce. Those regulatory standards are included in the IKB ei scheme. Certification bodies also include these regulatory standards in their audits. So certification bodies inspect farmers using public standards. They share their findings with public inspectorates. Public regulators retain responsibility for the enforcement of laws and regulations. Public inspectorates continue to inspect companies that are not associated with IKB ei.
2. There are extra conditions for certification bodies, some of them anticipating EN45011 accreditation. There is, for example, a standard for the amount of time an audit visit should take, in order to prevent audits from being rushed.
3. The CPE and AID conduct verification audits for the poultry farmers to check whether the certificates have been awarded correctly.

Elaborating TOC further in an arrangement has been quite a challenge. It took place in a period between the original issue of TOC in 2005 and the introduction of TOC in the sector on 1 January 2008. The Ministry of Agriculture has managed this process. All actors mentioned have been involved. They faced some issues that hide typical conflicts between the domains as mentioned above. I selected three key issues below.

13.6.2   Issue 1. Addition of Unannounced Inspections: Regulators versus Industry

The recognised system between clients and suppliers is for the certification bodies to announce the audits. The principle of announced audits, however, conflicts with practices of the inspectorates AID and CPE. Their philosophy is that poultry farmers should be prevented from preparing for inspections. To facilitate this, the CPE has insisted on unannounced inspections, backed by European regulations.[11]

At the instigation of the Ministry of Agriculture, the industry therefore requires certification bodies to audit an extra 50 per cent of their client base unannounced. The costs of these extra audits are included in the contributions to IKB ei, which are increasing accordingly. This leaves the poultry farmers in doubt as to whether TOC is actually in their best interests. One interviewee remarked: 'I have always resisted this. Either "they" [the government, HV] trust us or they do not. If they don't, TOC should not be adopted (interview industry).'

In the first instance the industry did not seem to be very keen to initiate such unannounced audits. In 2008, the certification bodies did not receive the requests for unannounced audits until November, and in 2009 not until July. In 2010, while awaiting an evaluation of TOC and IKB ei by the Ministry, the number of unannounced audits was unilaterally reduced by the industry representatives.

13.6.3   Issue 2. The Use of Fines as Sanctioning Instruments: Public versus Private Regulators

Just before the introduction of TOC, self-regulation became an issue in the media. The media paid a lot of attention to the quality of self-regulatory regimes within the agriculture sector. In his reaction, the Minister planned to use fines to enforce some laws on animal welfare.[12] This step indicated that there was not much political support for trusting private quality systems. The difficulty was that the instruments available to private inspectors were either too lax (i.e. revisiting) or too harsh (revocation of a certificate). There would be little incentive for private inspectors to withdraw a certificate where the violation of regulations was not too serious. The use of fines would empower inspections, because fines are less severe than revocation but more serious than revisiting. The ministry was sensitive to this new political sentiment and included the fine in the TOC arrangement. However, who would enforce these fines? Following the TOC philosophy, the self-regulating industry should do this, based on information provided by the certification bodies.

The sector did not support the use of fines. IKB ei is a voluntary arrangement and the sector was particularly concerned that IKB ei members would be at a disadvantage compared to non-members.

> The fine is problematic. We can fine immediately, while governmental sanctions are very slow, if they get enforced anyway. Sometimes fines don't make it to the farmer's bank account. They get stuck in the bureaucratic administrative processes (interview industry).

This suggests that the use of fines by the private industry would be quicker and more reliable than state fines. The members of IKB ei fear that the 'tit-for-tat' effect of fines would alienate farmers from their association and that they would try to find buyers without having to fulfil the quality rules of IKB ei, which could weaken the reputation of Dutch eggs.

The certification and accreditation bodies were also fierce opponents of the use of fines, for different reasons. They were reluctant to do more than specify whether a scheme or organization is conforming to private regulations or not, for this is their raison d'être.

> It is one of the accreditation requirements that we as certifying body can do our job only with the aim to tell what is. Not more. The addition of enforcement tasks would be like 'I have told what is, and now I fine you'. That's absolutely not allowed in the accreditation world (interview private regulator).

The RvA labelled the fine as 'highly unusual' in 2009 and 'unacceptable' in 2010. It suggested not accrediting IKB ei for product certification (EN45011) if the fine was included. A fine would be too alien to the roles and tasks of a certification body.

> If the fine would be implemented, the certification bodies would become some kind of collecting agent. They are not organized for such a task. This implies just too many requirements that are non-typical to certification bodies (interview private regulator).

These non-typical requirements could lead to a drop in quality for the audits, because if the consequences of the audit reports was an immediate fine, the certifiers could be tempted to mitigate their audit reports and thus serve the client by doing so. Note that the farmers are still the certifier's customers that pay for their services.

Therefore, an odd situation has emerged, in that the RvA might not accredit IKB ei. This would threaten the international reputation of IKB ei. At the same time TOC (instigated by government) requires accreditation. TOC and the political wish to include the possible imposition of fines seem incompatible. The sector feels supported by the RvA in its resistance to the fine and therefore deleted corresponding provisions from the IKB ei scheme unilaterally.

13.6.4   Issue 3. Verification Audits: Public versus Private Regulators

TOC requires the CPE and AID to conduct verification audits. They do these audits on site at the farms, with the purpose of auditing the jobs that the certification bodies have already done. If the farmer has a certificate, but still violates the norm, this will be reported as a non-conformity by the certification body.

In the first year, 15 per cent of the farmers would receive a verification audit.

By July 2008, the CPE has found non-conformities and claimed that this proved the necessity for these verification audits. The PPE, together with certification bodies, did not agree. They suggested that the CPE had an interest in finding non-conformities, because the certification bodies do the jobs CPE used to do. In this way, TOC, is damaging CPE financially. This would provide incentives to CPE to find non-conformities to discredit TOC.

The verification audits are seen as a direct threat to TOC. The sector finds the percentage of 15 per cent too high. If it were to rise further, the advantage of TOC would be eroded. The attractiveness of TOC for them was that it would reduce the amount of audits.

Certification bodies are confronted with multiple principles. They see the RvA as their auditor and show little tolerance for other organizations meddling with how they do their jobs.

> The RvA audits us. We are 17020-accredited and now want to get accredited for EN45011, so the RvA tells us whether the system works well or not, whether we are independent enough, whether our employees are qualified enough, or whether there are enough auditors. We don't want the AID to do this job over again. (. . .) We want to meet 45011-requirements and keep the AID out or not meet 45011-requirements and get us audited by AID for a day. Otherwise we would face tensions between the findings of RvA and AID (interview private regulator).

The CPE states that it has full responsibility for auditing certification bodies as long as they are not EN45011 accredited.

As part of the agreement the ministry will evaluate TOC. Until the time the evaluation has been completed, the ministry and the sector (more specifically PPE) has agreed to share the costs of verification audits. That's a bit ironic, for the TOC philosophy was that the industry would take their own responsibility and government would retreat, but payment of verification audits by government suggests at least some government responsibility for the private quality system.

13.7 CONCLUSION: THE DYNAMICS OF CO-REGULATION

My main question was how introducing a 'metalevel' of governance might help in understanding the dynamics of co-regulation. Two meta-governance perspectives have been presented. I will answer the main question by framing the changes affected by TOC from both perspectives.

13.7.1   TOC as a Design: Government of Governance

The application of TOC to IKB ei meant a rendezvous between public inspections and private quality systems. This cooperation was prepared carefully and codified in an arrangement. Hence TOC is a good example of institutional design. After the design was completed, the poultry sector applied for its adoption. During the elaboration of the arrangement and its implementation, the three domains (government, industry and certification and accreditation bodies) met frequently and intensively. These 'meetings' were highly structured by the 'deliberate' character of TOC.

Coordination of activities between inspectorates and auditors was specified in the arrangement and carried out accordingly. In formal terms, this was it. The 'meta process' was the development of TOC and its application to IKB ei, that is, to the governance of the quality system.

The participants in this development, coordinated by the Ministry of Agriculture, operated at a 'meta-level'. They developed the institutional design according to the way they perceived governance. After finishing the design, the designers can leave governance as it is. Their job is done. Continuation of the governance processes as designed depends on formal evaluations. Currently, TOC is evaluated by involved actors, which will eventually result in a decision as to whether to continue or not.

13.7.2   TOC as an Emergent Phenomenon: Governance of Governance

This case is a good example of institutional design. However, the confrontations between government and the two other domains show that many of the interactions and their results were unforeseen. The ministry assumed the 'meta-level' intentionally and explicitly, but often had to tolerate other actors climbing and descending the meta-chair. Their interventions determined the actual execution of the arrangement significantly. Examples are the controversies over the use of fines, the requirements for EN45011, and the verification audits. They indicate that TOC has not been completed as intended. There is no accreditation yet and there is an ongoing discussion about the necessity of unannounced audits and verification audits. It is questionable whether the design will ever be finished.

It is hard to pinpoint the key topics on a meta-level and when and where they are decided upon. (This might only be possible for a scholar or evaluator to do, with hindsight.) That is because they are about issues and interventions, which subsequently had a strong effect on cooperation between inspectorates and auditors. The outcomes of these discussions, e.g. regarding the use of fines, resulted in a structural change to the interactions. Also individual strategies, such as the CPE trying to expand its role as verifier, may have consequences on a 'meta'-level. It could, for example, provide incentives to other actors to stop supporting TOC.

So every actor can make 'meta-interventions' at any moment, whether intentionally or not. The purposes for meta-governance interventions are not that evident anyway. The way actors value regulation and inspections may vary per domain. Hence, there is no central idea for the optimization of meta-governance, because it is not clear which goals would guide such optimizations.

From this perspective actors enter and leave the meta-level. Interaction is a continuous process. It is heavily influenced by the designers, but not in a definitive way. This implies that there is no formal beginning or end of meta-governance, as implied by the perspective of institutional design.

13.7.3   Discussion: A Shift from 'Government of Governance' to 'Governance of Governance'?

The answer to the main question is 'yes, introducing a meta-level has helped in the understanding of the dynamics of co-regulation'. Still, the conclusions are a bit schizophrenic: two perspectives on meta-governance have resulted in two explanations of dynamics of co-regulation. What can we learn about meta-governance, when we apply it to a specific case of co-regulation?

It seems that the explanatory value of the second model of meta-governance (governance of governance) is higher than that of the first model, at least for this case. The perception of the Ministry of Agriculture is illustrated in the left column of Table 13.1. The Ministry seems, however, to face the reality of the right column. From a single domain, let alone from a single actor, it seems a very hard job to oversee it all. Indeed, it seems impossible for a designer to distance himself from his own perspective. For example, was it possibile for the government, as the author of the institutional design, to ignore the political support for fines and get the quality system accredited? Was it possible to please the sector by leaving requirements from European and Dutch regulation uncodified in the arrangement? The likely answers are 'no'. That is, not without severe political and legal damage.

The irony here is that the very same reasons why there would be a shift from 'government' to 'governance' seem to be applicable on the meta-level. Government of governance requires a position that just does not hold in a multi-actor environment. A conscious design will be the subject of confrontation between actors from different domains. The designer does not have the hierarchical position to maintain the design as intended, because of his dependency on other actors. If we assume relations between government and industry to be more horizontal, we inevitably see a shift from 'government to governance' as well as a shift from 'government of governance' to 'governance of governance'.

I think this implies a warning against all-too-instrumental thinking about regulation in which regulators are seen as the ultimate owners of the problem of the regulatory regime. Seeing co-regulation as an instrument for government would ignore the efforts, values and perspectives of the regulated and private regulators. They could see co-regulation as an instrument for their purposes and values as well. This requires a more modest approach to the organization and evolution of co-regulation.

NOTES

1. I realize that the term 'private regulators' is often used in a broader sense. It could refer to any private actor imposing regulations, such as banks, insurance companies or trade organizations (Baggott 1989; Hutter 2006; Dorbeck-Jung et al. 2010). In this chapter I focus on certification and accreditation bodies as actors that are explicitly hired by the industry for regulation.
2. It is important to remember that the boundaries mentioned above still exist. It would be simplistic to view the various actors involved in a co-regulation regime as merely 'networks', without taking into account hierarchical relations and markets that might also be apparent in co-regulatory regimes. Both hierarchy and market imply different rules of interaction from networks (Powell 1991).
3. It should be emphasized that this will not do justice to the nuances most authors show in their writing. The function of the table is to clarify perspectives, not to categorize work of specific authors.
4. Dutch Ministry of Internal Affairs, 'Minder last, meer effect; Zes principes van goed toezicht, Tweede kaderstellende visie op toezicht', 2005.
5. Dutch Ministry of Agriculture, Policy framework 'Beleidskader Toezicht op Controle', 2005.
6. Translates into 'Integral Chain Management of Eggs'.
7. AID and VWA have been merged into the new nVWA (Food and Consumer Product Safety Authority).
8. European Directive EU 589/2008.
9. Report 'Maat houden', MDW – werkgroep doorberekening handhavingskosten', June 1996.
10. Wet Aanwijzing Accreditatie-Organisatie, BWBR 0026591.
11. European Directive EU 589/2008.
12. Letter from the Minister of Agriculture, TK 2008–2009, 26991, 10 October 2008; the laws are 'Gezondheids- en welzijnswet voor dieren en wetsvoorstel Dieren' (TK 2007–2008, 31 389).

REFERENCES

Baggott, R. (1989), 'Regulatory Reform in Britain: The Changing Face of Self-Regulation', *Public Administration*, 67, 435–455.

Barkay, T. (2009), 'Regulation and Voluntarism: A Case Study of Governance in the Making', *Regulation & Governance*, 3, 360–375.

Barnett, M. and M. Finnemore (2004), *Rules for the World: International Organizations in Global Politics*, Ithaca: Cornell University Press.

Bartle, I. and P. Vass (2005), 'Self-Regulation and the Regulatory State; A Survey of Policy and Practice', Centre for the Study of Regulated Industries (CRI), Research Report 17, Bath: University of Bath.

Castells, M. (1996), *The Rise of the Network Society*, Oxford: Blackwell.

Dean, M. (2010), *Governmentality: Power and Rule in Modern Society*, 2nd edition, London: Sage.

De Bruijn, H., E.F. Ten Heuvelhof and R. In 't Veld (2002), *Process Management: Why Project Management Fails in Complex Decision Making Processes*, Dordrecht: Kluwer.

De Bruijn, H. and E.F. Ten Heuvelhof (2008), *Management in Networks: On Multi-actor Decision Making*, London: Routledge.

DeMarzo, P.M., M.J. Fishman and K.M. Hagerty (2005), 'Self-Regulation and Government Oversight', *Review of Economic Studies*, 72, 687–706.

Dorbeck-Jung, B.R., M.J. Oude Vrielink, J.F. Gosselt, J.J. Van Hoof and M.D.T. De Jong (2010), 'Contested Hybridization of Regulation: Failure of the Dutch Regulatory System to Protect Minors from Harmful Media', *Regulation & Governance*, 4, 154–174.

Foucault, M. (1991), 'Governmentality', in G. Burchell, C. Gordon and P. Miller (eds), *The Foucault Effect*, Hertfordshire: Harvester Wheatsheaf, pp. 87–104.

Garcia Martinez, M., A. Fearne, J.A. Caswell and S. Henson (2007), 'Co-regulation as a Possible Model for Food Safety Governance: Opportunities for Public-Private Partnerships', *Food Policy*, 32, 299–314.

Garcia Martinez, M., P. Verbruggen and A. Fearne (2013), 'Risk-based Approaches to Food Safety Regulation: What Role for Co-regulation?', in *Journal of Risk Research*, 16(9), 1101–1121.

Grabosky, P.N. (1995), 'Using Non-Governmental Resources to Foster Regulatory Compliance', *Governance: An International Journal of Policy and Administration*, 8(4), 527–550.

Gunningham, N. and P. Grabosky (1998), *Smart Regulation: Designing Environmental Policy*, Oxford/New York: Clarendon Press/Oxford University Press.

Gunningham, N. and J. Rees (1997), 'Industry Self-Regulation: An Institutional Perspective', *Law and Policy*, 19(4), 363–414.

Howlett, M. and J. Rayner (2004), '(Not So) "Smart regulation"? Canadian Shellfish Aquaculture Policy and the Evolution of Instrument Choice for Industrial Development', *Marine Policy*, 28(2), 171–184.

Hutter, B. (2006), 'The Role of Non-State Actors in Regulation', Discussion Paper 37, The Centre for Analysis of Risk and Regulation (CARR), London: London School of Economics.

Jessop, B. (2002), *The Future of the Capitalist State*, Cambridge: Polity.

Jessop, R. (2003), 'Governance, Governance Failure, and Meta-Governance', paper presented on the International Seminar 'Policies, Governance and Innovation for Rural Areas', Università della Calabria, 21–23 November.

Jessop, B. (2004), 'Multi-level Governance and Multi-level Meta-governance', in I. Bache and M. Flanders, *Multi-level Governance*, Oxford: Oxford University Press.

Kelly, J. (2006), 'Central Regulation of English Local Authorities: An Example of Meta-Governance?', *Public Administration*, 84(3), 603–621.

Kickert, W.J.M., E.H. Klijn and J.F.M. Koppenjan (eds) (1997), *Managing Complex Networks*, London: Sage.

King, A.A. and M.J. Lenox (2000), 'Industry Self-Regulation without Sanctions: The Chemical Industry's Responsible Care Program', *Academy of Management Journal*, 43(4), 698–716.

Klijn, E.H. and J. Edelenbos (2007), 'Meta-governance as Network Management', in E. Sörensen and J. Torfing, *Theories of Democratic Network Governance*, New York: Palgrave MacMillan.

Kooiman, J. (ed.) (1993), *Modern Governance: New Government-Society Interactions*, London: Sage.

Kooiman, J. (2003), *Governing as Governance*, London: Sage.

Kooiman, J. and S. Jentoft (2009), 'Meta-Governance: Values, Norms and Principles, and the Making of Hard Choices', *Public Administration*, 87(4), 818–836.

Koppenjan, J., M. Kars and H. Van der Voort (2009), 'Vertical Politics in Horizontal Policy Networks: Framework Setting as Coupling Arrangement', *Policy Studies Journal*, 37(4), 769–792.

O'Rourke, D. (2003), 'Outsourcing Regulation: Analyzing Nongovernmental Systems of Labor Standards and Monitoring', *Policy Studies Journal*, 31(1), 1–29.

O'Toole, L.J. (2007), 'Governing Outputs and Outcomes of Governance Networks', in E. Sörensen and J. Torfing, *Theories of Democratic Network Governance*, New York: Palgrave MacMillan.

Parker, C. and V. Nielsen (2009), 'The Challenge of Empirical Research on Business Compliance in Regulatory Capitalism', *Annual Review of Law and Social Sciences*, 5, 45–70.

Pierre, J. (ed.) (2000), *Debating Governance*, Oxford: Oxford University Press.

Powell, W.W. (1991), 'Neither Market, nor Hierarchy: Network Forms of Organization', in G. Thompson, J. Frances, R. Levàoic and J. Mitchell, *Markets, Hierarchies and Networks: The Coordination of Social Life*, London: Sage, pp. 265–274.

Power, M. (2003), 'Evaluating the Audit Explosion', *Law and Policy*, 25(3), 185–202.

Rametsteiner, E. and M. Simula (2002), 'Forest Certification – An Instrument to Promote Sustainable Forest Management?', *Journal of Environmental Management*, 67, 87–98.

Rhodes, R.A.W. (1997), *Understanding Governance*, Buckingham: Open University Press.

Schepel, H. (2005), *The Constitution of Private Governance: Product Standards in the Regulation of Integrating Markets*, Oxford and Portland: Hart Publishing.

Sörensen, E. and J. Torfing (2007), *Theories of Democratic Network Governance*, New York: Palgrave MacMillan.

Triantafillou, P. (2007), 'Governing the Formation and Mobilization of

Governance Networks', in E. Sörensen and J. Torfing, *Theories of Democratic Network Governance*, New York: Palgrave MacMillan.

Whitehead, M. (2003), 'In the Shadow of Hierarchy: Meta-Governance, Policy Reform and Urban Regeneration in the West Midlands', *Area*, 35(1), 6–14.

Index